M000310299

DECLARATION OF THE AMERICAN MIND

America's True & Lasting Character

Richard Stuby

PRESS

NEW TRIPOLI

Copyright © 2020 by Richard G. Stuby Jr.

Published in the United States by Jordan Ridge Press, an imprint of Jordan Ridge LLC, New Tripoli, PA.

Unless noted, all Scripture quotations are taken from the New American Standard Bible® (NASB), Copyright © 1960, 1962, 1963, 1968, 1971, 1972, 1973, 1975, 1977, 1995 by The Lockman Foundation Used by permission. www.Lockman.org.

Scripture quotations from The Holy Bible, English Standard Version® (ESV®), copyright © 2001 by Crossway, a publishing ministry of Good News Publishers. Used by permission. All rights reserved.; Green's Literal Translation (LITV). Scripture quoted by permission. Copyright 1993 by Jay P. Green Sr. All rights reserved. Jay P. Green Sr., Lafayette, IN. U.S.A. 47903.

All rights reserved. No part of this book may be reproduced or transmitted in any form or by any means without written permission from the author.

ISBN 978-1-7347314-0-8

Library of Congress Control Number: 2020905373

Printed in the United States of America

For my children and posterity

Contents

The sacred rights of mankind are not to be rummaged for among old parchments or musty records, they are written, as with a sunbeam, in the whole volume of human nature, by the hand of the Divinity itself; and can never be erased or obscured by mortal power.

Alexander Hamilton

No people can be bound to acknowledge and adore the invisible hand, which conducts the affairs of men, more than the people of the United States. Every step by which they have advanced to the character of an independent nation, seems to have been distinguished by some token of providential agency.

George Washington

I have lived, sir, a long time; and the longer I live, the more convincing proofs I see of this truth, that God governs in the affairs of men! And if a sparrow cannot fall to the ground without his notice, is it probable that an empire can rise without his aid?

Benjamin Franklin

Preface

Declaration of the American Mind was written because the purpose for the American experiment and its godly roots have never been more questioned than today. Despite the ready availability of information, much of America's founding history is no longer taught in schools. Additionally, most Americans have neither the time nor inclination to comb through old documents to understand America's founding principles. Even with unimpeded access to historical documents on websites like Google Books, JSTOR and Yale Law School's Avalon Project, for many the postmodern worldview of "You have 'your truth,' I have 'my truth,'" is stronger than the facts.

Therefore, some may wonder if there is any reason to spend time presenting American history and culture through *Declaration of the American Mind.* There is, at the very least, the need to set out the truth regarding the American founders. For most of America's 240 or so years, the founders' truth has been *the* truth. That truth needs to be restored, in context, by leveraging quotations from founders, leaders and philosophers of the time, and illuminating the godly basis by which the American founding came for the good of all.

However, the real goal of *Declaration of the American Mind,* is to go beyond delivering simple facts on the American founding, and uncover the fantastic painted-over portrait of America that has just as much importance now as when it was created, and to rediscover the foundational American culture as established in America's founding documents.

Audience

Declaration of the American Mind has a definite focus on the American founding and purpose from a God-believing moral perspective, but the information is also relevant for any open-minded person interested in how America came to be and what America is meant to be. This is not a book promoting a special religious status or advocating Christian dominance in government. America was founded for liberty, not oppression, and equality, not elitism. However, Christianity and godly morals, virtues and ethics are entrenched deeply in America's founding and American culture, and this reality is reflected in the discussion of this book, not to the exclusion of anyone, but as a blessing, a gift, to all.

For the religious believer, the purpose is education, that they can take their place in securing "the Blessings of Liberty to ourselves and our Posterity," which includes the liberty to live in relationship with God. The time has passed, and never really was, for Christians to keep Christianity in church while living a secular public life. The very foundation of America is built upon recognition of God, not as a theocratic ruler, but as a benevolent provider offering freedom and abundant life to all. Christians must return to that recognition, live it, and share it:

> You are the light of the world. A city set on a hill cannot be hidden. Nor do people light a lamp and put it under a basket, but on a stand, and it gives light to all in the house. In the same way, let your light shine before others, so that they may see your good works and give glory to your Father who is in heaven. (Matthew 5:14-16)

For the non-religious person, the purpose is to likewise take part in securing liberty through the morality built into the founding American culture, and perhaps do so by developing an understanding of why religious people may think the way they do about America. Some of this will be expressed through verses from the Bible which should be relatable simply as philosophy, a source for morals and ethics. Indeed, this is the very reason the underlying principles applied in our founding documents were not offensive to those founders and citizens who may have not been religious.

Past Performance Not a Guarantee of Future Results

Much of the impact, or lack thereof, of this book will be based on the attitude of the reader. Like a pre-game speech from a coach describing how the team is equipped for a win, the effect of this book on an individual will be based on motivation and present effort, and not on impressive statistics of the past. An openness to ideas and honesty in the search for truth is required, as it was in the Age of Enlightenment from which America arose. In short, do Americans still want to be patriots and part of God's plan for good? And are Americans willing to make the effort to renew American virtue and blessings?

Heritage, not Nostalgia

Declaration of the American Mind is not a fantasy about going back in time to become something America once was. This book *is* about living the foundational culture of who Americans have always been. The use of sources and quotations contemporary to the institution of America is intended to reduce the fog of reinterpretation of events over time. One may consider that the author is making interpretation in some instances, but any such interpretation should be judged against original words and concepts.

The sources are cited[1], and most are readily available with web addresses provided. The reader is encouraged to check the context for themselves. A glossary is provided to define words in the context used.

Political Correctness

Effort has also been made to avoid setting stumbling blocks for the reader. Consider the Bible verse,

---

[1] Citations are generally of the form (Author, Short Title, page).

> But take care that this liberty of yours does not somehow
> become a stumbling block to the weak. (1 Corinthians 8:9)

While seeking to avoid being a stumbling block, this book will not confuse discussions by chasing after "politically correct" dialog. Terminology in the book may include references to "man" covering "men and women," as well as "sons" meaning "sons and daughters" or similar simplifications that have been norms of English language and the Bible for centuries. Similarly, the United States of America is typically addressed as "America" throughout this book. The hope is that the reader will consider the content and not seek out offenses which are not at all intended.

Keeping in Context

The "stumbling block" verse has its biblical context in regard to eating certain foods, but it also provides an appropriate general reminder of the responsibility to be thoughtful of others. However, this extensibility is not the case for all quotations. Removed from the original context, quotations can be, and often are, twisted to alter their meaning[2]. Some quotations stand well in multiple contexts, while some may be thoughtfully applied to an argument in another context as part of analogy or reference to character. Others do not apply in any context other than that in which it was originally presented. In many cases the correct response to context may require one's own discernment[3].

Organization

Declaration of the American Mind is organized into two parts. Part One establishes the historical context of the American experiment and develops the foundational American culture through the Declaration of Independence, Constitution and Bill of Rights. Part One also looks at the

---

[2] See the discussion on "separation of church and state" in Part Two, under *The First Amendment*.

[3] Matthew 11:13-14. "For all the prophets and the Law prophesied until John. And if you are willing to accept it, John himself is Elijah who was to come."

perspective of thinking and living the foundational American culture. Part Two applies the understanding from Part One to provide a deeper look at American rights and the issues of culture that affect them. An Appendix is also included, offering insight into political structures and philosophies that affect American culture, relevant historical background and background on Christian beliefs that relate to government.

PART ONE –
THE AMERICAN
MIND

Introduction

America is an experiment in culture and government, the first of its kind in the history of the world (Tocqueville, vol. 1, 23).

America was called into existence by circumstances hundreds of years in the making. John Quincy Adams, sixth President of the United States, and son of John Adams, who signed the Declaration of Independence, said it well that America was,

> chartered by adventurers of characters variously diversified, including sectarians, religious and political, of all the classes which for the two preceding centuries had agitated and divided the people of the British islands—and with them were intermingled the descendants of Hollanders, Swedes, Germans, and French fugitives from the persecution of the revoker of the Edict of Nantes. … In the bosoms of this people, thus heterogeneously composed, there was burning, kindled at different furnaces, but all furnaces of affliction, one clear, steady flame of LIBERTY. (Adams, J.Q., 7)

Oppressed by their British brethren, these intermingled American colonists were forced on a journey of philosophical discovery to discern the meaning and mechanisms of sound civil government based in liberty. Pressed beyond toleration through many colonial calls upon Britain for reconciliation, no relief was offered, and the colonies rebelled. They fought battles and declared their rationale for the uptake of arms against the British king. Despite small victories, the patriotic colonists were losing the war. Then the representatives of the colonial American people gathered to openly and fully debate their lifelong learnings on government. Taking stock of the oppression they endured, these men envisioned the future of freedom that they desired for themselves and their posterity. And they sought the favor of Divine Providence. From it all, the Declaration of Independence crystallized into more than just a proclamation of liberty, but a vision and culture statement for America.

The battles continued to rage for seven years, but the die was cast in liberty, truth, and justice; America achieved its declared independence from Britain. What emerged was the freest society and greatest economy the world has ever seen. The Declaration of Independence made America the champion for the enlightened civilized world.

Like all heroes, America is imperfect. Because of human faults, society and government can never be perfect. There will always be periods of failure and sometimes grotesque mistakes. America's greatest sin was the institution of slavery. Its impact remains an open wound in society; sometimes almost healed, only to fester until it again bursts open in pain and sorrow. But America declared that all men are created equal. Where America failed to implement equality correctly at the outset, America has desired to make it so from its founding. Herein lies the importance of understanding the foundational American vision and culture. The intent is lasting, the failures, though painful, are fleeting. Those who are truly patriots are the ones who overcome the faults and mistakes of a nation, advancing it toward its vision.

Few people understand patriotism. Patriotism is not national loyalty. It is not the same as being a sports fan, supporting a favorite team, win or lose, irrespective of changes in lineup, coaching or ownership. True patriotism requires reasoned, moral, and principled sacrifice for one's countrymen. Anything else is just nationalism or simple party spirit. Thomas Paine famously wrote,

> These ARE THE TIMEs THAT TRY MEN's souls. The summer-soldier and the sun-shine patriot will, in this crisis, shrink from the service of their country; but he that stands it

now, deserves the thanks of man and woman. (Paine, *American Crisis,* 12)

Most Americans don't understand the founding documents and principles of the nation to which they claim citizenship. Most American Christians don't understand the truth regarding Christian religion in America's founding and their place in achieving America's God-ordained purposes. Without such knowledge, informed consent to patriotically stand for the American vision is impossible. Founder, Benjamin Rush, placed patriotism as a virtue, far above party spirit:

> The obligations of patriotism are as universal and binding, as
> those of justice and benevolence … (Rush, 357)

The maxim, "We do not rise to the level of our expectations, we fall to the level of our training[4]" rings true for American patriotism. Most consider themselves patriots because they love what they personally believe America to be, or what it should be by their own imaginings. Nationalists believe this way. Socialists believe this way. Many professing Christians believe this way. They imagine that they will resist evil or fight for what their feelings tell them is right for America. Yet few are educated in what America fundamentally is, making their patriotism hollow, often misguided, nationalism; and their effectiveness in the moral and principled cause for America unlikely.

Just as the Christian who accepts Jesus as their Savior should understand the inheritance they receive in Christ,[5] those who accept, or at least consider, that America has been shepherded by God for good in the world should understand the history from which America arose, and the "Blessings of Liberty to ourselves and our Posterity[6]" that we can expect when remaining faithful to the American cause.

---

[4] Widely attributed to ancient Greek philosopher, Archilochus.
[5] See *Who Christians are in Christ* in the Appendix.
[6] U.S. Constitution.

Those driven by other standards of morality likewise should understand America as it was founded and how it relates to their principles. Essentially any moral, just, liberty-loving, belief system can thrive in foundational American culture. America was founded for that purpose, and with that requirement.

It would be easy to lose focus and ask, "What then do we do with immorality and principles that do not align with American Culture?" That is a valid question. But it seems better to think like the American founders, who considered that Divine Providence had that question answered, believing that society would do best by aligning with the "Supreme Judge of the World[7]" to create a nation for which the question of managing immorality and lack of principles should become moot within the lives of its liberty-loving populace.

The founding documents of America establish such a system, a culture and government, for society to thrive in liberty and with a moral compass that sustains this liberty for posterity. Simply reading across the preambles of the Declaration of Independence, Constitution and Bill of Rights provides the one-minute introduction to that American notion of Liberty:

The Declaration of Independence attests that God-given rights exist implicitly in humankind, and that the purpose of government is to secure these rights.

> that all men are created equal, that they are endowed by their Creator with certain unalienable Rights, that among these are Life, Liberty, and the pursuit of Happiness. That to secure these rights, Governments are instituted among Men …

The Constitution was written to provide a framework to secure unalienable rights for all time.

> in Order to … secure the Blessings of Liberty to ourselves and our Posterity.

---

[7] Declaration of Independence.

And the Bill of Rights was written to specifically declare a number of those unalienable rights to ensure a good government and prevent abuse of power.

> in order to prevent misconstruction or abuse of its powers, that further declaratory and restrictive clauses should be added: And as extending the ground of public confidence in the Government, will best ensure the beneficent ends of its institution.

Unlike any other government in the history of the world, the American Republic was established with acknowledgement of, and appeal to, the Creator of mankind to secure the Blessings of Liberty. And that government was specifically developed to prevent domination and tyranny by the majority, powerful individuals, political parties, or a religious order.

Thomas Paine believed an even greater place for America in world history,

> The cause of America is in a great measure the cause of all mankind. Many circumstances have, and will arise, which are not local, but universal, and through which the principles of all Lovers of Mankind are affected, and in the Event of which, their Affections are interested. The laying of a Country desolate with Fire and Sword, declaring War against the natural rights of all Mankind, and extirpating the Defenders thereof from the Face of the Earth, is the Concern of every Man to whom Nature hath given the Power of feeling ... (Paine, *Common Sense*, 4)

Americans must take stock of that which we know and believe to ensure we are not fighting against our own cause. Christians must further consider their place as ambassadors of Christ[8] in American life. All must set aside party spirit, uphold truth and justice, and,

---

[8] 2 Corinthians 5:11-21.

Let the names of Whig and Tory[9] be extinct; and let none other be heard among us, than those of *a good citizen, an open and resolute friend, and a virtuous supporter of the* RIGHTS *of* MANKIND *and of the* FREE AND INDEPENDENT STATES OF AMERICA. (Paine, *Common Sense*, 90)

---

[9] The British political factions to which colonists generally ascribed at the time of the American Revolution.

Chapter 1 –

The Fullness of Time for America

The American vision and culture expressed in the Declaration of Independence defines an inflection point in history culminating from a chain of events that bears the handwriting of Divine Providence[10]. This "fullness of time" for America's creation deserves attention, as do events of the preceding hundreds of years that led to it. In a world filled with willing and unwilling participants, God works in the kingdoms of men to achieve His purposes while allowing individuals to exercise free will. Only the world's Creator is capable of such mastery, akin to completing a complex jigsaw puzzle while the shapes of the pieces are constantly changing. At key points in time, various sections of the puzzle are completed, and the results are striking to consider.

In a manner much like the history that aligned to bring the fullness of time for Jesus Christ,[11] it can be contended that God arranged and ordained the founding of America. Whether or not one chooses to believe this, it is apparent that many of the founders believed it and they were all educated using the Bible so as to understand it. They appealed to "the Supreme Judge of the world for the rectitude" of their Declaration of Independence and expressed "a firm reliance on the protection of divine Providence" for their lives, fortunes, and sacred honor. They believed in America as the

---

[10] "Divine Providence" is invoked in the Declaration of Independence and a wealth of other founding documents, the importance of which will be developed throughout Part One of this book.

[11] Refer to *The Fullness of Time – The Advent of Jesus Christ* in the Appendix.

fulfillment of hundreds of years of developing philosophies, sufferings under tyrants, and religious persecution.

Thomas Jefferson, facing armed resistance with Britain, understood the "Divine favour" of timing and preparation a year before authoring the Declaration of Independence when he wrote *A Declaration by the Representatives of the United Colonies of North-America, Now Met in Congress at Philadelphia, Setting Forth the Causes and Necessity of Their Taking Up Arms*, saying,

> We gratefully acknowledge, as signal instances of the Divine favour towards us, that his Providence would not permit us to be called into this severe controversy, until we were grown up to our present strength, had been previously exercised in warlike operation, and possessed of the means of defending ourselves. (Continental Congress, 9)

John Jay, future first Chief Justice of the United States, writing *Federalist 2* to support the new Constitution, recognized the result of the "fullness of time" for America,

> With equal pleasure I have as often taken notice, that Providence has been pleased to give this one connected country to one united people; and a people descended from the same ancestors, speaking the same language, professing the same religion, attached to the same principles of government, very similar in their manners and customs; and who, by their joint counsels, arms, and efforts, fighting side by side, throughout a long and bloody war, have nobly established their general liberty and independence. (Hamilton, *Federalist*, 12)

Even Abraham Lincoln, when facing dissolution of the Union some 85 years after the nation's founding, understood this timeless significance. As president-elect, speaking to a joint session of the New Jersey legislature in February of 1861, Lincoln said,

I recollect thinking then, boy even though I was, that there must have been something more than common that those men [George Washington and the American revolutionaries] struggled for; that something even more than National Independence; that **something that held out a great promise to all the people of the world to all time to come**; I am exceedingly anxious that this Union, the Constitution, and the liberties of the people shall be perpetuated in accordance with the original idea for which that struggle was made, and **I shall be most happy indeed if I shall be an humble instrument in the hands of the Almighty, and of this, his almost chosen people, for perpetuating the object of that great struggle**. (Lincoln, 383, emphasis added)

From Printing Press to the American Founding

A clear starting point for the timeline of the "fullness of time" for America begins with the development of the printing press, and the Gutenberg Bible circa 1455. The printing press helped end the Middle Ages and usher in the Renaissance and the Age of Discovery. The mass production (relatively speaking) of the Bible created an opportunity for more people, at least the well-educated, to read and interpret Scripture unimpeded by intermediaries, eroding the political control of the Church[12] by opening minds to discovery.

Just a few decades later, in 1492, Christopher Columbus opened the "New World" to exploration, colonization, commerce, and the spread of the gospel. Columbus was a hero in America for hundreds of years, yet is much maligned today for claims that others discovered the Americas before him, and accusations that he mistreated the aboriginal[13] Americans,

---

[12] Church, capitalized, refers to the universal Christian church and not any particular sect or denomination.

[13] "Aboriginal" is used rather than the popular term "native" because "aboriginal" accurately reflects the pre-colonial incumbency of these peoples in North America, whereas "native" implies a place of birth which, today, also applies to generations of non-aboriginal peoples.

and established the Atlantic slave trade.[14] Regardless of any validity in such claims, Christopher Columbus' voyages of discovery set in motion the colonization of America by Western civilization. And, in his mind, he did it by God's grace (Columbus, *Will*, 193), for the glory of God, and to convert people to the Christian faith (Columbus, *Journal*, 16, 90, 91). Columbus was followed by other explorers during this Age of Discovery, many, if not all, with less godly intent. The point being, America would have eventually been opened to the civilized world with, or without, Columbus, but with Columbus, America was opened for God and not just gold.

The world of religion also changed in Europe as the New World was being opened. In 1517, Martin Luther wrote his "95 Theses" disputing corrupt practices of the Roman Catholic Church and seeking to reform it in conformity with the Holy Scriptures (Luther, 3). Luther's actions ushered in the Protestant Reformation, reforming Christian theology to reflect an individual acceptance of Jesus Christ as the path to salvation. Throughout the Reformation, the Bible became more available to the public. The Tyndale Bible was the first New Testament printed in English in 1526 (Lewis, 75). Tyndale was later executed for his "heretical" efforts, but not until completing a full translation of the Bible.

In 1534, Great Britain severed ties with the Catholic church and established the Church of England as a Protestant state-sponsored church. The Church of England leveraged the Tyndale Bible as the basis of its own version of the scriptures, followed by the Geneva Bible in 1560, until, in 1611 the King James version of the Bible (Lewis, 323-324), written in plain English of the time to be read aloud in church, became the Authorized Version of the Church of England and the leading Bible for private use. The availability and English simplicity of the King James Bible (*The Holy Bible*, King James Version) enabled it to also become a

---

[14] Columbus surely did not set out to establish a slave trade, nor did he effectively establish one. He did transport 500 prisoners from battle to be sold as slaves in Spain as had become customary from Spanish wars with the Moors (Irving, 105).

ubiquitous religious tool outside of the Church of England during the Reformation, and later the basis for education among colonial American families.

Over the next 100 years, Reformation leaders such as John Calvin and John Wesley established new church doctrines as the Bible was opened to study and interpretation apart from the Catholic priesthood and the papacy. The various doctrines that arose during the Reformation also ushered in religious persecution and wars across Europe. In 1618 the Thirty-Years War began, resulting in the death of some eight million people. It, and many other persecutions, created religious refugee groups who sought asylum across Europe. Religious migration to America began in 1620 with the separatist "Pilgrims" establishing Plymouth Plantation in Massachusetts. Eight years later, the first Calvinist Reformed church began in Dutch New York. In 1630 the Puritans settled in Massachusetts. In 1634 the first Catholic churches were started in Maryland, and in 1636 Roger Williams started the first Baptist church in Rhode Island, which was also proclaimed to be a place of religious freedom.

Another Christian group, the Quakers were persecuted throughout Europe and some American colonies. In 1681, William Penn, an English Quaker, was granted title in the American colonies to a large tract of land, which came to be known as Pennsylvania,[15] as payment by the king who owed a debt to Penn's father. William Penn had been persecuted in England, being unjustly jailed in Newburg Prison in 1670 for "contempt of court" after being found not guilty of "preaching and speaking" in public, leading to a disturbance. During Penn's trial, the judge expressed his desire for even greater religious persecution of the Quakers, saying, "Till now I never understood the Reason of the Policy and Prudence of the Spaniards, in suffering the Inquisition among them: And certainly, it will never be well

---

[15] Penn preferred "New Wales" but the king ordered the name, meaning Penn's Woods (Weems, 119-120).

with us, till something like the Spanish Inquisition be in England" (Penn, 17).

William Penn desired to make Pennsylvania a place of religious freedom, calling his plan for Pennsylvania a "holy experiment" (Janney, 175). He opened Pennsylvania to settlement and created a Charter of Privileges that included radical liberties including an elected representative Assembly and explicit religious freedom for monotheistic believers. The final version of the Charter of Liberties, written in 1701 and serving as the constitution for Pennsylvania until 1776, reads, in part:

> BECAUSE no People can be truly happy, though under the greatest Enjoyment of Civil Liberties, if abridged of the Freedom of their Consciences, as to their Religious Profession and Worship: And Almighty God being the only Lord of Conscience, Father of Lights and Spirits; and the Author as well as Object of all divine Knowledge, Faith and Worship, who only doth enlighten the Minds, and persuade and convince the Understandings of People, I do hereby grant and declare, That no Person or Persons, inhabiting in this Province or Territories, who shall confess and acknowledge One almighty God, the Creator, Upholder and Ruler of the World; and profess him or themselves obliged to live quietly under the Civil Government, shall be in any Case molested or prejudiced, in his or their Person or Estate, because of his or their conscientious Persuasion or Practice, nor be compelled to frequent or maintain any religious Worship, Place or Ministry, contrary to his or their Mind, or to do or suffer any other Act or Thing, contrary to their religious Persuasion.

> FOR the well governing of this Province and Territories, there shall be an Assembly yearly chosen, by the Freemen thereof, to consist of Four Persons out of each County, of most Note for Virtue, Wisdom and Ability, ... Which Assembly shall have Power to choose a Speaker and other their Officers; and shall be Judges of the Qualifications and Elections of their own Members; sit upon their own Adjournment; appoint Committees; prepare Bills in order to pass into Laws; impeach

Criminals, and redress Grievances; and shall have all other
Powers and Privileges of an Assembly, according to the
Rights of the free-born Subjects of England, and as is usual in
any of the King's Plantations in America. (Pennsylvania, 413-
414)

These were fantastic rights for the time, conferred directly on the people
by Penn, in accordance with British rule, yet they were also very much in
opposition to the practice of British rule in America and in contrast to the
religious sectarianism of the other colonies, Rhode Island excepted.

Mutual religious persecution between Catholics, Protestants and other
sects continued throughout Europe into the 18th century. Many of the
groups found a foothold of religious freedom in America, especially under
the religious freedom of Pennsylvania. Thomas Paine, in *Common Sense*,
noted that

This new world hath been the asylum for the persecuted lovers
of civil and religious liberty from every part of Europe.
(Paine, *Common Sense*, 36)

He also expressed an understanding of the plans of Divine Providence
when he wrote:

The time likewise at which the continent was discovered, adds
weight to the argument, and the manner in which it was
peopled encreases the force of it. The reformation was
preceded by the discovery of America, as if the Almighty
graciously meant to open a sanctuary to the persecuted in
future years, when home should afford neither friendship nor
safety. (Paine, *Common Sense*, 40)

Early on, there was considerable religious persecution within American
colonies. By the time of King George III, however, the colonies were well
established, and the principles of freedom of religious conscience had
taken hold due to the Enlightenment and Great Awakening, which
lessened the harshness of divides between Christian religious
denominations.

The Enlightenment was contemporaneous with much of the Reformation, beginning in the later 1600s. Also called the Age of Reason, the Enlightenment leveraged the reason and process of science to tie together the natural world with the accepted truth of God in Natural Law. The Enlightenment ended shortly after the founding of America, at a point sometimes considered to be coincident with the start of the French Revolution in 1789. However, the "Law of Nature and Nature's God," as goes the phrase from the American Declaration of Independence, was a prevalent basis for political philosophy continuing well past America's founding.

Within the timeframe of the Enlightenment, from 1730 to 1750 and tailing into the 1760s, there was the rise of the First Great Awakening in America as a social and religious counterbalance to the faithless reason purveyed by some Enlightenment philosophers. The First Great Awakening was characterized by Christian clergymen such as Jonathan Edwards[16] and George Whitfield who preached the need for a personal relationship with Jesus Christ for salvation and reduced focus on the "works" of religious liturgy and traditions of the church.

The First Great Awakening was a return to foundational belief as a natural response to the pendulum of popular culture having swung away from the faith aspect of religion during the Enlightenment. The result of the Great Awakening was to bring about a common basis for American unity in Christian faith and morality[17] with a strong foundation in reason and belief in freedom of conscience from the Enlightenment, together tempering mankind's natural tendencies to oppress others via both religious and secular power. Emblematic of this change taking hold in America was John Witherspoon, the only theologian to sign the Declaration of

---

[16] A classic sermon of the time is "Sinners in the Hands of an Angry God" by Jonathan Edwards (Edwards), which paints a horrifying picture of the wrath of God in the final judgement for those choosing to remain apart from the grace and forgiveness provided through Jesus Christ.

[17] Unity in culture does not imply uniformity in beliefs.

Independence, who proclaimed in his May 17, 1776 sermon entitled, "The Dominion of Providence over the Passions of Men,"

> If your cause is just—you may look with confidence to the Lord and intreat him to plead it as his own. You are all my witnesses, that this is the first time of my introducing any political subject into the pulpit. At this season however, it is not only lawful but necessary, and I willingly embrace the opportunity of declaring my opinion without any hesitation, that the cause in which America is now in arms, is the cause of justice, of liberty, and of human nature. So far as we have hitherto proceeded, I am satisfied that the confederacy of the colonies, has not been the effect of pride, resentment, or sedition, but of a deep and general conviction, that our civil and religious liberties, and consequently in a great measure the temporal and eternal happiness of us and our posterity, depended on the issue. The knowledge of God and his truths have from the beginning of the world been chiefly, if not entirely, confined to those parts of the earth, where some degree of liberty and political justice were to be seen, and great were the difficulties with which they had to struggle from the imperfection of human society, and the unjust decisions of usurped authority. There is not a single instance in history in which civil liberty was lost, and religious liberty preserved entire. If therefore we yield up our temporal property, we at the same time deliver the conscience into bondage. (Witherspoon, 36-37)

In 1760, King George III came to power in Britain which was in the midst of the European Seven Years War and its North American counterpart, the French and Indian War. With British victory against France in North America in 1763, King George III turned his focus to reigning in the growing call for self-governance in the American colonies. The King's attempts at regaining control of governance and recouping war losses increasingly turned American thoughts from self-governance with loyalty to the King to American independence. In a few short years, the run up to conflict climaxed and American Independence was declared.

The oppression throughout the world and subsequent opportunity for independence of the American colonies from King George III, was the completion of the fullness of time for America. *Common Sense* expresses, throughout, a well-accepted view of America at its fullness of time, ordained for a purpose, independent of Great Britain,

> Every spot of the old world is overrun with oppression. Freedom hath been hunted round the globe. Asia, and Africa, have long expelled her. Europe regards her like a stranger, and England hath given her warning to depart. O! receive the fugitive, and prepare in time an asylum for mankind. (Paine, *Common Sense*, 58)

> Youth is the seed time of good habits, as well in nations as in individuals. It might be difficult, if not impossible, to form the Continent into one government half a century hence. (Paine, *Common Sense*, 69)

> The present time, likewise, is that peculiar time, which never happens to a nation but once, VIZ. the time of forming itself into a government. Most nations have let slip the opportunity, and by that means have been compelled to receive laws from their conquerors, instead of making laws for themselves. (Paine, *Common Sense*, 70)

> we have every opportunity and every encouragement before us, to form the noblest purest constitution on the face of the earth. We have it in our power to begin the world over again. A situation, similar to the present, hath not happened since the days of Noah until now. (Paine, *Common Sense*, 87)

The American Colonies sat thousands of miles from their tormentor with legislative, or at least deliberative, bodies comprising learned men, with a common European history and a general affinity for one another, along with a growing animosity toward the British King and Parliament. This alignment provided America the opportunity of which Thomas Paine wrote, the opportunity to peacefully, deliberately and through open debate, create the Declaration of Independence while yet under a Monarchy, and when the war was won, to write the Constitution without splintering into warring factions. The first shot of the American Revolution was fired in 1775 and independence declared in 1776, but the first revolution, one of enlightenment leading to a government of, by, and for, the people truly won American independence. The Colonies would not have stood against Britain in armed revolution without it.

The Close to America's Fullness of Time

The events happening just after the founding of America also provide proof points for America's fullness of time. Thirteen years after a declaration of independence, and as the Constitution was being ratified by the American states, revolution arose in France. The French Revolution of 1789 began, on paper, in the mold of the American Revolution. The French declared Liberty, Equality and Fraternity, an end to monarchy, and government by the people. But individual liberty quickly gave way to populist collectivism under the guise of guaranteeing individual rights. The error being the desire for liberty, equality and fraternity without the express basis of principle; without the "Law of Nature and Nature's God" as the source of the rights of the people. Without that immutable truth, the French Revolution was doomed to be subservient to the "truth" of whomever held power: briefly the People, then the Committee of Public Safety and Robespierre, who cleansed the revolution by guillotine, and finally by dictatorship under Napoleon. In just ten years France traded a monarch for an Emperor. Had America waited for independence, the French would not have been there to help defeat the British and may have signaled an end to the consideration for American independence by their failed example.

In America, westward expansion would continue. Settlers in the new territories would naturally have interest in survival, commerce and local government. They would be less concerned, for a time, about how they succeeded in achieving that life, whether by way of a federated America, state government, or even foreign intervention. As the British Quebec

Act[18] had shown in 1774, present benefits often outweighed a principled future. With expansion came a dilution in the level of education previously attendant in representative bodies as well as continued calls for the expansion of slavery. If not held in check by the vision of the Declaration of Independence, the rule of law in the Constitution, and a determined cadre of founders in government, the American colonies would likely have dissolved into a weak confederation or completely reverted to being foreign vassals of European masters.

Eventually, technology would have closed the window on America's fullness of time. With the invention of the telegraph, railroad, and steamships by the mid-eighteen hundreds, the grievances in the Declaration of Independence resulting from the remoteness of the British King to the American colonies may not have existed to create the same intolerable oppressive environment that lead the colonies to shed British authority in 1776.

Finally, as if to say that the close had come to the Providential fullness of time for establishing the foundational American culture, two of the most prominent, yet philosophically different, American founders died on the very same day. John Adams and Thomas Jefferson both died on July 4, 1826, the 50th anniversary of the Declaration of Independence. The 50th year of the Declaration had occurred, the Jubilee celebration of American liberty was over, and symbolically, the declaration of the American vision and culture was bequeathed in trust to posterity.

With America established in the "Law of Nature and Nature's God," time would see America grow to be the economic and military power of the world. While Europe suffered from the French Revolution and developed social and political philosophies that continued to drive unrest and more war, America grew in area and resources, and, after paying a heavy price in the American Civil War for its sin of slavery, was poised to save liberty

---

[18] See *The Cause of Revolution* in the Appendix.

from the coming return to totalitarianism in Western Civilization during the two world wars of the twentieth century.

Justice and the Fullness of Time

It was noted at the outset that God achieves His purposes through people, willing and unwilling. Some, not knowing the God of the Bible, might ask why God would allow, or prescribe, someone to perform evil in His name. This seems particularly important when considering today's view of Christopher Columbus as a villain. If one asks this about Columbus, the same question must be asked of people and circumstances throughout time; of the Assyrians and Babylonians who executed the Jewish diasporas, of the conquests of Alexander the Great, of the evil within the Roman empire, and of any evil that happens today. The answer to all these is that God never prescribes or desires evil, but He did give mankind free will – part of the liberty that defines America – knowing that some people will use their liberty in evil and for evil.

God has plans and purposes for His Creation. God seeks people to do His righteous will and to live morally, but when they fail, in themselves or by the intervention of others, God still finds a way to effect His purposes within the free will of others. In the Bible, Joseph was sold into slavery by his brothers but rose to become second in power only to Pharaoh in Egypt, ultimately saving his family, and all of Egypt, from famine. When Joseph's brothers begged his forgiveness he said, "As for you, you meant evil against me, but God meant it for good in order to bring about this present result, to preserve many people alive" (Genesis 50:20). God did not create the evil of Joseph's brothers, or in Columbus' voyages. Nor did God condone it. God did foresee it and made good of it without altering His gift of free will. This is the back story to the Fullness of Time for Christ, and it is also true for the "fullness of time" for America.

Chapter 2 –

The Declaration of Independence is the American Mind

When in the Course of human events, it becomes necessary for one people to dissolve the political bands which have connected them with another, and to assume among the powers of the earth, the separate and equal station to which the Laws of Nature and of Nature's God entitle them, a decent respect to the opinions of mankind requires that they should declare the causes which impel them to the separation.

We hold these truths to be self-evident, that all men are created equal, that they are endowed by their Creator with certain unalienable Rights, that among these are Life, Liberty and the pursuit of Happiness. That to secure these rights, Governments are instituted among Men, deriving their just powers from the consent of the governed …

Preamble of the Declaration of Independence

How the Declaration of Independence Came to Be

The American Declaration of Independence resulted from years of patient suffering among the American colonists,[19] and painstaking soul-searching and debate in America's Continental Congresses. In July, 1774, Thomas Jefferson wrote *A Summary View of the Rights of British America*, which might be described as a "long form" version of the complaints to the King that ended up in the Declaration of Independence. Jefferson's pamphlet was provided to the Virginia delegates to the first Continental Congress to guide their engagement with the other representatives. The pamphlet was debated by the Continental Congress which rejected it as being too bold for the time. However, in October of 1774, the Continental Congress sent a softened complaint, often called the *Declaration and Resolves of the First Continental Congress* (Force, *Archives*, ser. 4, vol. 1, 910-912), to King George III. The document reads like an unpolished, subdued draft of the Declaration of Independence, but maintained loyalty to the King. The King never responded (Morse, 181-184). Then, on April 19, 1775, the "shot heard round the world" (Cooke, 39) occurred in Massachusetts with the battles of Lexington and Concord (Lee, 140), causing the Continental Congress to strongly move in the direction of self-governance for the Colonies, with many preferring outright independence. Again, by the pen of Thomas Jefferson, on July 6, 1775, they produced *A Declaration by the Representatives of the United Colonies of North-America, Now Met in Congress at Philadelphia, Setting Forth the Causes and Necessity of Their Taking Up Arms* (Continental Congress, 3) as an explanation of their preparations for war. By August, King George declared his American subjects to be engaged in open and avowed rebellion against the Crown.

Beginning in January of 1776, the pamphlet, *Common Sense* (Paine, *Common Sense*), did much to draw the public to the cause of independence. George Washington commented on it in one of his letters to Col. Joseph Reed, writing,

---

[19] Refer to *The Cause of Revolution* in the Appendix

and by private letters, which I have lately received from Virginia, I find '*Common Sense*' is working a powerful change there in the minds of many men. (Sparks, 347)

With some 120,000 copies distributed (Moncure, 136), *Common Sense* made many arguments for independence and against a useless reconciliation with Britain, as well summarized in the phrase,

> Our present condition, is, Legislation without law; wisdom without a plan; constitution without a name; and, what is strangely astonishing, perfect Independance contending for dependance. (Paine, *Common Sense*, 84)

Paine even expressed the general process by which the Declaration would ultimately be outlined and circulated:

> Were a manifesto to be published, and despatched to foreign courts, setting forth the miseries we have endured, and the peaceable methods we have ineffectually used for redress; declaring, at the same time, that not being able, any longer, to live happily or safely under the cruel disposition of the British court, we had been driven to the necessity of breaking off all connections with her; at the same time, assuring all such courts of our peacable disposition towards them, and of our desire of entering into trade with them: Such a memorial would produce more good effects to this Continent, than if a ship were freighted with petitions to Britain. (Paine, *Common Sense*, 75-76)

As the second Continental Congress convened in May of 1776, the time was ripe for the call for American independence. On May 10th (Adams, C. F., *Letters*, 173-174), Congress adopted a resolution from John Adams encouraging States not having a government sufficient and able to stand apart from Britain to adopt a form of government to "best conduce to the happiness and safety of their constituents in particular and America in general" (Force, *Mahon*, 23-24). A week later, Adams wrote his wife, noting the completion of the resolution[20] in relationship to the readiness of the colonies for independence by relating to a sermon he heard on May 17th,

> I have this morning heard Mr. Duffield upon the Signs of the Times. He ran a parallel between the case of Israel and that of America, and between the conduct of Pharaoh and that of George. Jealousy that the Israelites would throw off the Government of Egypt made him issue his edict that the midwives should cast the children into the river, and the other edict that the men should make a large revenue of bricks without straw. He concluded that the course of events indicated strongly the design of Providence that we should be separated from Great Britain. (Adams, C. F., *Letters*, 173)

Then, with considered rationale from the independence-minded leaders, Richard Henry Lee of Virginia, made the motion on June 7, 1776 to declare independence. John Adams seconded the motion (Bancroft, vol. 4, 423). Lee's resolution read,

> Resolved, That these United Colonies are, and of right, ought to be, free and independent States; that they are absolved from all allegiance to the British Crown; and that all political connexion between them and the State of Great Britain is and ought to be totally dissolved. That it is expedient forthwith to take the most effectual measures for forming foreign alliances. That a plan of confederation be prepared and transmitted to the respective Colonies for their consideration and approval. (Force, *Mahon*, 33)

The resolution was debated, and on June 10th discussion was postponed until July 1st. However, Congress agreed that "meanwhile, that no time may be lost, in case Congress agree thereto, that a committee be appointed to prepare a declaration to the effect of the said first resolution" (Force, *Mahon*, 34), and on June 11, a committee comprising John Adams,

---

[20] Released with preamble on May 15th.

Thomas Jefferson, Benjamin Franklin, Roger Sherman of Connecticut and Robert Livingston of New York was appointed to draft a declaration of independence (Lanman, 523). A draft of that declaration was first read in Congress on June 28th and was reported to the Committee of the Whole for the resolution on independence on July 1, 1776. On July 2nd, Congress again took up debate of Lee's resolution for independence, debated it, then finally adopted it. The Continental Congress resolved for independence but had not yet declared it to the public (Force, *Mahon*, 38). The difference between the Resolution of Independence and the Declaration of Independence has largely been lost to history. Historian, Peter Force, spoke of the difference this way:

> the Resolution of Independence, and the Declaration of Independence, were separate and distinct measures before Congress, proposed at different times, considered at different times, and decided at different times; that the Resolution was the great question of American Independence—the Declaration was the announcement of American Independence to the world. (Force, *Mahon*, 38)

John Adams, writing to his wife on July 3, 1776, summed up the effect of independence,

> The hopes of reconciliation which were fondly entertained by multitudes of honest and well-meaning, though weak and mistaken people, have been gradually, and at last totally extinguished. Time has been given for the whole people maturely to consider the great question of independence, and to ripen their judgment, dissipate their fears, and allure their hopes, by discussing it in newspapers and pamphlets, by debating it in assemblies, conventions, committees, of safety and inspection, in town and county meetings, as well as in private conversations, so that the whole people, in every colony of the thirteen, have now adopted it as their own act. (Adams, C. F., *Letters*, 193)

Debate on the Declaration of Independence continued on July 3rd, and the final draft was approved by the Continental Congress on July 4, 1776. In the same letter to his wife, John Adams reacted to the passage of the Resolution of Independence on July 2nd with remarkable prescience, except that his prediction proved true for the Declaration of Independence on July 4th rather than the Resolution of Independence:

> The second day of July, 1776, will be the most memorable epocha in the history of America. I am apt to believe that it will be celebrated by succeeding generations as the great anniversary festival. It ought to be commemorated as the day of deliverance, by solemn acts of devotion to God Almighty. It ought to be solemnized with pomp and parade, with shows, games, sports, guns, bells, bonfires, and illuminations, from one end of this continent to the other, from this time forward forevermore. (Adams, C. F., *Letters*,193-194)

The Declaration was hurriedly printed by John Dunlap the night of July 4th, and a copy inserted into the "rough journal" of the Continental Congress for July 4 (Department of State, 90) with the printed text followed by the words "Signed by Order and in Behalf of the Congress, John Hancock, President. Attest. Charles Thomson, Secretary" (Force, *Mahon*, 61).

While Lee, Adams and the rest of the Congress had resolved for independence and voted to approve the Declaration of Independence, only Hancock's signature appeared underneath the approved declaration while the Declaration was "fairly engrossed on parchment," creating the durable parchment version known today (Force, *Mahon*, 61). The other delegates began to sign the engrossed parchment Declaration upon the return of Congress beginning August 2, 1776, with all signatures not being obtained until as late as November. The Declaration was open to signing by all members of Congress, not just those voting for it on July 4th. Only a few never signed, including Robert Livingston, member of the committee to draft the Declaration of Independence. Livingston was recalled to New York before enjoying the opportunity, and then was seated in the New

York Convention rather than returning to Congress. Only one man refused to sign, John Alsop of New York. He resigned Congress instead (Force, *Mahon*, 61, 65). The Declaration was closed to signatures at the end of 1776, but Thomas McKean, absent for military duty, followed by service in the Delaware Constitutional Convention, signed by resolution of Congress when he returned in December of 1777 (Force, *Mahon*, 63, 65).

The July 4th approval of the Declaration came with a resolution that copies "be sent to the several assemblies, conventions, and committees, or councils of safety, and to the several commanding officers of the Continental troops; that it be proclaimed in each of the United States, and at the head of the army" (Lanman, 527). The first public readings of the Declaration occurred at 12 noon on July 8, 1776, the Declaration being read simultaneously in the Pennsylvania cities of Easton and Philadelphia, and at Trenton, New Jersey. Acceptance of the Declaration by the colonists, as was predicted by John Adams' letter on July 3rd, is exemplified by the response to its reading in Easton, Pennsylvania, about 50 miles north of Philadelphia. The Declaration of Independence was read on the courthouse steps by Robert Levers (Deshler, 168),

> This day, the Declaration of Independence was received here, and proclaimed in the following order: the Colonel, and all other field officers of the First Battalion repaired to the courthouse, the light infantry company marching there with drums beating, fifes playing, and the standard (the device for which is the thirteen united colonies) which was ordered to be displayed; and after that the Declaration was read aloud to a great number of spectators, who gave their hearty assent with three loud huzzas, and cried out, "May *God* long preserve and unite the Free and Independent States of *America*." (Force, *Archives*, 5th ser., vol. 1, 119)

In Baltimore, Maryland, a similar scene played out at the July 29th reading, which lead into a more raucous "celebration" in the evening,

> Baltimore, July 30. Yesterday, by order of the Committee of this town, the declaration of Independency of the United

States of America was read at the Court House to a numerous
and respectable body of Militia and the company of Artillery,
and other principal inhabitants of this town and county, which
was received with general applause and heart-felt satisfaction.
And at night the town was illuminated and, at the same time,
the Effigy of our late King was carted through the town and
committed to the flames amidst the acclamations of many
hundreds – the just reward of a Tyrant. (Deshler, 182-183)

Similar responses were recorded throughout the colonies (Deshler, 165-
187). It was done. America had united in the Declaration of Independence.

As John Quincy Adams put it sixty-three years later,

Independence was declared. The colonies were transformed
into States. Their inhabitants were proclaimed to be one
people, renouncing all allegiance to the British crown;
(Adams, J. Q., 9)

In the completion of the fullness of time for the Declaration of
Independence, America won the war for independence with Britain, and
King George III signed *The Definitive Treaty of Peace between the United
States of America and His Britannic Majesty* on November 30, 1782,
which included the phrase,

His Britannic Majesty acknowledges the said United States
… to be free, sovereign and independent States; that he treats
with them as such; and for himself, his heirs and successors,
relinquishes all claims to the government, propriety and
territorial rights of the same, and every part thereof. (United
States, 479)

The King of Britain did not grant independence to America, he
acknowledged it, confirming that independence had existed from the
moment it was resolved and declared in the American Declaration of
Independence.

Structure of the Declaration

The Declaration of Independence is structured with a preamble, a statement of natural rights, a summary of the proper role of government and the conditions for abolishing and replacing government, followed by the list of grievances against the British King, then a statement of separation, and is closed with a statement of commitment and signatures. The King, only, is held directly responsible for the grievances of the Declaration, not the parliament or the British citizenry. The reason is well-expressed by Daniel Webster in his eulogy for John Adams and Thomas Jefferson:

> The king was known, indeed, to have acted, as in other cases, by his ministers, and with his parliament; but as our ancestors had never admitted themselves subject either to ministers or to Parliament, there were no reasons to be given for now refusing obedience to their authority. This clear and obvious necessity of founding the declaration on the misconduct of the king himself, gives to that instrument its personal application, and its character of direct and pointed accusation. (Webster, *Eulogy*, 162)

In creating this structure for the Declaration of Independence, Thomas Jefferson drew from his own, *A Summary View of the Rights of British America*, and the *Declaration and Resolves of the First Continental Congress*. In so doing, he maintained continuity with those prior appeals as British subjects and the final case for independence. Jefferson also simplified the document, designing the Declaration to provide a straightforward rationale and argument for independence while laying out the very philosophy and principles on which the foundational culture and new government for America could be laid.

The Declaration of Independence

The text of the engrossed parchment Declaration of Independence reads:

A DECLARATION BY THE REPRESENTATIVES OF THE UNITED STATES OF AMERICA, IN CONGRESS ASSEMBLED.

When, in the course of human events, it becomes necessary for one people to dissolve the political bands which have connected them with another, and to assume, among the powers of the earth, the separate and equal station to which the laws of nature and of nature's God entitle them, a decent respect to the opinions of mankind requires that they should declare the causes which impel them to the separation.

We hold these truths to be self-evident, that all men are created equal; that they are endowed by their Creator with certain unalienable rights; that among these are life, liberty, and the pursuit of happiness. That to secure these rights, governments are instituted among men, deriving their just powers from the consent of the governed; that whenever any form of government becomes destructive of these ends, it is the right of the people to alter or to abolish it, and to institute a new government, laying its foundation on such principles, and organizing its powers in such form, as to them shall seem most likely to effect their safety and happiness. Prudence, indeed, will dictate that governments long established, should not be changed for light and transient causes; and accordingly, all experience hath shown, that mankind are more disposed to suffer, while evils are sufferable, than to right themselves by abolishing the forms to which they are accustomed. But when a long train of abuses and usurpations, pursuing invariably the same object, evinces a design to reduce them under absolute despotism, it is their right, it is their duty, to throw off such government, and to provide new guards for their future security. Such has been the patient sufferance of these Colonies, and such is now the necessity which constrains them to alter their former systems of government. The history of the present king of Great Britain is a history of repeated injuries and usurpations, all having, in direct object, the establishment of an absolute tyranny over these States. To prove this, let facts be submitted to a candid world: —

He has refused his assent to laws the most wholesome and necessary for the public good.

He has forbidden his Governors to pass laws of immediate and pressing importance, unless suspended in their operation till his assent should be obtained; and, when so suspended, he has utterly neglected to attend to them.

He has refused to pass other laws for the accommodation of large districts of people, unless those people would relinquish the right of representation in the Legislature; a right inestimable to them, and formidable to tyrants only.

He has called together legislative bodies at places unusual, uncomfortable, and distant from the depository of their public records, for the sole purpose of fatiguing them into compliance with his measures.

He has dissolved representative houses repeatedly, for opposing, with manly firmness, his invasions on the rights of the people.

He has refused, for a long time after such dissolutions, to cause others to be elected; whereby the legislative powers, incapable of annihilation, have returned to the people at large for their exercise; the State remaining, in the mean time, exposed to all the danger of invasion from without, and convulsions within.

He has endeavored to prevent the population of these States; for that purpose, obstructing the laws for naturalization of foreigners; refusing to pass others to encourage their migration hither, and raising the conditions of new appropriations of lands.

He has obstructed the administration of justice, by refusing his assent to laws for establishing judiciary powers.

He has made judges dependent on his will alone, for the tenure of their offices, and the amount and payment of their salaries.

He has erected a multitude of new offices, and sent hither swarms of officers to harass our people and eat out their substance.

He has kept among us, in times of peace, standing armies, without the consent of our legislature.

He has affected to render the military independent of, and superior to, the civil power.

He has combined, with others, to subject us to a jurisdiction foreign to our constitution, and unacknowledged by our laws; giving his assent to their acts of pretended legislation.

For quartering large bodies of armed troops among us:

For protecting them, by a mock trial, from punishment, for any murders which they should commit on the inhabitants of these States:

For cutting off our trade with all parts of the world:

For imposing taxes on us without our consent:

For depriving us, in many cases, of the benefits of trial by jury:

For transporting us beyond seas to be tried for pretended offences:

For abolishing the free system of English laws, in a neighboring province, establishing therein an arbitrary government, and enlarging its boundaries, so as to render it at once an example and fit instrument for introducing the same absolute rule into these Colonies:

For taking away our charters, abolishing our most valuable laws, and altering, fundamentally, the powers of our governments:

For suspending our own legislatures, and declaring themselves invested with power to legislate for us in all cases whatsoever.

He has abdicated government here, by declaring us out of his protection, and waging war against us.

He has plundered our seas, ravaged our coasts, burnt our towns, and destroyed the lives of our people.

He is, at this time, transporting large armies of foreign mercenaries to complete the works of death, desolation, and tyranny, already begun, with circumstances of cruelty and perfidy scarcely paralleled in the most barbarous ages, and totally unworthy the head of a civilized nation.

He has constrained our fellow-citizens, taken captive on the high seas, to bear arms against their country, to become the executioners of their friends and brethren, or to fall themselves by their hands.

He has excited domestic insurrections among us, and has endeavored to bring on the inhabitants of our frontiers, the merciless Indian savages, whose known rule or warfare is an undistinguished destruction of all ages, sexes, and conditions.

In every stage of these oppressions, we have petitioned for redress in the most humble terms; our repeated petitions have been answered only by repeated injury. A prince, whose character is thus marked by every act which may define a tyrant, is unfit to be the ruler of a free people.

Nor have we been wanting in attention to our British brethren. We have warned them, from time to time, of attempts made by their legislature to extend an unwarrantable jurisdiction over us. We have reminded them of the circumstances of our emigration and settlement here. We have appealed to their native justice and magnanimity, and we have conjured them, by the ties of our common kindred, to disavow these usurpations, which would inevitably interrupt our connections and correspondence. They, too, have been deaf to the voice of justice and consanguinity. We must, therefore, acquiesce in the necessity which demands our separation, and hold them, as we hold the rest of mankind, enemies in war, in peace friends.

We, therefore, the Representatives of the United States of America, in General Congress assembled, appealing to the Supreme Judge of the world for the rectitude of our intentions, do, in the name and by the authority of the good people of these Colonies, solemnly publish and declare, That these United Colonies are, and, of right, ought to be, *free and independent States*; that they are absolved from all allegiance to the British crown, and that all political connection between them and the State of Great Britain is, and ought to be, totally dissolved; and that, as *free and independent States*, they have full power to levy war, conclude peace, contract alliances, establish commerce, and to do all other acts and things which *independent States* may of right do. And, for the support of this Declaration, with a firm reliance on the protection of Divine Providence, we mutually pledge to each other, our lives, our fortunes, and our sacred honor.

John Hancock.

New Hampshire.

| Josiah Bartlett, | William Whipple, | Matthew Thornton. |

Massachusetts Bay.

| Samuel Adams, | Robert Treat Paine, | Elbridge Gerry. |
| John Adams, | | |

Rhode Island.

| Stephen Hopkins, | William Ellery. |

Connecticut.

| Roger Sherman, | William Williams, | Oliver Wolcott. |
| Samuel Huntington, | | |

New York.

| William Floyd, | Francis Lewis, | Lewis Morris. |
| Philip Livingston, | | |

New Jersey.

Richard Stockton,	Francis Hopkinson,	Abraham Clark.
John Witherspoon,	John Hart,	

Pennsylvania.

Robert Harris,	John Morton,	George Taylor,
Benjamin Rush,	George Clymer,	James Wilson,
Benjamin Franklin,	James Smith,	George Ross.

Delaware.

Caesar Rodney,	George Reed,	Thomas McKean.

Maryland.

Samuel Chase,	William Pace,	Thomas Stone.
Charles Carroll, of Carrollton,		

Virginia.

George Wythe,	Benjamin Harrison,	Francis Lightfoot Lee,
Richard Henry Lee,	Thomas Nelson, Jr.,	Carter Braxton.
Thomas Jefferson,		

North Carolina.

William Hooper,	Joseph Hewes,	John Penn.

South Carolina.

Edward Rutledge,	Thomas Lynch, Jr.,	Arthur Middleton.
Thomas Heywood, Jr.,		

Georgia.

Button Gwinnett,	Lyman Hall,	George Walton.

Resolved, That copies of the Declaration be sent to the several assemblies, conventions, and committees, or councils of safety, and to the several commanding officers of the Continental troops; that it be proclaimed in each of the United States, and at the head of the army. (Lanman, 524-527)

The Declaration Defines the "American Mind"

The Declaration of Independence was something new at the time of its writing, yet it comprised principles and ideals that were commonly known to the people, if not timeless. It was more than a complaint letter to the colonial authorities. The colonies had appealed many times to the King's governors and to the King himself. It also was never a declaration of war on Britain. Nor was it a ploy to bring the King to the negotiating table for reconciliation. The Continental Congress did not expect this document to change the mind of any British oppressor. They had already made those appeals and the case for taking up arms in defense of their rights. The Declaration of Independence simply stated the facts and effected the parting of company with Britain as the Continental Congress had resolved, while establishing the social compact for the people of the new United States of America. No begging, no threats, no ultimatum, no timeframe for reconsideration, no amendment process. The Declaration of Independence was final and irrevocable.

The Declaration of Independence provides the vision statement for America. It says what America is to be about and why. No one had yet created the structure for America, other than knowing it consisted of the disparate States engaged in the Continental Congress. There was no Constitution, not even the Articles of Confederation. It was just two months before the Declaration was finalized that the Continental Congress had resolved to tell the colonies that they should prepare their own governments. Still, men had gathered from thirteen independent colonies and created a vision that united them as Americans, with a common purpose that went beyond throwing off the oppression and paternalism of the Britannic King.

Thomas Jefferson, in a letter written in 1825, just a year before his death, confirmed this vision,

> But with respect to our rights, and the acts of the British government contravening those rights, there was but one opinion on this side of the water. All American whigs thought alike on these subjects. When forced, therefore, to resort to arms for redress, an appeal to the tribunal of the world was deemed proper for our justification. This was the object of the Declaration of Independence. Not to find out new principles, or new arguments, never before thought of, not merely to say things which had never been said before; but to place before mankind the common sense of the subject, in terms so plain and firm as to command their assent, and to justify ourselves in the independent stand we are compelled to take. Neither aiming at originality of principle or sentiment, nor yet copied

from any particular and previous writing, **it was intended to be an expression of the American mind**, and to give to that expression the proper tone and spirit called for by the occasion. All its authority rests then on the harmonizing sentiments of the day, whether expressed in conversation, in letters, printed essays, or in the elementary books of public right, as Aristotle, Cicero, Locke, Sidney, &c. The historical documents which you mention as in your possession, ought all to be found, and I am persuaded you will find, to be corroborative of the facts and principles advanced in that Declaration. (Jefferson, *Writings*, vol. 7, 407, emphasis added)

The Declaration of Independence expressed common sense which commanded assent and was intended as an expression of the "American mind!"

The Declaration of Independence gained its authority from the "harmonizing sentiments of the day," the common-sense truths gained across time, and the trials of history that led to America's fullness of time; and those experiences in the Colonies and by the people contemporary to its writing. The Declaration was "self-evident" from history and experience. And it justified the Constitution and Bill of Rights that followed from its facts and principles.

The Declaration of Independence fully expresses the "American Mind," drawn from timeless principles and from the spirit of the American people. It is the master architect's vision from which the plans are drawn, supported by deep understanding of structures and aesthetics; appealing to the most common needs yet conveying a timeless sense of priceless value. An architect does not sit down to draw blueprints and select materials for a house without first understanding the purpose of the home. Will it support a small or large family? Is it intended for a warm or cold climate? Should it be expensive and extravagant, or cost-conscious and pedestrian? Only after these, and many more, questions, does the architect begin to draw up plans, select materials and ensure a solid foundation is specified to establish the vision. And, necessarily, the vision cannot significantly change mid-project without destroying the underlying plans, incurring great cost, and extending the time until the vision can be completed. Changes can always be made to keep the house contemporary and popular: an addition on the back, a new style of siding, or some new shrubs by the front door. If these changes fit the vision, they will enhance the value of the home while reflecting the individual taste of the current owner. But if they clash with the vision built into the house – like a hot tub on the front porch in a genteel neighborhood – they will reduce the home's value, draw contempt from the neighbors and cause strife within the household.

The Declaration of Independence is the cornerstone upon which the building of America stands. It can never change without undermining the foundation and risking collapse. It marks the date of the start of the construction, not its completion – America celebrates Independence Day from the date of the Declaration, not from the cessation of hostilities or peace with Britain in 1783 (United States, 477- 484), and not from the date of the Articles of Confederation ratified in 1781[21] or even the Constitution, the supreme law of America, which was not ratified until June 21, 1788.

The Declaration of Independence is like a biblical memorial[22] set for remembrance for generations to come. John Quincy Adams declared even more fervently,

> Fellow-citizens, the ark of your covenant is the Declaration of Independence. (Adams, J.Q., 119)

The ark of the covenant was an ornate vessel prescribed by God and built by the Israelites. It held the stone tablets of the Ten Commandments, a jar of manna from the Israelite's forty-year wandering in the desert, and the staff of Aaron, through whom God established the priesthood of the Israelites (Hebrews 9:4). On the lid of the ark was the mercy seat from which God met with Moses to give him commands for the Israelite people

---

[21] Adopted by Continental Congress on November 15, 1777, but not ratified until March 1, 1781
[22] For example, Joshua 4:6.

(Exodus 25:10-17). This remarkable metaphor by John Quincy Adams exhibits the understanding of the Declaration of Independence as being the mechanism by which American government could fulfill its godly purpose in liberty. It was built to espouse the laws of God, to show God's blessing on men like the providing of manna, and to define God's guidance as the source for righteous governance.

Like biblical memorials, the ideas and principles for which the Declaration of Independence stands are good, and timeless, regardless of subsequent failures to righteously address them. For this reason, some would have the Declaration forgotten and the Constitution raised as the banner of American culture. They want to be able to ignore or change the righteous vision of America's founding. The Constitution is to be hailed as the plan that has enabled America to weather many storms, but it could not have been, and likely would not have lasted, without the vision memorialized in the American Declaration of Independence; the American Mind.

Distilling Culture from the American Mind

The American Declaration of Independence, as the American Mind, is the guiding light of American law and defines America's foundational culture. The Declaration was written to explain the plight, actions, goals, responsibilities, beliefs, and aspirations of the colonial American people. Consider the following elements of the Declaration. All the other founding documents simply fill in the structure to protect and explain the culture that the Declaration envisions.

1. A decent respect to the opinions of mankind requires that they [who are separating from their former government] should declare the causes which impel them to the separation.

2. We hold these truths to be self-evident, that all men are created equal, that they are endowed by their Creator with certain unalienable Rights, that among these are Life, Liberty and the pursuit of Happiness.

3. That to secure these rights, Governments are instituted among Men, deriving their just powers from the consent of the governed ...

4. That whenever any Form of Government becomes destructive of these ends [of securing the unalienable rights of people], it is the Right of the People to alter or to abolish it, and to institute new Government ...

5. Governments long established should not be changed for light and transient causes; and accordingly all experience hath shewn, that mankind are more disposed to suffer, while evils are sufferable, than to right themselves by abolishing the forms to which they are accustomed.

6. When a long train of abuses and usurpations, pursuing invariably the same Object evinces a design to reduce them under absolute Despotism, it is their right, it is their duty, to throw off such Government, and to provide new Guards for their future security.

7. Appealing to the Supreme Judge of the world for the rectitude of our intentions ...

8. And for the support of this Declaration, with a firm reliance on the protection of Divine Providence, we mutually pledge to each other our Lives, our Fortunes and our sacred Honor.

Boiled down to their essence and written in more modern terms, the foundational American Culture, according to the Declaration of Independence, is:

Basic truths are self-evident and eternal, not created by man or government. (2)

Men have unalienable rights that come from God, not from man or government. (2)

All men are created equal by God. (2)

Rights have a duty aspect; respect the rights of others and offer rationale for actions that rightly concern them. (1, 2, 7)

Seek what is righteous according to God. (7)

Sacrifice all for right principles. (8)

Cover over the inconsequential mild transgressions of others. (5)

Governments are tools to secure God-given rights. (3)

Government power is only valid when just. (3, 4, 6)

Governments are temporary whereas people's rights are permanent. (2, 3, 4, 6)

People tend to, and should, be patient with the failings of government. (5)

Tyrannical government must be replaced. (4, 6)

Anarchy is not an alternative to government. (4)

This American Culture is one of individual liberty, truth, equality and duty, and seeks the preservation of these virtues for posterity. It is not prescriptive and legalistic in behavior or devised to control and subdue the people. Legalism and control belong to Confucianism, theocracies, and Mao's communist Cultural Revolution.[23] America relies on the peoples' love of the very liberty which allows an individual to act against American Culture to maintain American Culture. No other nation in time or place has been built on such a philosophy.

---

[23] Mao Zedong, the founding father of the communist People's Republic of China and Chairman of the Communist Party of China from 1949 to 1976 launched the "cultural revolution" to restore the Marxist/Leninist ideology of China and reassert his control, which was ebbing in the 1960s and 1970s.

Philosophy of the Declaration

The opening line of the Declaration of Independence proclaims the equality of mankind, and thus the basis of government, to be given by the "Law of Nature and Nature's God."

The "Law of Nature," or Natural Law is the philosophy which predominated colonial American political thought. Natural Law philosophy in the colonial era held the premise that there is no divine right of kings to rule, or to inherit rule, and that all men are equal in a state of nature. Natural Law recognizes God but, being a social philosophy and not a religion, does not expound the details of the character of God. The Law of Nature is based on reason in relationships between men in society and government. As philosopher John Locke put it,

> Reason, which God hath given to be the Rule betwixt Man and Man. (Locke, 301)

The laws of "Nature's God" refers to revealed or spiritual laws made known to man by God. Colonial American religion and education[24] was almost universally based on the Bible because the American colonies had largely been founded by European Christians seeking religious freedom. Therefore, whether Christian, Deist or atheist, the founders understood that the law of the civilized world through the ages was based on the laws of Nature's God as expressed in the Bible. John Locke put it very plainly,

> Thus the Law of Nature stands as an Eternal Rule to all Men, Legislators as well as others. The Rules that they make for other Mens Actions, must, as well as their own and other Mens Actions, be conformable to the Law of Nature, i.e. to the Will of God, of which that is a Declaration, and the fundamental Law of Nature being the preservation of Mankind, no humane sanction can be good, or valid against it.

---

[24] For example, *The American Spelling Book* by Noah Webster, 1793.

Humane Laws are measures in respect of Men whose actions they must direct, howbeit such measures they are as have also their higher Rules to be measured by, which rules are two, the Law of God, and the Law of Nature; so that Laws Humane must be made according to the general Laws of Nature, and without contradiction to any positive law of Scripture, otherwise they are ill made. (Locke, 270)

Therefore, the Declaration of Independence makes Natural Law, in close conjunction with the law of "Nature's God," the basis of American law and culture. Natural Law is not a political system. It is the underlying truth, the way things should be; in modern terms, the "worldview," for all political systems. Man, in the state of nature, has no politics, only personal beliefs. When men form societies and seek to combine their beliefs into laws to better effect their liberties and maintain their rights, only then do political systems come into play.

That Natural Law is the basis for American law and culture is fully supported in *An Analysis of the Laws of England*, in which Sir William Blackstone succinctly laid out the "Nature of Laws in General" in the very introduction. The Nature of Laws, as Blackstone headed the summary, is based in the Laws of Nature:

LAW is a Rule of Action, prescribed by a superior Power.

Natural Law is the Rule of human Action, prescribed by the Creator, and discoverable by the Light of Reason.

The divine, or revealed, Law (considered as a Rule of Action) is also the Law of Nature, imparted by God himself.

Society is formed for the Protection of Individuals; and States, or Government, for the Preservation of Society.

To interpret a Law, we must enquire after the Will of the Maker: Which may be collected either from the Words, the Context, the Subject-matter, the Effects and Consequence, or the Spirit and Reason of the Law. (Blackstone, *Analysis*, 2)

Blackstone further highlighted God's place in civil society that was well-established in English common law in his definitive source of English law in the latter 18th century, *Commentaries on the Laws of England*, stating:

> Man, considered as a creature, must necessarily be subject to the laws of his Creator, for he is entirely a dependent being. (Blackstone, *Commentaries*, vol. 1, 39)

and, considering the concepts of both the "Law of Nature and Nature's God:"

> Upon these two foundations, the law of nature and the law of revelation, depend all human laws; that is to say, no human laws should be suffered to contradict these. (Blackstone, *Commentaries*, vol. 1, 42)

Laws of Nature

These summary principles of the law laid out by Blackstone were derived from philosophers from Plato (Davis), Aristotle (Gillies), and Cicero (Cicero), to Thomas Aquinas[25], John Locke and Montesquieu, amongst others. John Locke is, perhaps, the most prominent and well-known 17th century Natural Law philosopher. Locke logically exposited the work of his predecessors in his tome, *Two Treatises of Government*. His first treatise addresses the divine right of kings, and the second develops natural law and the proper role of government in society.

Per Locke, Natural Law is the foundation of all society. The founders were in strong agreement. Consider how directly the Declaration of Independence borrows from Locke's *Two Treatises of Government*.

---

[25] Notably Acquinas' treatise on Law from *Summa Theologiae*.

Declaration of Independence	Locke's *Two Treatises of Government*
"We hold these truths to be self-evident, that all men are created equal, that they are endowed by their Creator with certain unalienable Rights, that among these are Life, Liberty and the pursuit of Happiness."	"The state of nature has a law of nature to govern it, which obliges every one: and reason, which is that law, teaches all mankind, who will but consult it, that being all equal and independent, no one ought to harm another in his life, health, liberty, or possessions." (169)
"That to secure these rights, Governments are instituted among Men, deriving their just powers from the consent of the governed,"	"for without this [legislative sanction of elected representatives] the law could not have that, which is absolutely necessary to its being a law, the consent of the society, over whom no body can have a power to make laws, but by their own consent, and by authority received from them." (267-268)

Declaration of Independence	Locke's *Two Treatises of Government*
"That whenever any Form of Government becomes destructive of these ends, it is the Right of the People to alter or to abolish it, and to institute new Government, laying its foundation on such principles and organizing its powers in such form, as to them shall seem most likely to effect their Safety and Happiness."	"whenever the legislators endeavour to take away, and destroy the property of the people, or to reduce them to slavery under arbitrary power, they put themselves into a state of war with the people, who are thereupon absolved from any farther obedience, and are left to the common refuge, which God hath provided for all men, against force and violence." (337)
"But when a long train of abuses and usurpations, pursuing invariably the same Object evinces a design to reduce them under absolute Despotism, it is their right, it is their duty, to throw off such Government, and to provide new Guards for their future security."	"using force upon the people without authority, and contrary to the trust put in him that does so, is a state of war with the people, who have a right to reinstate their legislative in the exercise of their power: … when they are hindered by any force from what is so necessary to the society, and wherein the safety and preservation of the people consists, the people have a right to remove it by force." (286)

These phrases, comprising almost the entirety of the preamble of the Declaration of Independence, are very recognizable in John Locke's work. This in no way demeans the work of Thomas Jefferson. He artfully collected the relevant philosophical points and crafted them into a concise and meaningful introduction in accord with the culture of colonial America. He and the drafting committee knew and lived by these principles, so it was not an undue challenge to bring them together. That Jefferson selected these key elements of Natural Law philosophy, and did not couch them in the Lockean language of being in a state of war, with rights to kill one's adversary, fully solidifies the precept that America was founded on the principles of the Law of Nature and of Nature's God with a desire for peace and prosperity.

While the preamble closely reflects Natural Law from John Locke's *Two Treatises of Government*, the list of grievances against the British King are also directly reflected in Locke's "bounds of trust" that are required for legitimate government:

> These are the bounds which the trust, that is put in them by the society, and the law of God and nature, have set to the legislative power of every common-wealth, in all forms of government. First, They are to govern by promulgated established laws, not to be varied in particular cases, but to have one rule for rich and poor, for the favourite at court, and the country man at plough. Secondly, These laws also ought to be designed for no other end ultimately, but the good of the people. Thirdly, They must not raise taxes on the property of the people, without the consent of the people, given by themselves, or their deputies. And this properly concerns only such governments where the legislative is always in being, or at least where the people have not reserved any part of the legislative to deputies, to be from time to time chosen by themselves. Fourthly, The legislative neither must nor can transfer the power of making laws to any body else, or place it any where, but where the people have. (Locke, 276-277)

It can fairly be said that all the listed grievances[26] of the Declaration of Independence regard law or application of law that is not designed for the good of the colonists, which is the second point in Locke's bounds of trust.

---

[26] Refer to *The Cause of Revolution* in the Appendix.

Relating to Locke's first point, the list of grievances cites many instances of the King governing outside of established law by ignoring laws established by colonial assemblies, and every charge involved his governing by different criteria for the colonists from other British subjects. The King was also guilty of violating Locke's fourth bound of trust by moving legislative assemblies to far locations. As for "taxation without representation," by the King, the breach of that bound of trust with the American colonists was likely the main grievance in the "long train of abuses" leading to the American Declaration of Independence.

Laws of Nature's God

The signers of the Declaration of Independence were well-educated and believed in, or assented to, the existence of a benevolent and just God actively ruling in the lives of mankind. John Quincy Adams corroborated this understanding of the founders in discussion of the Declaration of Independence in his 1839, *Jubilee of the Constitution*:

> That to secure the rights of life, liberty and the pursuits of happiness, governments are instituted among men, deriving their just powers from the consent of the governed. All this, is by the laws of nature and of nature's God, and of course presupposes the existence of a God, the moral ruler of the universe, and a rule of right and wrong, of just and unjust, binding upon man preceding all institutions of human society and of government. (Adams, J.Q., 13-14)

Adams also noted that the Declaration of Independence was written from a passion…

> ascending for the foundation of human government to the laws of nature and of God, written upon the heart of man. (Adams, J.Q., 17)

The devout faith with which Adams writes about the Declaration's appeals to Nature's God may not have been held with as great conviction by all of the signers, but by their signing it was surely acknowledged, just as it was acknowledged through a resolution of the Continental Congress calling for prayer and fasting (Continental Congress, Journal, 155) as the Congress assessed its war footing with Britain.

Comprehending the founders' acknowledgement of God, the Declaration of Independence stakes the fate and future of America on an appeal to God, establishing "Nature's God" as the source for America's law and culture. It also expands upon that call by stating that God is man's "Creator," the "Supreme Judge of the World," and "divine Providence." Each of these appellations for God as the source of revealed law is supported by the Bible.

> **Law of Nature** – "for it is not the hearers of the [Old Testament] Law [from God] who are just before God, but the doers of the Law will be justified. For when Gentiles who do not have the Law do instinctively the things of the Law, these, not having the Law, are a law to themselves, in that they show the work of the Law written in their hearts, their conscience bearing witness and their thoughts alternately accusing or else defending them." (Romans 2:13-15)

> **Nature's God** – "For since the creation of the world His invisible attributes, His eternal power and divine nature, have been clearly seen, being understood through what has been made, so that they are without excuse." (Romans 1:20)

> **Man's Creator** – "God created man in His own image, in the image of God He created him; male and female He created them." (Genesis 1:27)

> **Supreme Judge of the World** – "And the heavens declare His righteousness, For God Himself is judge." (Psalms 50:6)

> **Divine Providence** – "He established the earth upon its foundations, so that it will not totter forever and ever ... He sends forth springs in the valleys; they flow between the mountains; they give drink to every beast of the field; the wild donkeys quench their thirst. Beside them the birds of the

heavens dwell; they lift up their voices among the branches. He waters the mountains from His upper chambers; the earth is satisfied with the fruit of His works. He causes the grass to grow for the cattle, and vegetation for the labor of man, so that he may bring forth food from the earth, and wine which makes man's heart glad, so that he may make his face glisten with oil, and food which sustains man's heart ... They all wait for You to give them their food in due season. You give to them, they gather it up; You open Your hand, they are satisfied with good. You hide Your face, they are dismayed; You take away their spirit, they expire and return to their dust. You send forth Your Spirit, they are created; and You renew the face of the ground." (Psalm 104)

Each name for God in the Declaration of Independence also defines an interaction or relationship with mankind and therefore an expectation of God's participation in the America created through the Declaration. "Nature's God" acknowledges God's participation in all of nature and, with God as "Creator," that the Declaration not only declares independence, but assents that God is the creator of all things, irrespective of mankind's religious and sectarian lines. "Supreme Judge of the World" acknowledges the righteousness of God and establishes the law of God as the pinnacle of law and the benchmark for the laws of man. And God as "Divine Providence" is probably the most often used designation by the founders because it connotes the active participation of God in providing for the good of mankind.

Whether the Continental Congress intentionally expressed this multi-faceted character of God or did it unconsciously is debatable[27]. Either case expresses something fantastic about the founders' trust in the divine. If expressed intentionally, the Congress representing the whole of the people acknowledged and honored God as the guide and authority for America for all time. If expressed unconsciously, then the majesty and character of

---

[27] Congress added "Supreme Judge of the World" and "Divine Providence" to the text of Jefferson's Declaration of Independence (Jefferson, *Writings*, vol. 1, 19, 25-26).

God was so well-rooted in the founding American culture that God was implicitly sealed as the beacon for society and government in America. The net result is the same.

Law for a Moral and Religious People

The American colonies were founded by people principally seeking freedom to worship God and live according to the dictates of their consciences. They certainly did not all worship and believe the same way, in fact the colonies were often delineated by doctrinal differences. There also would have been some people who were agnostic or atheist. But, as backed by Blackstone and as secularly put by Jefferson, the common sense of the American culture was one of Christian morality and belief in a Creator God. These same people were also strongly behind the self-evident truths of the laws of nature as explained by Enlightenment philosophers, and none were seeking a priestly rule or theocratic government. Therefore, the moral, if not religious, foundation of Nature's God for the Declaration of Independence, and America's founding, was completely rational and consistent with the establishment of government. James Wilson, signer of the Declaration and later Supreme Court Justice, looked at civil law, reasoned from the law of nature, and religion this way:

> Far from being rivals or enemies, religion and law are twin sisters, friends, and mutual assistants. Indeed, these two sciences run into each other. The divine law, as discovered by reason and the moral sense, forms an essential part of both. (Wilson, 106)

This combination of Law of Nature and Nature's God may confound Christians and other religious believers who consider biblical law from God to be the sole source of law, and it may confound the irreligious who fear a theocratic government that weighs law against biblical standards. Yet the American founders unified behind these principles without concern for abridgment of individual liberty.[28] The morality of the Bible was unimpeachable in society.

This dual nature of colonial political thought should be of comfort to all. It affirms the freedom of religion as declared in the First Amendment of the Constitution. It provides room for people of all religions, and no religion, to relate to each other in peace through reason, or through the revelatory Natural Law of Thomas Aquinas and the Christian revivalist theologians of the Great Awakening.

Furthermore, for Christians and Jews, this understanding should drive acceptance of moral and righteous behavior of those who believe differently. The Bible speaks of religious "outsiders" who were accepted as allies by their righteous actions, without requiring a confession of faith.

Jesus instructed his disciples to leave a man alone in his good works, because those works made no affront to Jesus' ministry, and even helped to further it:

> John answered and said, "Master, we saw someone casting out demons in Your name; and we tried to prevent him because he does not follow along with us." But Jesus said to him, "Do not hinder him; for he who is not against you is for you." (Luke 9:49-50)

Rahab helped the Israelites conquer the city of Jericho because she recognized God's will in the effort. The Israelites accepted her into their midst and spared her and her family, despite the fact that she was not only of the enemy, but also a harlot.

> she [Rahab] came up to them on the roof, and said to the men, "I know that the Lord has given you the land, and that the terror of you has fallen on us, and that all the inhabitants of the land have melted away before you. ... for the Lord your

---

[28] Other than by preventing establishment of a single view of biblical understanding as the correct one.

God, He is God in heaven above and on earth beneath. (Joshua 2:8-9,11)

... Rahab the harlot and her father's household and all she had, Joshua spared; and she has lived in the midst of Israel to this day, for she hid the messengers whom Joshua sent to spy out Jericho. (Joshua 6:25)

This is not to say that all philosophical approaches are equal to the tenets of the Laws of Nature and Nature's God in sustaining a just government. But it does show that morality and recognition of Nature's God as the benevolent Creator and Provider is the nexus of culture upon which a just government supporting liberty can be built. There must always be an active fragment of the populace holding to this American culture or the system will fall apart. John Adams made that understanding clear in a letter to the Massachusetts Militia, October, 11, 1798:[29]

Because We have no Government armed with Power capable of contending with human Passions unbridled by morality and Religion. Avarice, Ambition, Revenge or Galantry, would break the strongest Cords of our Constitution as a Whale goes through a Net. Our Constitution was made only for a moral and religious People. It is wholly inadequate to the government of any other. (Adams, C. F., *Works*, vol. 9, 229)

American Commitment in the Declaration of Independence

The members of the Continental Congress who voted for, and signed, the Declaration of Independence were the original American culture-bearers. Signing the Declaration of Independence was an irrevocable act of treason by these men. The delegates were fully aware of the ramifications of what they had done. It was, in fact, indelibly included in the closing text:

---

[29] While this Adams quotation regards the Constitution, Chapter 3 – *The Constitution Frames the Vision of the American Mind* will show that the Constitution reflects the Declaration of Independence.

we mutually pledge to each other our Lives, our Fortunes and our sacred Honor.

This pledge was high treason against the British Crown. It carried specific penalties under British law that clearly affected the lives and fortunes of the revolutionaries.

Sir William Blackstone wrote in *Commentaries on the Laws of England*, about the punishment for high treason:

> THE punishment of high treason in general is very solemn and terrible. 1. That the offender be drawn to the gallows, and not be carried or walk; though usually a sledge or hurdle is allowed, to preserve the offender from the extreme torment of being dragged on the ground or pavement. 2. That he be hanged by the neck, and then cut down alive. 3. That his entrails be taken out, and burned, while he is yet alive. 4. That his head be cut off. 5. That his body be divided into four parts. 6. That his head and quarters be at the king's disposal. (Blackstone, *Commentaries*, vol. 4, 92)

With the sentence of treason came attainder – the forfeiture of rights and personal property (Blackstone, *Commentaries*, vol. 4, 374). Also, came Corruption of Blood, which prohibited children or other heirs from inheriting the convicted person's property. The signers of the Declaration were truly pledging their fortunes to the cause. Blackstone described it thusly:

> The consequences of attainder are forfeiture and corruption of blood.
>
> I. Forfeiture is twofold; of real and personal estates. First, as to real estates: by attainder in high treason a man forfeits to the king all his lands and tenements of inheritance, whether fee-simple or fee-tail, and all his rights of entry on lands and tenements, which he had at the time of the offence committed, or at any time afterwards, to be for ever vested in the crown: and also the profits of all lands and tenements, which he had in his own right for life or years, so long as such interest shall

subsist. This forfeiture relates backwards to the time of the treason committed ... (Blackstone, *Commentaries*, vol. 4, 374)

II. Another immediate consequence of attainder is the corruption of blood, both upwards and downwards; so that an attainted person can neither inherit lands or other hereditaments from his ancestors, nor retain those he is already in possession of, nor transmit them by descent to any heir ... (Blackstone, *Commentaries*, vol. 4, 381)

That the signers of the Declaration bothered to go beyond life and fortune to pledge their honor, describing it as "sacred," demonstrates the conviction that their timeless personal honor, what we might today think of as a legacy, was as important to them as the temporal prices that might be paid for independence. Between life, fortune and sacred honor, the signers and supporters of the Declaration of Independence offered all that they could possibly give for the vision, principles, and culture of America. These were America's original patriots.

The Pursuit of Happiness

One of the most well-known phrases from the Declaration of Independence lists the key unalienable rights of "life, liberty and the pursuit of happiness." Of these, the "pursuit of happiness" tends to be the most misunderstood and misapplied. John Locke in his Second Treatise on Government wrote,

no one ought to harm another in his life, health, liberty, or possessions. (Locke, 169)

which is very similar but speaks of possessions rather than happiness. Locke further wrote:

The great and chief end, therefore, of men's uniting into commonwealths, and putting themselves under government, is the preservation of their property. (Locke, 261)

> By property I must be understood here, as in other places, to
> mean that property which men have in their persons as well
> as goods. (Locke, 302)

Clearly the Lockean philosophy that Jefferson and the founders espoused
was that the right role of government was the preservation of life, liberty
and property, where property also includes one's own person and the fruits
of one's labor. Montesquieu, the key Natural Law philosopher following
Locke, who was a favorite of the founders because of his proposal for three
branches of government as a check on power, also spoke of the sanctity of
personal property:

> It is a paralogism to say, that the good of the individual should
> give way to that of the public; this can never take place, except
> when the government of the community, or, in other words,
> the liberty of the subject, is concerned; this does not affect
> such cases as relate to private property, because the public
> good consists in every one's having their property, which was
> given him by the civil laws, invariably preserved.
>
> Let us therefore lay down a certain maxim, that whenever the
> public good happens to be the matter in question, it is not for
> the advantage of the public to deprive an individual of his
> property, or even to retrench the least part of it by a law, or a
> political regulation. In this case we should follow the rigor of
> the civil law, which is the *Palladium* of property.
> (Montesquieu, 361, 362)

The *Declaration and Resolves of the First Continental Congress*,
forerunner to the Declaration of Independence, uses the term, "property"
rather than "pursuit of happiness:"

> Resolved, N.C.D. 1. That they are entitled to life, liberty and
> property: and they have never ceded to any foreign power
> whatever, a right to dispose of either without their consent.
> (Morse, 182)

Even the Virginia Declaration of Rights, from Thomas Jefferson's home state, adopted on June 12, 1776, just weeks before the Declaration of Independence, adds property to happiness.

> That all men are by nature equally free and independent and have certain inherent rights, of which, when they enter into a state of society, they cannot, by any compact, deprive or divest their posterity; namely, the enjoyment of life and liberty, with the means of acquiring and possessing property, and pursuing and obtaining happiness and safety. (Virginia, 25)

Why, then, does the Declaration of Independence not specifically mention acquiring and possessing property in its list of key unalienable rights? The answer rests in the great sin of chattel slavery in America. Jefferson, who called slavery an "abominable crime," (Jefferson, *Writings*, vol. 9, 276) (Bancroft, vol. 6, 118) wrote explicit mention of property out of the Declaration to ensure that slavery – holding human beings as personal property – would not become an unquestioned, or even sanctioned, element of American culture. By limiting the Declaration to "the pursuit of happiness," the acquiring and possessing of property became part of the pursuit, but so did a slave's pursuit of freedom. Given the lens of history, this is a dissatisfactory and insufficient differentiation. But at that moment when most of the world supported slavery, this, coupled with the phrase, "all men are created equal," was radical and as revolutionary as the idea of a cobbled alliance of poor colonies parting ways with the world's greatest military and economic power.

In time, the Constitution would address slavery, again insufficiently, but with a growing intent to eliminate it; and the Bill of Rights, in the Fifth Amendment to the Constitution, would directly address individual property rights, ensuring that people are not deprived of property without due process of law.

Equality in the Declaration of Independence

Equality means that no man is naturally subordinate to another. Equality of men is a key premise in the American Mind of the Declaration of Independence, as a premise of both the Law of Nature and of Nature's God.

John Locke summarized equality in the state of nature this way:

> The state of nature has a law of nature to govern it, which obliges every one: and reason, which is that law, teaches all mankind, who will but consult it, that **being all equal and independent**, no one ought to harm another in his life, health, liberty, or possessions. (Locke, 168-169, emphasis added)

The Bible, demonstrating God's equal love, equal offer of salvation, and surety of equal judgement, says:

> For God so loved the world, that He gave His only begotten Son, that **whoever believes** in Him shall not perish, but have eternal life. For God did not send the Son into the world to judge the world, but that the world might be saved through Him. (John 3:16-17, emphasis added)

> The Lord is not slow to fulfill his promise as some count slowness, but is patient toward you, **not wishing that any should perish, but that all should reach repentance.** (2 Peter 3:9, emphasis added)

> There will be tribulation and distress for every soul of man who does evil, of the Jew first and also of the Greek,[30] but glory and honor and peace to everyone who does good, to the

---

[30] Here "Greek" means "non-Jew." As noted in the *Fullness of Time – The Advent of Jesus Christ* discussion in the Appendix, the world at the time that the book of Romans was written was dominated by a Greek culture.

Jew first and also to the Greek. **For there is no partiality with God.**[31] (Romans 2:9-11, emphasis added)

What seems to have been lost today from the concept of equality in the "Law of Nature and Nature's God," is that equality means equality under law and justice, what amounts to equality of rights, opportunity and responsibility; not equality of outcomes. When the Declaration talks about the pursuit of happiness, it does not say, or mean, that everyone will reach a certain state of happiness or have a wealth of property. When Locke talks about life, health, liberty and possessions, he cannot guarantee that everyone will have the same length of life, quality of health, or extent of possessions. Liberty may be the closest unalienable right to which equality may be said to near equal outcome, but even then, one may unjustly be deprived of liberty, or make choices, resulting in the outcome of their life being different from the opportunity made available to them in nature or in society. John Locke speaks of liberty this way:

> THE natural liberty of man is to be free from any superior power on earth, and not to be under the will or legislative authority of man, but to have only the law of nature for his rule.
>
> The liberty of man, in society, is to be under no other legislative power, but that established, by consent, in the commonwealth; nor under the dominion of any will, or restraint of any law, but what that legislative shall enact, according to the trust put in it.[32] (Locke, 182)

Therefore, if a man is under the power of an employer as a condition of employment, or puts himself in debt to another, the outcome of his

---

[31] The scriptural context is that God will give each his due regarding judgement, irrespective of who they are. God has certainly imbued some with more talents, or health, or longer life, but God will not play favorites in the final judgement.

[32] "the trust put in it" does not equate to "because you are a representative of the people you are trusted to do right by the people." Rather it means the trust pertaining to right application of the Law of Nature and Nature's God to civil laws as previously discussed.

existence may not be equal to one who works for himself, or another who inherits a fortune.

Equality under law and justice was not a guarantee throughout the better part of history, and it was never certain under the capricious rule of a king. The concept of equality offered in the Declaration of Independence was revolutionary and remains foundational to America's culture. Regardless of any government failure to support equality, as had been the case with slavery, in dealings with aboriginal Americans, internment of Japanese Americans during wartime, suffrage for women, and other instances, there is no reason to suppose that America is not built upon the virtue of equality of all men. Rather these injustices via government serve as a reminder that equality for all men is the responsibility of all men; that as a government of "We the people," each person is responsible to support the principle of equality under law and justice as a duty and responsibility of liberty.

James Wilson summarized it, writing,

> But however great the variety and inequality of men may be with regard to virtue, talents, taste, and acquirements; there is still one aspect, in which all men in society, previous to civil government, are equal. With regard to all, there is an equality in rights and in obligations; there is that "jus aequum," that equal law, in which the Romans placed true freedom. The natural rights and duties of man belong equally to all. Each forms a part of that great system, whose greatest interest and happiness are intended by all the laws of God and nature. (Wilson, 308)

There is no way to protect the equality of man while trying to force an equality of outcomes in the lives of men. All men are responsible to one another for equality in rights, therefore, no man, being obligated to respect the rights of another man, can take that man's rights for the benefit of himself or another.

Natural Rights

> The sacred rights of mankind are not to be rummaged for among old parchments or musty records, they are written, as with a sunbeam, in the whole volume of human nature, by the hand of the Divinity itself; and can never be erased or obscured by mortal power. (Hamilton, *Papers*, 133)

The outflow of the "Law of Nature and Nature's God" is liberty, which Thomas Jefferson called a "gift from God" (Jefferson, *Writings*, vol. 8, 404), and that liberty is characterized by natural rights. The Declaration of Independence called them unalienable rights because they are not conferred by anyone, nor can they be taken, or given away, although they may be left unexercised. In the state of nature, liberty is absolute, including the liberty to do evil and overwhelm the rights of others, such as stealing from or killing another person. In the absence of society and government instituted to secure the blessings of liberty, an individual has the right to do as he pleases. Each person also has the right to respond to another person who is exercising liberty in a manner that infringes upon their own liberty.

Natural rights are claims on how things should be. All people have the right and liberty to justly acquire and keep property. All have the liberty to steal, but not the right to steal, because that liberty infringes on others' natural right to property. The way it should be is "live and let live." As Locke says,

> Men living together according to reason, without a common superior on earth, with authority to judge between them, is properly the state of nature. (Locke, 179)

This concept is where liberty meets equality in the Declaration of Independence. A personal right exercised to the detriment of the rights of another inherently denies the equality of the other person.

Therefore, to every natural right there is a duty or responsibility; a state of liberty is not a state of license (Locke, 168). Licentiousness is the wanton breach of duty; boundless liberty (Bellamy), the excess of which abridges the liberty of another. This is the corollary to James Wilson's statement that, "With regard to all, there is an equality in rights and in obligations," where the obligations are the positive duty to not take license. There is a natural right to property, and a duty not to steal from others. There is a natural right to live according to one's religious beliefs, and a duty to respect the religious conscience of another. There is a right to defend one's self and family from harm, and a duty not to cause harm to other people. There is a right to pursue happiness as one sees fit, and a duty to not have that pursuit interfere with the just pursuits of another. There is no end to the list of natural rights, but each comes with a duty or responsibility if man is to live above the "kill or be killed" state of nature. Duty is not a limitation of a right, it is simply an understanding that, all men being equal in rights, each has the obligation not to abridge the rights of another (Locke, 169). Although licentiousness will occur at times, it can only be addressed in its outcome, not by its mere possibility because that possibility is the very definition of the liberty to exercise a right. That is, if the right becomes limited apart from the obligation to the rights of another in a particular situation, it ceases to be a right. For example, people have the right to free speech, including yelling as loud as possible at the moon. To limit yelling at the moon would infringe the right to free speech. But to stand outside another person's window at night yelling at the moon likely breaches an obligation to the rights of the one trying to sleep.[33]

The duty concept has very often been misconstrued as a limitation in the legal discussion of natural rights. The duty aspect of a right is distinguishable from a limitation on that right by evaluating the justice of one exercising the right if no one else is harmed, or if the other party forgives the infraction. If there is harm in all circumstances, it is a limitation, or more appropriately, an absence of the right. Otherwise, "no

---

[33] Cases in which the line of obligation/licentiousness is unclear is where civility comes into play. These concepts are discussed further in Chapter 6 – *Living the American Mind*.

harm, no foul," as the maxim goes.[34] A point of clarification is in order here. The test is with respect to the rights of another, not the sensibilities of another. Offense taken by one in view of another exercising their rights is not an abridgement of the offended party's rights. The taking of offense is a choice based in popular culture and personal beliefs which very often, probably most often, do not align with actual injury to one's rights.

Biblical law also reflects the natural state of man and the revealed law of God to manage the affairs of mankind. The Bible expresses the understanding of natural rights in the story of Cain and Abel, the first people born in the state of nature. Cain murders Abel. Cain is confronted by God, and by his crime is cursed to be a vagrant and wander the earth. Cain cries in anguish to God, "I will be a vagrant and a wanderer on the earth, and whoever finds me will kill me" (Genesis 4:14). God did not tell Cain that people would seek to kill him. Cain naturally understood that, being a murderer, by the laws of nature he would be subject to retribution by all men. John Locke explained,

> Who so sheddeth man's blood, by man shall his blood be shed. And Cain was so fully convinced, that every one had a right to destroy such a criminal, that after the murder of his brother, he cries out, Every one that findeth me, shall slay me; so plain was it writ in the hearts of all mankind. (Locke, 173)

And

> every Man hath a Right to punish the Offender, and be Executioner of the Law of Nature. (Locke, 171)

There is consistency with the truth that, "Every Man hath a Right to punish the Offender, and be Executioner of the Law of Nature" in a state of nature, and Genesis 9:6, "Whoever sheds man's blood, by man his blood shall be shed, for in the image of God He made man." God is not requiring life for

---

[34] Examples are provided in the discussion around the Bill of Rights in Chapter 4 – *The Bill of Rights Clarifies the American Mind.*

life,[35] He is saying that in Creation, which is nature, taking the life of another makes one subject to forfeiture of one's own life at the hand of all others.

This concept is challenging, and at the same time, intuitively obvious. Men in society want to believe that they are above retribution in vengeance or in fear, yet it is the first natural reaction of most individuals, and more so groups, to extract vengeance and eliminate the potential threat of a murderer living alongside them.

While men have natural rights, protecting them in a state of nature is nearly impossible. Such a state is called uncivilized or anarchy. It is characterized by the cry, "every man for himself," and at the same time the cry of the mob to "get him!" And so, as Locke put it,

> Men unite into societies, that they may have the united strength of the whole Society to secure and defend their Properties …[36] (Locke, 271)

How government secures these rights is the role of the people who then lend to government the authority to exercise the natural retribution for infringement of natural rights. All natural rights are encapsulated in "liberty." The Declaration of Independence proclaims this liberty for America and declares security of these rights to be the proper role of government.

Liberty and Freedom

The Declaration of Independence describes liberty as an unalienable right, yet nowhere does it define liberty or differentiate it from, or even mention, freedom. "Freedom" is not found in the Declaration because there is a subtle, yet fundamental, difference between liberty and freedom in the context of the document, and liberty was understood in the context of the

---

[35] God shows it acceptable to kill at times, e.g. Deutermonomy 20:16, and proper not to shed the blood of one who has killed, e.g. Exodus 21:13.
[36] Where "properties" includes their lives and liberty.

Law of Nature and Nature's God as particularly expressed by John Locke.[37]

Liberty, as implied in the Declaration of Independence, is a slate of rights, a suite of reserved personal powers. Freedom is a state of being and the ability to exercise power. Liberty is the right to be free of coercive acts by other people; freedom is a state in which one can fully exercise liberty. In an ideal state of moral civil society, liberty and freedom should be the same.

John Locke characterizes this understanding in relation to law, where the law refers to the Law of Nature and Nature's God rather than civil law:

> the end of law is not to abolish or restrain, but to preserve and enlarge freedom: for in all the states of created beings capable of laws, where there is no law, there is no freedom: for liberty is, to be free from restraint and violence from others; which cannot be, where there is no law: but freedom is not, as we are told, *A liberty for every man to do what he lists*: (for who could be free, when every other man's humour might domineer over him?) but a liberty to dispose, and order as he lists, his person, actions, possessions, and his whole property, within the allowance of those laws under which he is, and therein not to be subject to the arbitrary will of another, but freely follow his own. (Locke, 206)

Montesquieu stated something similar in *The Spirit of Laws*,

> Liberty is a right of doing whatever the laws permit; and if a citizen could do what they forbid, he would be no longer possest of liberty, because all his fellow citizens would have the same power. (Montesquieu, 112)

---

[37] Let it be said that the concept of liberty itself, and in combination with the concept of freedom, is an age-old philosophical debate which reaches minutia in differences of opinion across multiple philosophical, social and legal contexts. This discussion is targeted to an overview of the usage in the Declaration of Independence.

Therefore, liberty and freedom do not, in reality, ever fully equate. A free person, one who is not in custody of authorities, or physically enslaved, may still be coerced to violate their beliefs or deprived of their rights – be deprived of liberty.[38] To the opposite point, a free person may exceed their liberty, breaching the obligations of their rights, thereby wielding unjust power over another person.

Thomas Jefferson, in personal correspondence with John Adams in 1819, defined liberty directly, and by characterizing it as *liberty*, and *rightful liberty*, implicitly made the distinction between freedom and liberty. He also separated liberty from the limit of law, tacitly recognizing that liberty resides within the Law of Nature and Nature's God.

> Of Liberty, then I would say, that in the whole plenitude of its extent, it is unobstructed action according to our will; but rightful liberty is unobstructed action according to our will within the limits drawn around us by the equal rights of others. I do not add 'within the limits of the law,' because law is often but the tyrant's will and always so when it violates the rights of an individual. (Jefferson, *Historical Magazine*, 251)

Consider just the first two of the five rights expressed in the First Amendment to the Constitution, "free exercise of religion" and "freedom of speech." The use of "freedom of," versus "liberty of," implies the power and capability to act on the liberty. It also implies the ability to wrongly use the freedom, which would then be subject to law for the breach of duty aspect of the liberty.

The Declaration of Independence canonizes liberty because of this fundamental distinction between liberty and freedom, and the congruence of the terms in the ideal culture that it establishes. The founders understood that liberty was derived from the unalienable rights in the Law of Nature

---

[38] Noted by Tocqueville as, "…in democratic republics; there the body is left free, and the soul is enslaved" (Tocqueville, vol. 2, 260).

and Nature's God and they laid it at the base of the foundation for American society and government.

On the Loss of Liberty

Liberty is at the foundation of the American Mind, ingrained in foundational American culture that is not fleeting nor permanently changed by changes in customs or the whims of popular culture. These components of culture, at any given time, are like the level of the ocean; whereas the foundational culture is like the average level of the ocean, stable and true. Customs are like the tides, modestly variable, reasonably predictable and, on average, at the foundational level; and popular culture is like the ocean waves, unpredictable in timing, amplitude and direction, with an element driven by external catastrophic events of the moment.

That the thirteen colonies, and the states they became, ever joined together in union is a testament to the truth of liberty being at the foundation of American Culture. At the same time, no society has lasted for all time, and those that were best capable of standing the test of time have generally been destroyed from within. Liberty, once lost, is impossible to regain without societal pain, perhaps even revolution, if it can be regained at all. Christopher Gadsden, creator of the well-known Gadsden "Don't Tread on Me" flag (Editor, *Harpers*, vol. 47, 177, 180), and representative to the Continental Congress from South Carolina said,

> Our houses being constructed of brick, stone and wood, though destroyed, may be rebuilt; but liberty, once gone, is lost forever! (Davies, 17)

Benjamin Franklin concurred when he famously stated,

> They who can give up essential liberty to obtain a little temporary safety, deserve neither liberty nor safety. (Franklin, *Memoirs*, 142, 270)

John Adams said much the same to his wife, Abigail in his letter dated July 7, 1775:

> Our consolation must be this, my dear, that cities may be rebuilt, and a people reduced to poverty may acquire fresh property. But a constitution of government, once changed from freedom, can never be restored. Liberty, once lost is lost forever. (Adams, *Letters*, 76)

Certainly the most famous admonition on the preservation of liberty was given after the American Revolution by Patrick Henry, who stated to the Constitutional Convention in June of 1783,

> Guard with jealous attention the public liberty. Suspect every one who approaches that jewel. Unfortunately, nothing will preserve it, but downright force. Whenever you give up that force, you are inevitably ruined. (Wirt, 194)

And Patrick Henry also spoke the most famous words about liberty, perhaps the most famous quote from the American Revolution, given at the Second Virginia Convention on March 23, 1775,

> Is life so dear, or peace so sweet, as to be purchased at the price of chains and slavery? Forbid it, Almighty God! — I know not what course others may take; but as for me, give me liberty, or give me death! (Wirt, 94-95)

The message is clear from the American founders who studied, toiled in Congress, fought in war, and pledged all they had to the cause of American liberty. Hold on to liberty at the expense of property, safety, and even life. Hold on to liberty for posterity, for love of those who will be in the future, and out of obligation to those who sacrificed for today.

The foundational culture of the Declaration of Independence is sustained by the many identifying themselves with its precepts, even if they are not practiced, and the personal conviction and discipline of a smaller segment, the patriotic, that brings the best elements of American culture into actual practice. The American culture of equality and liberty ends, not when broader society ceases to identify themselves with it, but only when the patriotic culture-bearers concede that it is lost.

Commerce

Aside from protecting individual liberty, equality, and the security function of government, the Declaration of Independence uses just two words to express a concept that provides the sustenance to maintain both liberty and security: "establish Commerce." In more detail, "as Free and Independent States, they have full Power to levy War, conclude Peace, contract Alliances, establish Commerce, and to do all other Acts and Things which Independent States may of right do." The only explicit act expressed as a duty of Free and Independent States besides political management of foreign powers is for them to establish commerce.

Commerce is the interchange of goods. On a large scale, commerce generally comprises exchange of a product or commodity for money. On the smallest level, commerce is the act of people freely trading and exchanging by barter or use of instruments of value such as gold coinage or government currency which are durable and do not spoil. The economic atmosphere in which such commerce occurs is the so-called "free market," regulated only by an "invisible hand" as expressed by Adam Smith (Smith, *Sentiments*, 273). The understanding of economics as philosophy and science was up-and-coming during the time of America's founding, and it was recognized that commerce, by the people, supported by government, was the way to build individual and societal wealth and sustain the function of government. *Wealth of Nations,* the first, and seminal, treatise on modern economics, was published in Scotland in March of 1776 by Adam Smith, and built on the base of his philosophical work, *Moral Sentiments. Wealth of Nations* was too late to have been read by the committee that produced the Declaration, but many concepts it expressed were already naturally in practice in America, and understood by the educated leaders of the time.

Government in Commerce

Commerce is the interchange of goods between people, yet the Declaration of Independence talks about states establishing commerce. Therefore, there must be a role for government in the free interchange of goods between people. Principally, government has the same role that it has outside of commerce: to protect the rights of its citizens.

At the time of the Declaration of Independence, the British economic model was mercantilism. Mercantilism is an economic system designed to build a wealthy and powerful state through charters of monopoly proffered to favored businesses with protection by the army and navy in return for payment to the monarch and government. It is, therefore, inherently designed to produce national wealth and protectionism rather than individual prosperity. Because mercantilism was established and protected by the might of monarchs and governments, it was also inherently crony and corrupt. Exemplified by the British East India Company,[39] Britain had been under the economic system of mercantilism for roughly two hundred years by the time of the American founding.

The American colonial governments had naturally developed commerce within, and amongst, the colonies without the mercantile system. But America was not viewed as an economic trading partner by King George III. Rather, America and its people were viewed as a resource to be harvested for the betterment of England as demonstrated by the charge in the Declaration of "imposing Taxes on us without our Consent." It was the passage of the Tea Act of 1773, giving the East India Company the exclusive right to sell tea in the American colonies, thereby precluding American efforts to import and sell tea and enjoy the economic opportunities associated with developing that trade, that led to the Boston Tea Party in December of 1773.[40]

The British East India Company highlighted everything that people generally consider to be wrong with commerce then, and today. The company was in debt from unsound business practices. They had

---

[39] The British East India Company was established by Queen Elizabeth I in 1600 as a merchant company.
[40] See *The Cause of Revolution* in the Appendix.

plundered the East Indies.[41] They immorally courted and purchased favor from the King. They were even an active participant in the slave trade, principally between Africa and the East Indies (British National Archives). In a comparison of the economics of mercantilism and the open commerce practiced in America, Adam Smith found no need for extensive analysis of the prosperity of America versus the East Indies:

> The difference between the genius of the British constitution, which protects and governs North America, and that of the mercantile company which oppresses and domineers in the East Indies, cannot, perhaps, be better illustrated than by the different state of those countries. (Smith, *Wealth*, vol. 1, 89)

Adam Smith also described the right role for government to play in commerce,

> Commerce and manufactures can seldom flourish long in any state which does not enjoy a regular administration of justice, in which the people do not feel themselves secure in the possession of their property, in which the faith of contracts is not supported by law, and in which the authority of the state is not supposed to be regularly employed in enforcing the payment of debts from all those who are able to pay. Commerce and manufactures, in short, can seldom flourish in any state in which there is not a certain degree of confidence in the justice of government. (Smith, *Wealth*, vol. 2, 537-538)

And Smith described what government should not do, even using the example of British interference in Colonial American commerce,

> The statesman who should attempt to direct private people in what manner they ought to employ their capitals would not only load himself with a most unnecessary attention, but assume an authority which could safely be trusted, not only to no single person, but to no council or senate whatever, and

---

[41] Maritime Southeast Asia, essentially modern Malaysia, Brunei, Philippines, Singapore and Indonesia.

which would nowhere be so dangerous as in the hands of a man who had folly and presumption enough to fancy himself fit to exercise it. (Smith, *Wealth*, vol. 2, 36)

To prohibit a great people, however, from making all that they can of every part of their own produce, or from employing their stock and industry in the way that they judge most advantageous to themselves, is a manifest violation of the most sacred rights of mankind.[42] (Smith, *Wealth*, vol. 2, 179-180)

Therefore, when the Declaration of Independence stated that "... Free and Independent States, they have full Power to ... establish Commerce," it was revolutionary, meaning that government should leave people to freely engage in moral commerce, that government should not decide what commerce is best for the State or any persons, and that government should support commerce through consistent and just laws, equal application of law, and security from general threats to commerce.

Basic Economics in Commerce

Commerce is an outgrowth of liberty and the Law of Nature and Nature's God. In nature, one must "scrounge for nuts" (Locke, 199-200) to survive. As mankind forms society, people specialize in their efforts to survive and thrive based on their talents and resources. People then trade with others having different specializations to advance the needs of both. The result is more opportunity for wealth for each party. The specialization process is called "division of labor." As Adam Smith said,

The division of labour, however, so far as it can be introduced, occasions, in every art, a proportionable increase of the productive powers of labour. (Smith, *Wealth*, vol. 1, 7)

---

[42] The context is in relation to British laws regarding import and export restrictions on the American Colonies, notably, The Iron Act of 1750.

With government, trade largely gives way to payment by coin and currency, which further facilitates interaction because one need not seek a trade partner who has what is needed *and* wants what is offered in trade. James Wilson, discussing equality and the role of man in society, spoke of the economic benefits of inequality and interdependence in society,

> When we say, that all men are equal; we mean not to apply this equality to their virtues, their talents, their dispositions, or their acquirements. In all these respects, there is, and it is fit for the great purposes of society that there should be, great inequality among men. In the moral and political as well as in the natural world, diversity forms an important part of beauty; and as of beauty, so of utility likewise. That social happiness, which arises from the friendly intercourse of good offices, could not be enjoyed, unless men were so framed and so disposed, as mutually to afford and to stand in need of service and assistance. Hence the necessity not only of great variety, but even of great inequality in the talents of men, bodily as well as mental. ... Society supposes mutual dependence: mutual dependence supposes mutual wants: all the social exercises and enjoyments may be reduced to two heads–that of giving, and that of receiving: but these imply different aptitudes to give and to receive. (Wilson, 306-307)

The beauty and utility in the diversity of abilities and talents of mankind naturally drives division of labor. In turn, this division of labor enables a multiplication effect in "every art" from which men increase individual wealth and improve society.

Capitalism

Wilson's description of mutual dependence and mutual wants driving a natural system of economic interaction is a definition of free enterprise or the free market, also known as capitalism. Capitalism does not create liberty or freedom, it derives from them, and is therefore aided by a civil government which supports liberty. With capitalism, one may choose greater, lesser, or no participation with others in the free market.

Capitalism does not require a specific set of religious or social beliefs, or limit them. Capitalism is not a political system because it exists under the Law of Nature and Nature's God, apart from government, and it functions within or under any form of government.[43]

Adam Smith, like James Wilson, had insights into this natural form of economic interaction in a society based in liberty without ever calling it capitalism, or even defining it as an economic system.

> The natural effort of every individual to better his own condition, when suffered to exert itself with freedom and security, is so powerful a principle, that it is alone, and without any assistance, not only capable of carrying on the society to wealth and prosperity, but of surmounting a hundred impertinent obstructions with which the folly of human laws too often encumbers its operations; though the effect of these obstructions is always more or less either to encroach upon its freedom, or to diminish its security. (Smith, *Wealth*, vol. 2, 127-128)

Capitalism is nothing more than the everyday interaction of people, each looking to their self-interest, and finding a common point of self-interest with another person that results in mutual benefit. We are all capitalists. Adam Smith wrote of this as differentiation of man from animal in the state of nature:

> Nobody ever saw a dog make a fair and deliberate exchange of one bone for another with another dog. Nobody ever saw one animal by its gestures and natural cries signify to another, this is mine, that yours; I am willing to give this for that ... But man has almost constant occasion for the help of his brethren, and it is in vain for him to expect it from their benevolence only. He will be more likely to prevail if he can interest their self-love in his favour, and show them that it is for their own advantage to do for him what he requires of them. Whoever offers to another a bargain of any kind,

---

[43] The "black market" naturally exists for commerce prohibited by government.

proposes to do this. Give me that which I want, and you shall have this which you want, is the meaning of every such offer; and it is in this manner that we obtain from one another the far greater part of those good offices which we stand in need of.[44] (Smith, *Wealth*, vol. 1, 26)

The "Ills of Capitalism"

In the present, "capitalism" seems, for many people, to conjure up a vision of things that are not commerce. The term brings to mind price fixing, monopolies, greed and "crushing the competition." These are all faults of human nature that are sometimes expressed in capitalism and every other economic system. As John Adams stated, America was designed for "a moral and religious People." The ills of human nature become most evident, most visible, but are not necessarily most prominent, in an economic system based in moral individual liberty. Furthermore, these ills are generally made worse by laws and norms when society is unjust, or the culture is immoral. Price fixing, the practice of competing sellers conspiring to hold prices above the natural clearing price of demand, for example, would be met in a state of nature with aggression, and in a just society with legal action protecting individual liberty against a breached duty to respect the property of others. It is only in an immoral, unjust, society that such a practice is enabled by unjust laws or lax enforcement of good law. At the same time, mankind being in society establishes a prohibition of the "state of war" (Locke, 179) between the price fixers and buyers as prescribed by natural law. In a moral society, immoral market participants like price fixers are naturally weeded out and guarded against by the society as a whole. Therefore, any systemic occurrences of these ills are a sign of other immoral characteristics in society and culture, not the economic system. The mercantilism of 18th century Britain is a prime example: The British Crown supported an immoral monopoly by the East India Company for its own gain. Such systemic ills are endemic in

---

[44] This quote pertains to division of labor.

economic systems other than free market capitalism, and most often relate to some form of cronyism with the prevailing political system. Cronyism is also present in capitalism when business and corporate interests seek, and receive, favoritism (subsidy, price limits, special loans, loan guarantees, etc.) in the "free market" from political or government benefactors. This "crony capitalism" as it is often called, is really corporatism, a perversion of free market capitalism that is very much like the mercantilism described by Adam Smith. Whether for good intent or nefarious purposes, "impertinent obstructions" are detrimental to a free market economy.

In short, the "ills of capitalism" are expressions of immoral behavior in human nature that crop up in any economic system. They may show more clearly in capitalism because breaches of immorality are more clearly visible against the moral backdrop required for a society to exist in liberty. Any systemic occurrences of these ills are a sign of other concerns in society and culture, and not the economic system. More than likely, systemic ills are due to departure from free market capitalism, and a departure from liberty, to a system like mercantilism, or modern corporatism, which is a form of cronyism.

Chapter 3 –
The Constitution Frames the Vision of the American Mind

We the People of the United States, in Order to form a more perfect Union, establish Justice, insure domestic Tranquility, provide for the common defence, promote the general Welfare, and secure the Blessings of Liberty to ourselves and our Posterity, do ordain and establish this Constitution for the United States of America.

Preamble of the United States Constitution

Pathway to the Constitution

America was born with the Declaration of Independence, but its childhood was cut short by the need to fight for that declared independence. The American government was unable to advance its vision during the American Revolution, being constrained by the war and by the initial model of government; the deeply flawed Articles of Confederation. With the end of the Revolution a change was required to pursue the ideal of the American Mind; holding "these truths to be self-evident, that all men are created equal, that they are endowed by their Creator with certain unalienable Rights, that among these are Life, Liberty and the pursuit of Happiness." That change was the replacement of the Articles of Confederation with the United States Constitution and a federal form of government. The Constitution was the completion of the American Revolution that had started with the Declaration of Independence. As John Quincy Adams expressed,

> The revolution itself was a work of thirteen years— and had never been completed until that day. The Declaration of Independence and the Constitution of the United States, are parts of one consistent whole, founded upon one and the same theory of government, then new, not as a theory, for it had been working itself into the mind of man for many ages, and been especially expounded in the writings of Locke, but had never before been adopted by a great nation in practice. (Adams, J.Q., 40-41)

The Articles of Confederation

With Richard Henry Lee's proposed resolution for independence from Britain and the creation of a committee to draft a declaration, the Continental Congress recognized that the upstart United States of America would require rules of governance. Congress responded with the appointment of another committee, comprising one member from each colony, to prepare the form of confederation to be established between the Colonies (Adams, J.Q. 16). Just eight days after the issuance of the

Declaration of Independence, a draft of the Articles of Confederation was presented to the Continental Congress by John Dickinson, delegate from Pennsylvania, who had voted against the Declaration of Independence (Adams, J.Q., 17).

That an opponent to the Declaration of Independence was the presenter of the Articles of Confederation stands as a metaphor for the failure of the Articles of Confederation to represent the American culture embodied in the Declaration. John Quincy Adams explained it masterfully,

> There was thus no congeniality of principle between the Declaration of Independence and the Articles of Confederation. The foundation of the former were a superintending Providence—the rights of man, and the constituent revolutionary power of the people. That of the latter was the sovereignty of organized power, and the independence of the separate or dis-united States. The fabric of the Declaration and that of the Confederation, were each consistent with its own foundation, but they could not form one consistent symmetrical edifice. They were the productions of different minds and of adverse passions—one, ascending for the foundation of human government to the laws of nature and of God, written upon the heart of man— the other, resting upon the basis of human institutions, and prescriptive law and colonial charters. The corner stone of the one was right—that of the other was power. (Adams, J.Q., 17)

Failings of the Articles of Confederation

The Articles of Confederation were presented to the Continental Congress in July of 1776, but the final state needed for ratification, Maryland, did not sign until March of 1781. For many states, the Articles of Confederation provided little support, and in many cases were a hindrance to their needs. Despite referencing the "United States of America," the central government prescribed in the Articles of Confederation was designed to be weak. It had only one legislative chamber with a single representative from each state, each with a single vote. Nine of thirteen states were required to pass any law, there was no executive office to ensure operation of the government, and unanimous consent was required to amend the Articles, meaning that any one state could veto a proposal.

The central government under the Articles of Confederation had no authority to collect taxes, relying on the good will of the states to meet financial needs. It was supposed to have the authority to conduct foreign policy, but nothing prohibited states from practicing their own foreign engagements, leading to conflicting self-interested state policies that were readily exploited by foreign powers.

There were more issues with government under the Articles of Confederation: no means for settlement of Revolutionary War debt, inability to enact navigation law, lack of a common currency, and no central government power to regulate commerce within the Union. But the overarching failure of the Articles of Confederation was the incongruity of state sovereignty with the concept of "consent of the governed" from the Declaration of Independence. John Quincy Adams described it as an incurable disease:

> Its incurable disease was an apostacy from the principles of the Declaration of Independence. A substitution of separate state sovereignties, in the place of the constituent sovereignty of the people, as the basis of the confederate Union. (Adams, J.Q., 36)

Adams makes it clear that the United States of America, as expressed in the Declaration of Independence, was not a collection of confederated sovereign colonies, but a single union ordained "in the Name, and by Authority of the good People of these Colonies" organized as "Free and Independent States," but not sovereign states:

> Now the people of the Colonies, speaking by their delegates in Congress, had not declared each Colony a sovereign, free and independent State—nor had the people of each Colony so declared the Colony itself, nor could they so declare it, because each was already bound in union with all the rest; a

> union formed de facto, by the spontaneous revolutionary
> movement of the whole people, and organized by the meeting
> of the first Congress, in 1774, a year and ten months before
> the Declaration of Independence. (Adams, J. Q., 19)

Given the rivalries between the states and the veto power held by each, the Articles of Confederation made it impossible for the Union to adapt to peacetime governance after the war with Britain ended in 1783. These ongoing inter-state conflicts were brought to a head by the difficulty of the central government in putting down Shays' Rebellion (Holland, Massachusetts, 245) in 1786, leading the representatives of five states to call for a convention to address the deficiencies of the Articles of Confederation. In actuality, there were a number of delegates who sought not to repair, but to replace the Articles with a framework of government in the model of John Locke that "had never before been adopted by a great nation in practice." As John Quincy Adams recalled,

> In point of fact, the great measures by which the revolution
> was commenced, conducted, and concluded, were devised
> and prosecuted by a very few leading minds, animated by one
> pervading, predominating spirit. (Adams, J. Q., 42)

The Constitution

> The nation fell into an atrophy. The Union languished to the
> point of death. A torpid numbness seized upon all its faculties.
> A chilling cold indifference crept from its extremities to the
> centre. The system was about to dissolve in its own
> imbecility—impotence in negotiation abroad—domestic
> insurrection at home, were on the point of bearing to a
> dishonourable grave the proclamation of a government
> founded on the rights of man. (Adams, J. Q., 11)

This was, according to John Quincy Adams, the state of America at the outset of the Constitutional Convention at Philadelphia, Pennsylvania, in May of 1787. The convention was burdened in its objectives, having authority from state legislatures, but no direct authority from the people

(Adams, J. Q., 38). In this circumstance, those "few leading minds" sought to constitute a new government, abandoning the Articles of Confederation. They were opposed by a "highly respectable portion of the assembly" seeking to revive the Articles by granting additional powers to the Congress (Adams, J. Q., 39). "Never was a form of government so obstinately, so pertinaciously contested before its establishment" (Adams, J. Q., 48). By the close of the convention on September 17, 1787, the new constitutionalists had prevailed, and the Constitution was submitted to the States for approval. The Constitution,

> announced itself as the work of the people themselves; and as this was unquestionably a power assumed by the Convention, not delegated to them by the people, they religiously confined it to a simple power to propose, and carefully provided that it should be no more than a proposal until sanctioned by the confederation Congress, by the state Legislatures, and by the people of the several states, in conventions specially assembled, by authority of their Legislatures, for the single purpose of examining and passing upon it.
>
> And thus was consummated the work, commenced by the Declaration of Independence. A work in which the people of the North American Union, acting under the deepest sense of responsibility to the Supreme Ruler of the universe, had achieved the most transcendent act of power, that social man in his mortal condition can perform. (Adams, J. Q., 39-40)

John Quincy Adams outlined the great structural achievements of the Constitution:

> By the adoption and organization of the Constitution of the United States, these principles had been settled:—
>
> 1. That the affairs of the people of the United States were thenceforth to be administered, not by a confederacy, or mere league of friendship between the sovereign states, but by a government, distributed into the three great departments— legislative, judicial, and executive.

2. That the powers of government should be limited to concerns interesting to the whole people, leaving the Internal administration of each state, in peace, to its own constitution and laws, provided that they should be Republican, and interfering with them as little as should be necessary in war.

3. That the legislative power of this government should be divided between two assemblies, one representing directly the people of the separate states; and the other their legislatures.

4. That the executive power of this government should be vested in one person chosen for four years, with certain qualifications of age and nativity, re-eligible without limitation, and invested with a qualified negative upon the enactment of the laws.

5. That the judicial power should consist of tribunals inferior and supreme, to be instituted and organized by Congress, but to be composed of persons holding their offices during good behaviour, that is, removable only by impeachment. (Adams, J. Q., 60-61)

All of this was submitted to the people for approval. In keeping with the 9 of 13 majority requirement of the Articles of Confederation, the Constitution would go into effect following the approval of nine states. Delaware was the first state to approve it, on December 7, 1787. The ninth state to approve was New Hampshire, on June 21, 1788, thus ratifying the new Constitution. Rhode Island was the last of the thirteen original states to approve the Constitution, on May 29, 1790.

A Constitution Embodying the Declaration of Independence

Perhaps even more emphatically than the structural and legal considerations settled by the Constitution, John Quincy Adams highlighted the providential value of its passage:

Now the virtue which had been infused into the Constitution of the United States, and was to give to its vital existence the stability and duration to which it was destined, was no other than the concretion of those abstract principles which had been first proclaimed in the Declaration of Independence— namely, the self-evident truths of the natural and unalienable rights of man, of the indefeasible constituent and dissolvent sovereignty of the people, always subordinate to a rule of right and wrong, and always responsible to the Supreme Ruler of the universe for the rightful exercise of that sovereign, constituent, and dissolvent power. (Adams, J. Q., 54)

The well-known preamble to the Constitution provides clear connection to the Declaration of Independence, connecting the vision in the American Mind to the fulfillment of its purpose in law.

We the People of the United States, in Order to form a more perfect Union, establish Justice, insure domestic Tranquility, provide for the common defence, promote the general Welfare, and secure the Blessings of Liberty to ourselves and our Posterity, do ordain and establish this Constitution for the United States of America.

Each phrase maps back to the Declaration to ensure that the supreme law for America is an expression of the vision of the American Mind:

"We the people" is a fulfillment of the "Right of the people" of the Declaration.

The formation of "a more perfect union" fulfills the necessity to "dissolve the political bands" which was the object of explanation in the Declaration.

"Establish Justice" is the fulfillment of recognition that "all men are created equal, that they are endowed by their Creator with certain unalienable Rights" from the Declaration.

"Insure domestic Tranquility," "provide for the common defence," and "promote the general welfare" are the fulfillment of the Declaration's imperative "to institute new Government, laying its foundation on such principles and organizing its powers in such form, as to them shall seem most likely to effect their Safety and Happiness."

"Secure the Blessings of Liberty to ourselves and our Posterity" is the pronouncement of the intent of permanence of the Constitution to retain the "Right of the people," "appealing to the Supreme Judge of the world for the rectitude of our intention" professed in the Declaration.

This embodiment of the Declaration of Independence in the actual law and structure of America's Constitution took thirteen years of revolution and debate in America's Constitutional Convention to replace the failed Articles of Confederation. This fulfilment, enshrining the "Laws of Nature and Nature's God" from the Declaration in the Constitution, ensured that American law would have its foundation in liberty and justice, not for aristocracy, not for people of any special religious sect, not for people of particular states, but for all. John Quincy Adams understood what this fulfillment meant as he spoke at the Jubilee of George Washington's inauguration,

> The Declaration of Independence recognised the European law of nations, as practised among Christian nations, to be that by which they considered themselves bound, and of which they claimed the rights. This system is founded upon the principle, that the state of nature between men and between nations, is a state of peace. But there was a Mahometan law of nations, which considered the state of nature as a state of war — an Asiatic law of nations, which excluded all foreigners from admission within the territories of the state— a colonial law of nations, which excluded all foreigners from admission within the colonies— and a savage Indian law of nations, by which the Indian tribes within the bounds of the United States, were under their protection, though in a condition of undefined dependance upon the governments of the separate states. With all these different communities, the relations of the United States were from the time when they had become an independent nation, variously modified

according to the operation of those various laws. It was the
purpose of the Constitution of the United States to establish
justice over them all. (Adams, J. Q., 73)

There should never be an accusation, or threat, of theocracy in America.
The Constitution in no way requires adherence to any religion. There is no
requirement for religion in government. There is no State church. The
Constitution does, in accord with the Declaration of Independence, require
an acknowledgement, if not a full embrace, of the "Laws of Nature and
Nature's God," and there can be no prohibition of religion for those
serving in the public sphere. Such is the culture of the American mind and
the very soul of American history.[45]

Modern Patriotism – Defending the Constitution

Modern patriotism requires virtuous hearts and minds for the defense of
the Constitution and its principles incorporated from the Declaration of
Independence.

> This was the platform upon which the Constitution of the
> United States had been erected. Its VIRTUES, its republican
> character, consisted in its conformity to the principles
> proclaimed in the Declaration of Independence, and as its
> administration must necessarily be always pliable to the
> fluctuating varieties of public opinion; its stability and
> duration by a like overruling and irresistible necessity, was to
> depend upon the stability and duration in the hearts and minds
> of the people of that virtue, or in other words, of those
> principles, proclaimed in the Declaration of Independence,
> and embodied in the Constitution of the United States.
> (Adams, J. Q., 54)

John Quincy Adams affirmed the truth that patriotism requires rational
sacrifice. Patriotism requires virtue of heart and mind, and American

---

[45] Refer to *The First Amendment* in Part Two for discussion on "separation of
church and state."

patriots, acting sacrificially in virtue for their families, neighbors and for posterity, are necessary to maintain the American Mind in the law of the Constitution. Popular culture, the "fluctuating varieties of public opinion," will always apply pressure to prevailing law in one direction or another, away from its founding virtue in the Law of Nature and Nature's God. Only by the steadfastness of virtuous and sacrificial patriotism in the hearts and minds of the American people will the "stability and duration" of the Constitution remain.

A "Living" Constitution?

What seems to be one of the most prevalent and pressing questions about the Constitution today is, how does one interpret it? University courses and legal careers are dedicated to this subject. More than two hundred years after extensive recorded debate in the Constitutional Convention, after arguments published in the Federalist and Anti-federalist papers, after the debates in thirteen state legislatures over two and a half years, the method of interpretation of the Constitution continues to be argued.

James Madison, principal author of the Constitution, was asked to address the question of interpretation of the Constitution by anti-federalist and signer of the Declaration of Independence, Richard Henry Lee, in 1824. Madison replied,

> With a view to this last object, I entirely concur in the propriety of resorting to the sense in which the Constitution was accepted and ratified by the nation. In that sense alone it is the legitimate Constitution. And if that be not the guide in expounding it, there can be no security for a consistent and stable, more than for a faithful exercise of its powers. If the meaning of the text be sought in the changeable meaning of the words composing it, it is evident that the shape and attributes of the government must partake of the changes to which the words and phrases of all living languages are constantly subject. What a metamorphosis would be produced in the code of law if all its ancient phraseology were to be

taken in its modern sense. And that the language of our Constitution is already undergoing interpretations unknown to its founders will, I believe, appear to all unbiased inquirers into the history of its origin and adoption. Not to look farther for an example, take the word "consolidate" in the address of the convention prefixed to the Constitution. It there and then meant to give strength and solidity to the union of the states. In its current and controversial application it means a destruction of the states by transfusing their powers into the government of the union. (Madison, *Selections*, 52, emphasis added)

The truth in Madison's reply is self-evident, like the self-evident truths expressed in the Declaration of Independence from which the Constitution derives its right authority. No interpretation of the Constitution that does not comport with the Declaration of Independence can be valid, just as no law which does not comport with the "Laws of Nature and Nature's God" can be valid.

A "Text Without a Context"

It has been said that "a text without a context is only a pretext." This maxim, often used concerning biblical interpretation, applies equally well to the Constitution. It is a warning that there will always be people acting in ignorance or with an intent to confuse, distract, or deceive others by using a phrase out of the context in which it was written, or by reinterpreting the meaning of a word within a phrase. It is this latter case that Madison cites in his letter to Lee. Whether one misleads intentionally or in ignorance matters little if the one being misled is not equipped to understand the error. Even then, disingenuous intent or the wickedness of an "ends justify the means" mentality has the potential to overwhelm the intent of the text.

A classic biblical "text without a context" example is pacifists calling for Christians to "beat their swords into plowshares." This phrase is indeed scripture, from Isaiah 2:4. However, the context refers to a prophecy about a time when, under God's judgement, there will be no war and thus no need for weapons. Yet there also exists a prophecy in Joel 3:10 where there will be a time to "beat plowshares into swords." Therefore, a universal call for pacifism based on Isaiah 2:4 would be a pretext for using the "beat their swords into plowshares" text out of the context of the prophecy (text) in which it was given.

In regard to the Constitution, likely the most well-known "text without a context" is the phrase, "separation of church and state" in reference to the First Amendment.[46] This phrase was originally used to mean that the government should not interfere in religion. However, intentional misuse has turned the meaning around to incorrectly mean that religion has no place in government, or with people serving in government. America's founding documents and the words of most of the founders used in this book should make it clear that the moral foundation of religion is an essential element of the American Mind.

Washington's Final Word

George Washington spent two terms in office as the first President of the United States of America. As the first president, Washington had the job of establishing all of the executive functions for the nation which were both explicit and implicit, but undefined, in the Constitution. With that experience, he spoke in his farewell address to the proper understanding and operation of the Constitution as time and needs change:

> To the efficacy and permanency of your [the People's] Union, a government for the whole is indispensable. No alliance, however strict, between the parts can be an adequate substitute; they must inevitably experience the infractions and interruptions which all alliances in all times have experienced. Sensible of this momentous truth, you have improved upon your first essay, by the adoption of a constitution of government better calculated than your former for an intimate

---

[46] Thorough discussion of "separation of church and state" is available in *The First Amendment* in Part Two.

union, and for the efficacious management of your common concerns. This government, the offspring of our own choice, uninfluenced and unawed, adopted upon full investigation and mature deliberation, completely free in its principles, in the distribution of its powers, uniting security with energy, and containing within itself a provision for its own amendment, has a just claim to your confidence and your support. Respect for its authority, compliance with its laws, acquiescence in its measures, are duties enjoined by the fundamental maxims of true liberty. The basis of our political systems is the right of the people to make and to alter their constitutions of government. But the Constitution which at any time exists, till changed by an explicit and authentic act of the whole people, is sacredly obligatory upon all. The very idea of the power and the right of the people to establish government presupposes the duty of every individual to obey the established government. (Washington, *Farewell*, 16-17)

To change the Constitution by changing its context, by pretext of intent, by overreach of government entities, by State action or inaction, by anything apart from an "authentic act of the whole people," is a repudiation of the sacred. It is a usurpation of the honest acts of all American people, past and present, to establish a "more perfect union." It is a preemption of legitimate acts to "secure the Blessings of Liberty to ourselves and our Posterity." And it is a diminishing of the self-evident equality and intended liberty of the "Laws of Nature and Nature's God."

Madison and Washington have made it clear that there have always been those who have sought to subvert American law through misconstruction of the Constitution. It is for this reason, if no other, that the Constitution must be understood based on the origins of the American Mind of the Declaration of Independence. Should "We the People" decide that is no longer our vision, the People have the legal and upright processes to change it. But the People must never give it up in ignorance or apathy.

Republican Form of Government

Because present-day America has two major political parties, the Republican Party and the Democratic Party, people are often confused when "republican" or "democratic" are used to describe forms of government. The discussion around "republic" and "democracy" made here has nothing to do with present-day political parties. Nor is this discussion about a relative position on the continuum of political ideology *within* the American constitutional system.[47] This is a review of what the founders intended in creating a republican form of government with democratic elements, and their understanding of the failings of democracy as a form of government.

The Constitution, in Article 4, Section 4, guarantees a "Republican Form of Government" to the States, yet it never exactly defines what this means because that decision belongs to the individual states. However, the minimum expectation is the same as that defined for the Federal Government: a representative government comprising a freely elected legislature and executive, and a judiciary.

John Adams made clear at the time the American Constitution was proposed, the expected value of the checks and balances of republican government versus the turmoil of democracies in history,

> We shall learn to prize the checks and balances of a free government, and even those of the modern aristocracies, if we recollect the miseries of Greece which arose from their ignorance of them. The only balance attempted against the ancient kings was a body of nobles; and the consequences were perpetual altercations of rebellion and tyranny, and butcheries of thousands upon every revolution from one to the other. When the kings were abolished, the aristocracies tyrannized; and then no balance was attempted but between aristocracy and democracy. This, in the nature of things, could

---

[47] Refer to *Left, Center, Right – Framing Political Philosophies* in the Appendix.

be no balance at all, and therefore the pendulum was for ever on the swing. (Adams, *Defence*, xv)

And more than fifty years later, John Quincy Adams addressed the meaning of republican government by reinforcing the notion that democracy, as a form of government, was an intractable solution for American government, or as history showed, any government,

> The Constitution of the United States was republican and democratic— but the experience of all former ages had shown that of all human governments, democracy was the most unstable, fluctuating and short-lived; and it was obvious that if virtue—the virtue of the people, was the foundation of republican government, the stability and duration of the government must depend upon the stability and duration of the virtue by which it is sustained. (Adams, J. Q., 53)

Democracies and totalitarian regimes have always failed, usually in violent revolution and butchery. The Republican form of government established in the American Constitution has proved itself for more than 240 years, based in the "Laws of Nature and Nature's God" of the Declaration of Independence. Yet the past success of the American Constitution is no guarantee for the future. The continuance of the American Republic requires virtue in its people, that commitment to liberty, and duties in exercising liberty, as well as true patriotism, to hold on to the blessings of stability and longevity of the American Mind; the continuing gift to America's posterity.

Party Spirit

One of the great banes of America's Constitution, and to justice in general, is party spirit. Also called faction, "party spirit" better captures the base fault in the individual human spirit that drives the selfishness and love of power over principle. Faction in 1780 was defined essentially as today, "Party in general; party tumult; discord; dissension" (Webster, *American Dictionary*). It is remarkable that synonyms for a political party are "tumult, discord and dissension!"

Party spirit is not characterized by principled, logical, or thoughtful, disagreement. It is reactive, shallow, self-seeking, unconsidered and destructive. Unfortunately, it was in the founding era, and is now, the driving force in public politics – it is the lowest common denominator of political parties. Party spirit seeks to win at any cost, it trades principles for party success, believing that the ends justify the means and the "lesser of two evils" is acceptable. Party spirit does not support the truth of the "Laws of Nature and Nature's God" of the Declaration of Independence, or the separation of powers and Rule of Law of the Constitution. Party spirit only seeks to win and exert control over those who do not toe the party line; a line which often moves at the whim of party leaders.

Faction was well known prior to the American Constitution, and Alexander Hamilton described its place in history in *Federalist 9*.

> A FIRM Union will be of the utmost moment to the peace and liberty of the States, as a barrier against domestic faction and insurrection. It is impossible to read the history of the petty republics of Greece and Italy without feeling sensations of horror and disgust at the distractions with which they were continually agitated, and at the rapid succession of revolutions by which they were kept in a state of perpetual vibration between the extremes of tyranny and anarchy. (Hamilton, *Federalist*, 43-44)

James Madison, in *Federalist 10*, goes into much greater detail on how the Constitution would help manage faction via the republican form of government:

> A republic, by which I mean a government in which the scheme of representation takes place, opens a different prospect, and promises the cure for which we are seeking. ... the effect of [the republican form of government is] to refine and enlarge the public views, by passing them through the medium of a chosen body of citizens, whose wisdom may best discern the true interest of their country, and whose patriotism and love of justice will be least likely to sacrifice it to

temporary or partial considerations. (Hamilton, *Federalist*, 53)

Madison continued to describe the value of America's proposed compound republic, a federal republic of state republics, in providing as much a cure for faction as is possible in a country desirous of maintaining liberty,

> The influence of factious leaders may kindle a flame within their particular States, but will be unable to spread a general conflagration through the other States. ... [The effect of faction] will be less apt to pervade the whole body of the Union than a particular member of it; in the same proportion as such a malady is more likely to taint a particular county or district, than an entire State. (Hamilton, *Federalist*, 55)

Unfortunately, knowing George Washington's experience, the compound federal republic is not, of itself, enough to mitigate the ill effects of faction. George Washington was so beset by party spirit and the affliction of political parties during the term of his presidency that he extensively raised the issue in his *Farewell Address*. In part, Washington said,

> The alternate domination of one faction over another, sharpened by the spirit of revenge, natural to party dissension, which in different ages and countries has perpetrated the most horrid enormities, is itself a frightful despotism. But this leads at length to a more formal and permanent despotism. The disorders and miseries which result gradually incline the minds of men to seek security and repose in the absolute power of an individual; and sooner or later the chief of some prevailing faction, more able or more fortunate than his competitors, turns this disposition to the purposes of his own elevation, on the ruins of public liberty.

> Without looking forward to an extremity of this kind (which nevertheless ought not to be entirely out of sight), the common and continual mischiefs of the spirit of party are sufficient to make it the interest and duty of a wise people to discourage and restrain it. (Washington, *Farewell*, 20-21)

It is evident over the long history of political parties, and with today's extreme partisanship, that the Constitution, apart from the spirit of liberty and equality from the Declaration of Independence, is not enough to quash the ills of party spirit.

God in the Constitution

That God is not mentioned in the Constitution might mislead some regarding the importance of the foundation of the "Laws of Nature and Nature's God" that figured so prominently in the Declaration of Independence. Certainly, this is, in part, due to the Declaration being the builder's vision, while the Constitution is the blueprint which focuses on the details for implementation of laws by men. Yet, there is a major acknowledgement and reliance on God not only in the Constitution, but in the implementation of the Constitution's offices, for all time. This is found in the oath of office. Taking an oath,[48] or making an affirmation,[49] has the implication of consequences beyond the scope of human punishment should that oath be forsaken.

For the President, the oath is stated in Article II, Section 1, Clause 8 of the Constitution:

> Before he enter on the Execution of his Office, he shall take the following Oath or Affirmation:–"I do solemnly swear (or affirm) that I will faithfully execute the Office of President of the United States, and will to the best of my Ability, preserve, protect and defend the Constitution of the United States."

For members of Congress, the Judiciary, Executive officers, and members of state legislatures, the oath of office is in Article VI:

---

[48] An affirmation, negation, or promise corroborated by the attestation of the Divine Being (Sheridan).

[49] Some religious views treat an oath as taking the name of the Lord in vain, a breach of the command in Exodus 20:7, or based on the admonishment of Jesus in Matthew 5:33-37, which is the rationale for adding "or affirmation" in the Constitution.

> The Senators and Representatives before mentioned, and the Members of the several State Legislatures, and all executive and judicial Officers, both of the United States and of the several States, shall be bound by Oath or Affirmation, to support this Constitution; but no religious Test shall ever be required as a Qualification to any Office or public Trust under the United States.

By these oaths, the Constitution directly incorporates the acknowledgement of Nature's God from the Declaration of Independence. John Quincy Adams expressed the religious importance of the oath of office:

> The constitution had provided that all the public functionaries of the Union, not only of the general but of all the state governments, should be under oath or affirmation for its support. The homage of religious faith was thus superadded to all the obligations of temporal law, to give it strength; and this confirmation of an appeal to the responsibilities of a future omnipotent judge, was in exact conformity with the whole tenor of the Declaration of Independence— guarded against abusive extension by a further provision, that no religious test should ever be required as a qualification to any office or public trust under the United States. (Adams, J. Q., 62)

The General Welfare

The preamble of the Constitution expresses one of the goals to be to "promote the general Welfare." Today, this phrase has been used as rationale for an implicit grant of virtually unlimited powers not explicitly granted to the Federal Government by the Constitution. James Madison addressed this type of overreach in his rebuke of the Alien and Sedition

Acts of 1798[50] as part of the Virginia Resolutions (Elliot, *Debates*, vol. 4, 576-577):

> for it is evident that there is not a single power whatever which may not have some reference to the common defence or the general welfare; nor a power of any magnitude which, in its exercise, does not involve, or admit, an application of money. The government, therefore, which possesses power in either one or other of these extents, is a government without the limitations formed by a particular enumeration of powers; and, consequently, the meaning and effect of this particular enumeration is destroyed by the exposition given to these general phrases. (Elliot, *Debates*, vol. 4, 552)

Madison makes it clear that the term "general Welfare" must be used within the limitations and context of the enumerated powers of the Constitution, otherwise there are no boundaries within the Constitution.

Madison also discussed the fact that "general Welfare" was a term purposefully borrowed from the Articles of Confederation, Article VIII, with the idea that doing so would make it less likely to be misconstrued or misused,

> because it will scarcely be said, that in the former [Articles of Confederation] they were ever understood to be either a general grant of power, or to authorize the requisition or application of money, by the old Congress, to the common defence and general welfare, except in cases afterwards enumerated, which explained and limited their meaning; and if such was the limited meaning attached to these phrases in the very instrument revised and remodelled by the present Constitution, it can never be supposed that, when copied into this Constitution, a different meaning ought to be attached to them. (Elliot, *Debates*, vol. 4, 551)

---

[50] The Alien and Sedition Acts is covered in more detail in Chapter 4 – *The Bill of Rights Clarifies the American Mind*.

James Madison went on to thoroughly expound the concept that application of the phrase, "promote the general Welfare" exists within the context of the explicitly enumerated powers of the Constitution:

> The true and fair construction of this expression, both in the original and existing federal compacts, appears to the committee too obvious to be mistaken. **In both, the Congress is authorized to provide money for the common defence and general welfare. In both is subjoined to this authority an enumeration of the cases to which their powers shall extend.** Money cannot be applied to the general welfare, otherwise than by an application of it to some particular measure, conducive to the general welfare. When ever, therefore, money has been raised by the general authority, and is to be applied to a particular measure, a question arises whether the particular measure be within the enumerated authorities vested in Congress. If it be, the money requisite for it may be applied to it. If it be not, no such application can be made. This fair and obvious interpretation coincides with, and is enforced by, the clause in the Constitution which declares that "no money shall be drawn from the treasury but in consequence of appropriations made by law." An appropriation of money to the general welfare would be deemed rather a mockery than an observance of this constitutional injunction. (Elliot, *Debates*, vol. 4, 552, emphasis added)

Madison even more concisely made the point in 1792 while debating a cod fishery bill in Congress:

> I, sir, have always conceived—I believe those who proposed the constitution conceived—it is still more fully known, and more material to observe, that those who ratified the constitution conceived, that this is not an indefinite government, deriving its powers from the general terms prefixed to the specified powers—but, a limited government tied down to the specified powers, which explain and define the general terms. (Elliot, *Journal*, Cod Fishery Bill, 236)

> In short, … were the power of congress to be established in
> the latitude contended for, it would subvert the very
> foundation, and transmute the very nature of the limited
> government established by the people of America … (Elliot,
> *Journal*, Cod Fishery Bill, 238)

It seems there is also an implicit limitation on the constitutional provision
to "promote the general Welfare" in the very construction of the preamble.
Consider the verbs supporting each of the five functions of government.
"Establish," "insure," "provide," "promote," "secure." All but "promote"
connote strong ownership actions, but "promote" is a support action to the
ownership actions of all the others. Even at its strongest, "promote" is
ownership at a secondary level. Consider the role of a music or boxing
promoter today. The promoter is responsible for the marketing and set-up
of the event, but they do not play the music or participate in the fight which
is the real reason for the event. Promotion of the "general Welfare" is
similarly a secondary activity of government in support of The People
seeking "life, liberty and happiness," not the creation by the government
of life, liberty or happiness.

Finally, the closing of the preamble, "and secure the Blessings of Liberty
to ourselves and our Posterity," is really a wrap-up of the other four listed
functions of government. Securing the Blessings of Liberty constrains the
other functions of the preamble to what was expressed in the Declaration
of Independence – government is instituted to secure "life, liberty and the
pursuit of happiness." Therefore, if one were inclined to take "promote the
general Welfare" to excess, an honest, liberty-loving, person would
recognize it as infringing on the liberty of others and ratchet it back.

American Slavery

> Where slavery exists, the republican theory becomes still
> more fallacious.

> James Madison, Constitutional Convention, June 19, 1787
> (Madison, *Papers*, 899)

> They [slave masters] bring the judgment of Heaven on a country. As nations cannot be rewarded or punished in the next world, they must be in this. By an inevitable chain of causes and effects, Providence punishes national sins by national calamities.

> George Mason, Constitutional Convention, August 22, 1787
> (Madison, *Debates*, 458)

Slavery, in any form, is immoral, ungodly and must be abolished. The word "sin" derives from the biblical Greek meaning "missing the mark," and in the biblical sense, missing the mark of God's law and intent. Chattel slavery is America's great national sin.

American slavery was first British slavery. Britain embraced the Atlantic slave trade, but had no common law supporting slavery in Britain. For Britain, slavery was simply commerce. The American colonies and the West Indies were the object of much of the British slave trade (British National Archives). Slavery was, therefore, more of a public issue in the Colonies. Abolition of slavery was also a tremendous challenge in Britain and America because of the British support for the Atlantic slave trade, laws within many colonies supporting slavery, the early lack of a central government to drive uniform policy, and later the established bloc of slave-holding states in the Union exercising their democratic will within the central government.

While the Colonies were British, they were subject to British law, which supported slavery. With the Declaration of Independence, America declared "all men are created equal, that they are endowed by their Creator with certain unalienable Rights, that among these are Life, Liberty and the pursuit of Happiness." This was America's first national opportunity to morally address slavery. Jefferson tried to highlight the evil of the slave trade more fully as the final indictment of King George III in the first draft of the Declaration of Independence,

> He has waged cruel war against human nature itself, violating its most sacred rights of life and liberty in the persons of a

distant people who never offended him, captivating and carrying them into slavery in another hemisphere, or to incur miserable death in their transportation thither. This piratical warfare, the opprobium of INFIDEL powers, is the warfare of the CHRISTIAN King of Great Britain. Determined to keep open a market where MEN should be bought and sold, he has prostituted his negative for suppressing every legislative attempt to prohibit or to restrain this execrable commerce. And that this assemblage of horrors might want no fact of distinguished die, he is now exciting those very people to rise in arms among us, and to purchase that liberty of which he has deprived them, by murdering the people on whom he also obtruded them: thus paying off former crimes committed against the LIBERTIES of one people, with crimes which he urges them to commit against the Lives of another. (Linn, 49)

Tragically, the indictment was dropped from the final draft. Jefferson, in an 1818 letter to Robert Walsh, explained the reason for the demise of the charge,

When the Declaration of Independence was under the consideration of Congress, there were two or three unlucky expressions in it which gave offence to some members. ... Severe strictures on the conduct of the British king, in negotiating our repeated repeals of the law which permitted the importation of slaves, were disapproved by some Southern gentlemen, whose reflections were not yet matured to the full abhorrence of that traffic. Although the offensive expressions were immediately yielded, these gentlemen continued their depredations on other parts of the instrument. (Jefferson, *Writings*, vol. 8, 500)

Some delegates may have "not yet matured to the full abhorrence" of slavery, and excluded the black African slaves from being part of "all men," yet the heart of the nation was established in that principle of equality. During the Revolutionary War with Britain, under the bare bones American government of the Articles of Confederation, all focus was on defeating the British. There were movements to address slavery within some state governments, but there was no chance to address slavery as a nation.

Slavery Addressed by American States

As public understanding of the rights and equality of mankind grew leading up to the Declaration of Independence, and after the Revolutionary War freed the economies of the Northern states from British control, the desire and need for slaves changed in many of the new American states. By the time of the Constitution, ten states had made importation of slaves illegal and North Carolina law was silent on the topic. Only Georgia and South Carolina sanctioned the importation of slaves. Many of the Northern states had also ended slavery or adopted laws to gradually put an end to it.[51] By the time of constitutional discussions in 1787, Pennsylvania, Connecticut, Rhode Island, New York and New Jersey had provisions in place to abolish slavery.[52] Massachusetts and New Hampshire had constitutions declaring that all men are born free and equal, making abolition implicit, and ultimately explicit by a state supreme court ruling in Massachusetts.[53] Vermont, not one of the thirteen colonies, and not a state until 1791, also provided freedom from slavery in the colony's 1777 constitution.

Slavery Addressed in the Constitution

The first opportunity for America as a whole to functionally address the sin of slavery came with the Constitution. While functionally incomplete, the legal success of the Constitution in dealing with the evils of slavery is largely subject to personal interpretation. Debates in the federal and state

---

[51] The rationale for gradual emancipation was that it provided for slaveholder transition to alternative labor, staved-off a sudden negative impact to the economy and tempered the ill effects on all parties of releasing an uneducated, ill-equipped, poor, slave population to suddenly fend for themselves.

[52] Some states had better emancipation laws than others, with New York and New Jersey having the weakest abolition statutes.

[53] 1783, the Quock Walker case.

constitutional conventions express very differing perceptions of the very same clauses. For example, on the clause regarding importation of slaves into the existing states, there were these, amongst other, views:[54]

> With respect to the clause restricting Congress from prohibiting the *migration or importation of such persons* as any of the states now existing shall think proper to admit, prior to the year 1808 ... I will tell you what was done, and it gives me high pleasure that so much was done. Under the present Confederation, the States may admit the importation of *slaves* as long as they please; but by this article, after the year 1808, the Congress will have power to prohibit such importation, notwithstanding the disposition of any State to the contrary. I consider this as laying the foundation for banishing slavery out of this country; and though the period is more distant than I could wish, yet it will produce the same kind, gradual change, which was pursued in Pennsylvania. It is with much satisfaction I view this power in the General Government, whereby they may lay an interdiction on this reproachful trade;
>
> James Wilson, Pennsylvania Convention on the Constitution
> (Elliot, *Debates*, vol. 2, 452)

And,

> By this settlement we have secured an unlimited importation of negroes for twenty years; nor is it declared that the importation shall be then stopped; it may be continued — we have a security that the General Government can never emancipate them, for no such authority is granted, and it is admitted on all hands, that the General Government has no powers but what are expressly granted by the Constitution; and that all rights not expressed were reserved by the several States. ... In short, considering all circumstances, we have

---

[54] Both James Wilson and Charles C. Pinckney were vocal members of the federal Constitutional Convention.

made the best terms, for the security of this species of property, it was in our power to make. We would have made better if we could, but on the whole I do not think them bad.

Charles Pinckney, South Carolina Convention on the Constitution
(Elliot, *Debates*, vol. 4, 286)

The original ratified Constitution, prior to amendment, addressed slavery in four locations: Article 1, Section 2; Article 1, Section 9; Article 4, Section 2; and Article 5 stated that Article 1, Section 9 could not be changed by amendment. Although it can definitively be said that the representatives of most states were, in mind, if not also in policy, opposed to slavery, all of the constitutional clauses relating to slavery benefitted the slave-holding states. Therefore, it is easy to suggest that the majority Northern and Eastern (mostly free) states could have cut off the southern slave-holding states and formed the Constitution with firm anti-slavery language without consideration for South Carolina and Georgia, the two states strongly supporting slavery. However, it must be recalled what John Quincy Adams said of the state of the Union under the Articles of Confederation throughout the Revolution:

> Instead of resorting to the source of all constituted power [Declaration of Independence], they had wasted their time, their talents, and their persevering, untiring toils, in erecting and roofing and buttressing a frail and temporary shed to shelter the nation from the storm, or rather a mere baseless scaffolding on which to stand, when they should raise the marble palace of the people, to stand the test of time. (Adams, J. Q., 18)

The Articles of Confederation had been just sufficient enough for wartime, all thirteen states had fought together for independence and remained a single nation in union under the Declaration of Independence. However, the Articles would not long sustain America, and there were clear signs that the slavery issue could scuttle a new Constitution[55] (Phillips, 30, 34, 35, 43). Georgia and South Carolina, in particular, viewed slavery as their only means of recovery from the human and economic losses incurred during the Revolution. And for the other states, the idea of jettisoning multiple states from the Union just after surviving an existential national crisis was outside the scope of consideration for the Constitutional Convention. Furthermore, to concede an insurmountable difference and abandon the southern states would have been to concede slavery in the south forever. Such a concession would have also tacitly condoned slavery, at least to the same extent that the constitutional compromises can be viewed to condone slavery, without recourse, short of another war to eliminate it. America would have been in a position not much different than allowing the south to secede at the time of the Civil War, but without a constitution to deal with it, or funds and people to be able to fight for the Union. This is a position from which America would never have recovered, resulting in war, rather than debate in Congress as pioneers moved westward; and continuous foreign interference on the Atlantic coast as Europe vied to regain influence and control of the disunited states. The anti-slavery majority of the Constitutional Convention intentionally, rightly or wrongly, provided an allowance for time to eliminate slavery in the United States rather than dissolving the new Union and creating a weaker United States alongside an equally weak permanent confederation of slave-holding states (Elliot, *Debates*, vol.4, 283). Perhaps the words of Thomas Paine on the fullness of time were echoing in their minds:

> The present time, likewise, is that peculiar time, which never happens to a nation but once, VIZ. the time of forming itself into a government. Most nations have let slip the opportunity, and by that means have been compelled to receive laws from their conquerors, instead of making laws for themselves. (Paine, *Common Sense*, 70)

---

[55] At the Constitutional Convention. Mr. Davie of NC, July 12, 1787, Mr. Butler of SC on July 13, General Pinckney of SC on July 23.

None of this rationale for constitutional compromise is intended as absolution for continuing to enable slavery at a point when it might have, to the very same point made by Thomas Paine, been the most opportune time to end it. It is, rather, a rebuke to those long-separated in time and condition from the founders in lightly passing judgement on them, and consideration for future leaders in America to trust in Divine Providence for support in doing what is right.

The 3/5 Clause

Article 1, Section 2 of the unamended Constitution is known as the 3/5 Clause. It stated,

> Representatives and direct Taxes shall be apportioned among the several States which may be included within this Union, according to their respective Numbers, which shall be determined by adding to the whole Number of free Persons, including those bound to Service for a Term of Years, and excluding Indians not taxed, three fifths of all other Persons.

By process of elimination, "all other persons," refers to slaves. This clause did not say that black people are worth three-fifths of a white person. A free black person was counted as any other free person. This clause was about compromise regarding the influence of slave-holding states in the Congress and on taxation. The question vacillated between treating slaves as freemen or property when it came to taxation and representation in Congress, which often had a subtext in debate of whether that question was to be evaluated from a perspective of humanity or simple politics. All possible views were expressed throughout the debate. Some sought more power in the Federal Government by disingenuously calling for "equality" in the Constitution by including black slaves, who could not hold property or vote, in the number used to apportion seats in the House of Representatives. Others argued that slaves should not be included in representation at all, that they were merely property. After a month of rancorous debate, a compromise was proposed. Based on a ratio established by Congress under the Articles of Confederation (Madison,

Writings, vol. 3, 143), it was proposed to count slaves at three-fifths of other persons for purposes of representation in Congress and taxation.[56] The southern slave-holding states were happy to deal with the potential for taxation, given the absolute power advantage of increased "representation" and the social claims they could make in terms of characterizing slaves as property. The agreement was complete, but the bitterness of it was retained by many. Gouverneur Morris of Pennsylvania on August 8, 1787, bemoaned as constitutional debate continued,

> The admission of slaves into the representation, when fairly explained, comes to this,– that the inhabitant of Georgia and South Carolina who goes to the coast of Africa, and, in defiance of the most sacred laws of humanity, tears away his fellow-creatures from their dearest connections, and damns them to the most cruel bondage, shall have more votes in a government instituted for protection of the rights of mankind, than the citizen of Pennsylvania or New Jersey who views with a laudable horror so nefarious a practice. (Elliot, *Debates*, vol. 5, 393)

The 3/5 Clause was removed from the Constitution as part of the Fourteenth Amendment ratified in 1868.

Importation Clause

Article 1, Section 9 of the Constitution includes the clause,

> The Migration or Importation of such Persons as any of the States now existing shall think proper to admit, shall not be prohibited by the Congress prior to the Year one thousand eight hundred and eight, but a Tax or duty may be imposed on such Importation, not exceeding ten dollars for each Person.

---

[56] Debate ran from May 29 through July 12, 1787. Mr. King and Mr. Wilson made the proposals which ultimately passed on June 11, 1787 (Madison, Writings, Vol. 3).

This clause is an exception to the power granted to Congress to regulate commerce (Elliot, *Debates*, vol. 3, 541). The importation clause was developed by committee after an inability for the entire convention to come to agreement. The same committee was coincidentally chartered to work on an act for the regulation of navigation relating to commerce. In committee, the Eastern states essentially agreed to slave importation until 1800, later changed to 1808 in full session, in exchange for a concession from the South supporting the requirement of only a simple majority, rather than a 2/3 vote in Congress, to regulate commerce and navigation (Phillips, 72-74, 91-92). Many in the Constitutional Convention, including some from Southern states, believed that slave importation would naturally decline, since all but Georgia and South Carolina had already halted the practice, making them lukewarm on pressing the issue in the Constitution. Therefore, the recommendation of the committee was adopted (Phillips, 45).

As noted in the earlier quotation from James Wilson, this compromise has the great benefit of clearly establishing a date after which the importation of new slaves could be stopped by act of Congress if not already ended by the states. No such power had been granted under the Articles of Confederation. To the contrary view, as expressed by Charles C. Pinckney, the clause does not require a moratorium on the importation of slaves, and it can be viewed as having the effect of sanctioning the importation of slaves until 1808, while precluding the opportunity for a federal government to halt the practice before this date.[57] Perhaps the wording made a perfect compromise, no one was fully happy with it but it was acceptable to all. However, James Madison expressed his understanding of the worst of it during debate, saying,

> Twenty years will produce all the mischief that can be
> apprehended from the liberty to import slaves. So long a term
> will be more dishonorable to the American character than to

---

[57] Article V of the Constitution precluded the amendment of the Importation Clause, ensuring that it would remain until 1808.

say nothing about it in the Constitution[58]. (Madison, *Debates*, 477)

Another issue with the Importation Clause is that it only addressed importation to existing states and not new states that might potentially be added to the union. The issue of slavery had already been addressed with new territories seeking statehood in America's "Northwest." The Northwest Ordinance (Authority, iii) was passed in the Congress of the Confederation on July 13, 1787 while the Constitutional Convention was debating. It created a government for the Northwest Territory, a bill of rights for the territory, and provided a method for admitting new states to the Union from the territory. The Northwest Ordinance also prohibited slavery in the Northwest Territory and any of the three to five states that might eventually join the union from it. This was a coup for American abolitionists. Drafter of the Ordinance, Nathan Dane, recalled in a letter written just days after its adoption,

> When I drew the ordinance which passed (in a few words excepted) as I originally formed it, I had no idea the States would agree to the sixth Art. prohibiting Slavery. (Cutler, 372)

But, being mere legislation, the provisions of the Northwest Ordinance could be readily changed in the future if not defined in the Constitution. The debate in the Constitutional Convention was clearly focused on establishing a constitution to maintain the union of the original thirteen colonies and did not reach into the prospect of future states despite Madison's implication of "mischief" during the twenty-year sanction for slave importation.

---

[58] Madison, the Constitution having been completed including the 3/5 Clause, and sent to the states for ratification, takes a more pragmatic tone in discussing the importation of slaves in the Virginia ratifying convention (Elliot, *Debates* vol. 3, 453) and *Federalist 42* (Hamilton, *Federalist*, 228).

Fugitive Slave Clause

Article 4, Section 2 of the unamended Constitution contained the clause,

> No Person held to Service or Labour in one State, under the
> Laws thereof, escaping into another, shall, in Consequence of
> any Law or Regulation therein, be discharged from such
> Service or Labour, but shall be delivered up on Claim of the
> Party to whom such Service or Labour may be due.

This compromise also relates to the Northwest Ordinance prohibiting slavery in the Northwest territory and new states admitted from it. The price for the prohibition of slavery in Article 6 of the Northwest Ordinance was a requirement for the return of escaped slaves. It is this clause which the slave-holding states pressed in negotiation on the Constitution during the convention.

What is particularly pernicious is that the fugitive slave clause treats slaves only as property and obliges non-slave states to treat them as such. Furthermore, there was no strong prohibition of slavery in the Constitution for counterbalance, as had been achieved in the Northwest Ordinance. The Fugitive Slave Clause was accepted by the Convention because South Carolina and Georgia would agree to nothing less, intimating that they would renege on their agreed concessions on regulation of commerce as agreed in the committee that discussed the importation clause.[59] These states feared that their property, and thus the means to sustain their state economies,[60] would be systematically drained from them if a slave was considered to be free upon reaching a free state.

The Fugitive Slave Clause was eliminated from the Constitution in 1865 with the Thirteenth Amendment to the Constitution which ended slavery.

---

[59] August 28, 1787 (Phillips, 53-55).
[60] Such was the degree of "property value" in the slaves compared to other means of economic production in the South.

Fallout of Slavery and the Constitution

Following ratification of the Constitution, there were several important Federal acts to curtail the slave trade. The Slave Trade Act of 1794 (Congress, *Laws*, vol. 2, 383) prohibited the fitting of ships by Americans or in American ports for the purposes of the slave trade in foreign countries, subject to fines, loss of the slaves, and forfeiture of the vessel. This act outlawed the export of slaves from America.

In 1807, both America and the British Empire abolished the slave trade.[61] In America, President Thomas Jefferson called for legislation prohibiting the importation of slaves as part of his 1806 state of the union address (Cobbett, vol. 11, 156). Congress took up the call and passed *An Act to Prohibit the Importation of Slaves* ... (Congress, *Laws*, vol. 4, 94) in March of 1807, which became effective on January 1, 1808, fulfilling the expectations of many in the Constitutional Convention that 1808 would see the end of importation of slaves into America.

Tragically, despite the hopes of most, none of these measures led to emancipation for slaves. Even with the end of the slave trade in 1808, the invention of the cotton gin in 1793 had made slavery more economically attractive in the South and the system spread to new southern states throughout the 1800s. It took another 81 years and some 500,000 American lives lost in the Civil War (U.S. Dept. of Veterans Affairs) for the Thirteenth Amendment to the Constitution to formally end slavery in America in 1865 (Baldwin, 37), and blot its stain from the Constitution, placing it in harmony with the intent of the Declaration of Independence. Even then, the effects of slavery, in the form of bigotry and prejudice, remained as scars of America's great national sin.

While the Declaration and Constitution were great accomplishments by the founders in their time, the true tone of the American founding is one of hope in posterity to fulfill the vision of the American Mind. The

---

[61] For Britain, it was the *Abolition of the Slave Trade Act of 1807*.

founders were like Moses, who led the Israelites out of bondage in Egypt and into the promised land. While Moses was praised and honored by God, he was also denied entry to the promised land for his failings (Numbers 20:6-12), and he was required to put his trust in future generations, under the leading of God, to complete that which he began. Such seems to be the case with the American founders. They led the Colonies into a union of statehood, fought for them, pledged all to them, but are denied the full glory of their accomplishment because of the taint of slavery. But the stain of slavery does not undo the many righteous accomplishments, nor eliminate the laud which they are due. Rather, each one was called to account to God for their individual responsibility in not completing the job, and American posterity was, and is, responsible to take care of the rest. As Abraham Lincoln closed his second presidential inaugural address at the close of the Civil War,

> With malice toward none, with charity for all, with firmness in the right as God gives us to see the right, let us strive on to finish the work we are in, to bind up the nation's wounds, to care for him who shall have borne the battle and for his widow and his orphan, to do all which may achieve and cherish a just and lasting peace among ourselves and with all nations. (Holland, *Lincoln*, 504)

It is the call of all Americans to cover over the lasting effects of slavery in love,[62] and stand in the truth of the Declaration of Independence that "all men are created equal" in the foundation of the "Laws of Nature and Nature's God."

Benjamin Franklin's Call for Prayer

While not manifest within the Constitution, Benjamin Franklin's call for prayer during the Constitutional Convention is notable in the final establishment of America's Republic. Without it, there may not have been

---

[62] 1 Peter 4:8

a Constitution, or America may have been founded with only nine states and a less robust system of government.

As has often been the case with mankind, reliance on Divine Providence and focus on prayer tend to fade during times of security and plenty.[63] Such was the case at the Constitutional Convention. The war with Britain was over, and, despite the need to overcome the challenges of the Articles of Confederation and war debt, the promise of American liberty and a republican government never before seen in history loomed on the horizon.

The development of the Constitution was moving along with much debate, but also with regular agreement and progress. Then the question of representation in the new government came under consideration. Representation in the House of Representatives was one of the stickier points between factions of the Northern and Southern states. And the question of how to apportion representation in the Senate entailed a battle between the large and smaller states, with the large states calling for representation based on population while the smaller states argued that the concept of the Senate was representation of the states in the Federal Government and should therefore treat all states equally. The smaller states threatened to exit the Convention if not accommodated in state-oriented representation. The floor of Congress was beset by rancorous debate and then Benjamin Franklin took the floor:

> Mr. President – The small progress we have made, after four or five weeks' close attendance and continued reasonings with each other – our different sentiments on almost every question, several of the last producing as many noes as ayes – is methinks a melancholy proof of the imperfection of the human understanding. We indeed seem to feel our want of political wisdom, since we have been running all about in search it. We have gone back to ancient history for models of government, and examined the different forms of those

---

[63] For example, Judges 8:28-34, 1 Kings 11:1-8, Exodus 32, 2 Kings 17:7-17.

republics which, having been originally formed with the seeds of their own dissolution, now no longer exist. And we have viewed modern states all round Europe, but find none of their constitutions suitable to our circumstances.

In this situation of this assembly, groping as it were in the dark to find political truth, and scarcely able to distinguish it when presented to us, how has it happened, sir, that we have not hitherto once thought of humbly applying to the Father of lights to illuminate our understandings? In the beginning of the contest with Britain, when we were sensible of danger, we had daily prayer in this room for the divine protection. Our prayers, sir, were heard, and they were graciously answered. All of us, who were engaged in the struggle, must have observed frequent instances of a superintending Providence in our favor. To that kind Providence we owe this happy opportunity of consulting in peace on the means of establishing our future national felicity. And have we now forgotten that powerful Friend? Or do we imagine we no longer need his assistance? I have lived, sir, a long time; and the longer I live, the more convincing proofs I see of this truth *that God governs in the affairs of men*! And if a sparrow cannot fall to the ground without his notice, is it probable that an empire can rise without his aid? – We have been assured, sir, in the sacred writings, that "except the Lord build the house, they labor in vain that build it." I firmly believe this; and I also believe, that without his concurring aid, we shall succeed in this political building no better than the builders of Babel. We shall be divided by our little, partial, local interests; our projects will be confounded; and we ourselves shall become a reproach and a bye-word down to future ages. And what is worse, mankind may hereafter, from this unfortunate instance, despair of establishing government by human wisdom, and leave it to chance, war, and conquest.

I therefore beg leave to move, That, henceforth, prayers imploring the assistance of Heaven, and its blessing on our deliberations, be held in this assembly every morning before we proceed to business, and that one or more of the clergy of

this city be requested to officiate in that service. (Madison,
Debates, 253-254)

Discussion followed within the committee of the whole, with some noting
that there was no money to pay for a chaplain to lead prayer as was
customary, that it was late in the proceedings to begin such a practice, and
that such a change might concern the public about dissention within the
proceedings (Madison, *Debates*, 254). No vote was taken on Franklin's
proposal. Franklin, in a footnote to his published letters containing his
speech, wrote that "the Convention, except three or four persons, thought
prayers unnecessary" (Madison, *Debates*, 597).

Debate continued on the voting structure of the Senate for two days until,
on June 30, Benjamin Franklin suggested a compromise be made and
provided a draft rather than just a suggestion. Franklin prefaced his draft
with some simple wisdom,

> When a broad table is to be made, and the edges of planks do
> not fit, the artist takes a little from both, and makes a good
> joint. In like manner, here, both sides must part with some of
> their demands, in order that they may join in some
> accommodating proposition. (Madison, *Debates*, 266)

The proposition was (in part, regarding the Senate),

> That in the appointment of all civil officers of the general
> government, in the election of whom the second branch may
> by the constitution have part, each state shall have equal
> suffrage. (Madison, *Debates*, 266)

Franklin's compromise was not voted on and rancorous debate continued.
On July 2, Charles C. Pinckney stated that he liked Franklin's motion and
proposed a committee consisting of one member from each state to report
on a compromise (Madison, *Debates*, 270). The special committee was
agreed, and the committee of the whole adjourned for three days over the
Independence Day holiday, allowing for candid discussion between a
special compromise committee of delegates apart from party spirit on the
floor of Congress. As a result, minds were changed, seeing the path

forward to the "Great Compromise" and the great end of the Constitution in having a Senate with equal representation for the States.[64] The Great Compromise is also known as the Connecticut Compromise because of a motion made in special committee by Roger Sherman from Connecticut, who had seconded Benjamin Franklin's motion for prayer. Yet, history records that it was Benjamin Franklin's motion in committee and not that of Sherman that established Senate representation as each state having an equal vote (Madison, *Debates*, 274).

While some might focus on the abandonment of Benjamin Franklin's motion calling for prayer, it may be better to focus on the fact that prayerful men made the motion in committee of the whole, and it was the motion in the special committee that led to a compromise that ultimately saved the Constitutional Convention. Benjamin Franklin was parsimonious in active debate at the Convention, yet, despite the rebuff of his call for prayer and his initial proposal for the Senate, it would seem substantive to argue that Divine Providence favored his input, swaying the Convention in establishing the compromise. Yet, what seems even more important is the truth that Franklin acknowledged prayer as key in establishing the Declaration of Independence and then connected it as necessary to the work the delegates were completing in establishing the Constitution to fulfill the vision of the Declaration of Independence.

---

[64] The special committee reported on July 5, but no vote was taken until July 16 when an amended report was put to vote that included other resolutions regarding the legislature. However, the resolution on an equal vote for each state in the Senate remained unchanged (Madison, *Debates*, 316-317).

Chapter 4 –
The Bill of Rights Clarifies the American Mind

THE Conventions of a number of the States, having at the time of their adopting the Constitution, expressed a desire, in order to prevent misconstruction or abuse of its powers, that further declaratory and restrictive clauses should be added: And as extending the ground of public confidence in the Government, will best ensure the beneficent ends of its institution.

Preamble to the Bill of Rights

Purpose of the Bill of Rights

What the Constitution implicitly says about the rights of The People, the Bill of Rights spells out with the clarity of authority that was demanded by founding antifederalist members of Congress and most of the state legislatures approving the Constitution (Elliot, *Debates*, vol. 4, 572). The Bill of Rights is intended to "prevent misconstruction or abuse of" the powers granted to the Federal Government by the Constitution. Abuse of power is fairly easy to understand and foresee. "Misconstruction" is something very different. It means the incorrect, whether accidental or malicious, application of the fundamental law of America. The very basic understanding of anything contained within the Bill of Rights is that it is intended to protect individuals and states from abuse and misuse of law by the Federal Government. Any other "interpretation" is the exact "misconstruction" that the Bill of Rights seeks to avert.

Backstory to the Bill of Rights

The English Bill of Rights was the direct ancestor of America's Bill of Rights. Its history began with England suffering under King Charles II, who returned to power from exile in 1671. Charles II faced lingering dissent following the de facto republic which existed under Oliver Cromwell. To defend his power, he took the means of defense and self-provision from the people under the guise of the Game Act (Chitty, 445). This act purported to regulate hunting and manage game in the kingdom by stripping people of their firearms and even their hunting dogs; and is known as the first recorded gun control law. The subsequent reign of King James II (1685-1688), who attempted to Catholicize an almost entirely Protestant England, took the oppression a step further by deploying a standing army and raiding homes to find hidden firearms. By 1688 the people revolted, James II abdicated in the face of the Glorious Revolution, and William and Mary came to power by agreement. That agreement included creation of the English Bill of Rights which was established in 1689 (Lancaster, 207-230). The influence of the English Bill of Rights on

America's founding documents is evident. Several very recognizable rights from it are (Ralph, 54):

> That the Freedom of Speech, or Debates, and Proceedings in Parliament, ought not to be impeach'd or question'd in any Court or Place out of Parliament.[65]

> That excessive Bail ought not to be requir'd, nor excessive Fines impos'd, nor cruel and unusual Punishments inflicted.[66]

> And that for Redress of all Grievances, and for the amending, strengthening, and preserving of the Laws, Parliaments ought to be held frequently.[67]

Development of the American Bill of Rights

A bill of rights was unnecessary under the Articles of Confederation because the Articles deferred all power to the States which, if desired, would declare particular rights for their citizens (McMaster, 112). With the coming of the Constitution, the antifederalists, those who believed the states should hold power with a loose affiliation between them, feared that a Federal Government superior to the States would quickly become a tyranny without having a specific bill of rights in place. At the time, five of thirteen state constitutions contained a bill of rights for their citizens (McMaster, 252) and antifederalists like Richard Henry Lee and George Mason were adamant that such a bill be part of a constitutional amendment should the Constitution be accepted. However, a bill of rights was not discussed until the Constitutional Convention had essentially completed its work, and even then, only in passing (McMaster, 253). Remarkably, at least in terms of today's politics, the antifederalists waited on development of the Bill of Rights by "gentleman's agreement" until after adoption of the Constitution.[68] Were it not for James Madison faithfully introducing a

---

[65] Similar to First Amendment to the U.S. Constitution.
[66] Similar to Eighth Amendment to the U.S. Constitution.
[67] Similar to First Amendment to the U.S. Constitution.
[68] As acknowledged in the preamble of the accepted Bill of Rights.

list of amendments in Congress as he felt "bound in honor and duty" to do (Lloyd, 414), the Bill of Rights might not have ever become "important" business addressed by Congress.

The Virginia Declaration of Rights (Virginia, 25), written by George Mason in May of 1776 just prior to completion of the Declaration of Independence, became the base, along with elements from the constitutional debates, for Madison's introduction of seventeen constitutional amendments to the House of Representatives on June 8, 1789. At that point, Rhode Island and North Carolina had not yet ratified the Constitution and joined the Union, in part due to the lack of a bill of rights. Congress sent Madison's proposal to committee and, after debate, passed the seventeen amendments and sent them to the Senate. The Senate addressed the House bill of rights, and in reconciliation between the houses of Congress, the seventeen amendments were reduced to twelve (Cobbett, vol. 26, 510-512) and forwarded President George Washington. Washington then sent the list of amendments to the state executives, including North Carolina and Rhode Island, on September 28, 1789. The proposed bill of rights, although yet unratified, helped bring North Carolina and Rhode Island into the Union on November 21, 1789 and May 29, 1790, respectively. Ten of those proposed amendments, what is now known as the Bill of Rights, reached ratification by three quarters of the states, per Article V of the Constitution, on December 15, 1791.

Argument Surrounding a Bill of Rights

Throughout the debates leading to passage, and in debates at the state level, there were many valid arguments against a bill of rights (Story, *Commentaries*, vol. 3, 713-721). James Wilson cited the main arguments during Pennsylvania's debates on ratifying the Constitution,

> ... New Jersey has no bill of rights, New York has none, Connecticut has none, and Rhode Island has none. Thus, Sir, it appears from the example of other states, as well as from principle, that a bill of rights is neither an essential nor a necessary instrument in framing a system of government,

since liberty may exist and be as well secured without it. But it was not only unnecessary, but on this occasion it was found impracticable—for who will be bold enough to undertake to enumerate all the rights of the people?—and when the attempt to enumerate them is made, it must be remembered that if the enumeration is not complete, everything not expressly mentioned will be presumed to be purposely omitted. So it must be with a bill of rights, and an omission in stating the powers granted to the government, is not so dangerous as an omission in recapitulating the rights reserved by the people. ... Thus, Mr. President, an attention to the situation of England will show that the conduct of that country in respect to bills of rights, cannot furnish an example to the inhabitants of the United States, who by the revolution have regained all their natural rights, and possess their liberty neither by grant nor contract. In short, Sir, I have said that a bill of rights would have been improperly annexed to the federal plan, and for this plain reason that it would imply that whatever is not expressed was given, which is not the principle of the proposed constitution. (McMaster, 253-4)

Madison adds to this set of arguments with another that had been expressed during debates on the Constitution,

It has been said, that in the Federal Government they [declared rights] are unnecessary, because the powers are enumerated, and it follows, that all that are not granted by the constitution are retained; that the constitution is a bill of powers, the great residuum being the rights of the people; and, therefore, a bill of rights cannot be so necessary as if the residuum was thrown into the hands of the Government. (Gales, 455)

Madison also noted the argument that "the intermediate existence of the state governments between the people and that [federal] government" would be a bulwark of "vigilance with which they would descry the first symptoms of usurpation, and to the promptitude with which they would sound the alarm to the public" (Elliot, *Debates*, vol. 4, 580), so they, the People, could rise to preserve their liberty.

Yet, the arguments for a bill of rights were also strong. In Madison's introduction of his amendments to the House of Representatives, he outlined them in detail,

> It will be a desirable thing to extinguish from the bosom of every member of the community, any apprehensions that there are those among his countrymen who wish to deprive them of the liberty for which they valiantly fought and honorably bled. And if there are amendments desired of such a nature as will not injure the constitution, and they can be ingrafted so as to give satisfaction to the doubting part of our fellow-citizens, the friends of the Federal Government will evince that spirit of deference and concession for which they have hitherto been distinguished.

> if all power is subject to abuse, that then it is possible the abuse of the powers of the General Government may be guarded against in a more secure manner than is now done, while no one advantage arising from the exercise of that power shall be damaged or endangered by it. ... I shall not propose a single alteration but is likely to meet the concurrence required by the constitution.

> In some instances they [bills of rights] assert those rights which are exercised by the people in forming and establishing a plan of Government. In other instances, they specify those rights which are retained when particular powers are given up to be exercised by the Legislature. In other instances, they specify positive rights, which may seem to result from the nature of the compact. Trial by jury cannot be considered as a natural right, but a right resulting from a social compact which regulates the action of the community, but is as essential to secure the liberty of the people as any one of the pre-existent rights of nature. In other instances, they lay down dogmatic maxims with respect to the construction of the Government; declaring that the legislative, executive, and judicial branches

shall be kept separate and distinct. Perhaps the best way of securing this in practice is, to provide such checks as will prevent the encroachment of the one upon the other.

But whatever may be the form which the several States have adopted in making declarations in favor of particular rights, the great object in view is to limit and qualify the powers of Government, by excepting out of the grant of power those cases in which the Government ought not to act, or to act only in a particular mode. They point these exceptions sometimes against the abuse of the executive power, sometimes against the legislative, and, in some cases, against the community itself; or, in other words, against the majority in favor of the minority. (Gales, 449-450, 453)

It is notable that Madison reiterated his point that the positive value of a declaration of rights is not primarily protection from government, but protection of the minority from the majority body of the people,

Hence, so far as a declaration of rights can tend to prevent the exercise of undue power, it cannot be doubted but such declaration is proper. But I confess that I do conceive, that in a Government modified like this of the United States, the great danger lies rather in the abuse of the community than in the legislative body. The prescriptions in favor of liberty ought to be levelled against that quarter where the greatest danger lies, namely, that which possesses the highest prerogative of power. But this is not found in either the executive or legislative departments of Government, but in the body of the people, operating by the majority against the minority. (Gales, 455)

Madison went on to dispel the argument of enumerated powers in the Constitution as being a check on the infringement of peoples' rights, noting that the legislative branch has "the power to make all laws which shall be necessary and proper for carrying into execution all the powers vested in the Government of the United States," which could lead to laws abridging rights.

When the Constitution was under the discussions which preceded its ratification, it is well known that great apprehensions were expressed by many, lest the omission of some positive exception, from the powers delegated, of certain rights, and of the freedom of the press particularly, might expose them to danger of being drawn, by construction, within some of the powers vested in Congress; more especially of the power to make all laws necessary and proper for carrying their other powers into execution. (Elliot, *Debates*, vol. 4, 572)

Further, Madison noted,

The General Government has a right to pass all laws which shall be necessary to collect its revenue; the means for enforcing the collection are within the direction of the Legislature: may not general warrants be considered necessary for this purpose, as well as for some purposes which it was supposed at the framing of their constitutions the State Governments had in view? (Gales, 455-456)

Madison, using one of the amendments, also addressed the specific concern about people retaining the rights not explicitly declared in the Bill of Rights,

The powers not delegated by this constitution, nor prohibited by it to the States, are reserved to the States respectively. (Gales, 453)

With the passing of time and development of the American government, the Bill of Rights seems to have become a well-accepted set of clarifications to the Constitution. John Quincy Adams, looking through the lenses of his own presidency and that of his father as a Founder, had strong beliefs about the inclusion of a declaration of rights. Leveraging the "homebuilding" analogy of the founding documents[69] – considering the

---

[69] Initially discussed in Chapter 2 – *The Declaration of Independence is the American Mind*.

Declaration as the vision of the builder, showing what the character and use of the building will be; the Constitution as the blueprint for the building; and the Bill of Rights as a list of clarifying instructions beyond the basic needs of the contractor to ensure the best use of the structure by the homeowner – Adams noted,

> the omission of a clear and explicit Declaration of Rights, was a great defect in the Constitution as presented by the Convention to the people, and that it has been imperfectly remedied by the ten Articles of amendment proposed by the first Congress under the Constitution, and now incorporated with it.
>
> A Declaration of Rights would have marked in a more emphatic manner the return from the derivative sovereignty of the states, to the constituent sovereignty of the people for the basis of the federal Union, than was done by the words, "We the people of the United States," in the preamble to the Constitution. A Declaration of Rights, also, systematically drawn up, as a part of the Constitution, and adapted to it with the consummate skill displayed in the consistent adjustment of its mighty powers, would have made it more complete in its unity, and in its symmetry, than it now appears, an elegant edifice, but encumbered with superadditions, not always in keeping with the general character of the building itself.
>
> A Declaration of Rights, reserved by the constituent body, the people, might and probably would have prevented many delicate and dangerous questions of conflicting jurisdictions which have arisen, and may yet arise between the general and the separate state governments. The rights reserved by the people would have been exclusively their own rights, and they would have been protected from the encroachments not only of the general government, but of the disunited states. (Adams, J. Q., 45-46)

In short, John Quincy Adams recognized the power of the Bill of Rights in protecting "We the People," while also asserting that, had the Bill of

Rights been drafted by a committee during the Constitutional Convention, in the spirit of the Declaration of Independence rather than in the first general Congress of the new United States of America, it would have even better prevented abuse and misconstruction of the Constitution.

Structure of the Bill of Rights

The amendments comprising the Bill of Rights reflect several key principles. Firstly, the protection of natural (unalienable) rights that are implicit from the Declaration of Independence and the un-amended Constitution. Amendments I, II, IV and V address the preservation of unalienable rights, ensuring they remain beyond the scope of responsibilities delegated to government in the Constitution. Secondly, several of the amendments express rights that balance powers granted in the main body of the Constitution. For example, amendments VI, VII and VIII deal largely with limiting government overreach in legal proceedings for which government has legitimate purpose. The relationship of these provisions to the grievances against King George III in the Declaration of Independence is obvious. Finally, amendments IX and X wrap up the sentiment of the preamble, expressing that the declaration (as opposed to enumeration) of rights in the Bill of Rights does not deny or disparage other individual rights or the powers of the States or the people as society. Amendment X also highlights that the Bill of Rights, at least until after ratification of the Fourteenth Amendment, applied only to the Federal Government and not to states.[70]

The first ten amendments to the Constitution, accepted in whole, with a preamble, comprise the American Bill of Rights (Cobbett, vol. 26, 510). The first two articles of the Senate-passed Bill of Rights were not ratified by the States. The text here lists them as released by the Senate, with the original article number and the ratified amendment number in brackets [].

---

[70] See *The Tenth and Fourteenth Amendments* in Part Two.

The Bill of Rights

Congress of the United States

begun and held at the City of New-York, on

Wednesday the fourth of March, one thousand seven hundred and eighty nine.

THE Conventions of a number of the States, having at the time of their adopting the Constitution, expressed a desire, in order to prevent misconstruction or abuse of its powers, that further declaratory and restrictive clauses should be added: And as extending the ground of public confidence in the Government, will best ensure the beneficent ends of its institution.

RESOLVED by the Senate and House of Representatives of the United States of America, in Congress assembled, two thirds of both Houses concurring, that the following Articles be proposed to the Legislatures of the several States, as amendments to the Constitution of the United States, all, or any of which Articles, when ratified by three fourths of the said Legislatures, to be valid to all intents and purposes, as part of the said Constitution; viz.

ARTICLES in addition to, and Amendment of the Constitution of the United States of America, proposed by Congress, and ratified by the Legislatures of the several States, pursuant to the fifth Article of the original Constitution.

Article 1. [Not Ratified]

After the first enumeration required by the first article of the Constitution, there shall be one representative for every thirty thousand, until the number shall amount to one hundred, after which the proportion shall be so regulated by Congress, that there shall be not less than one hundred representatives, nor less than one representative for every forty thousand persons, until the number of representatives shall amount to two hundred; after which the proportion shall be so regulated by Congress, that there shall not be less than two hundred representatives, nor more than one representative for every fifty thousand persons.

Article 2. [Ratified in 1992 as Amendment XXVII]

No law varying the compensation for the services of senators and representatives shall take effect, until an election of representatives shall have intervened.

Article 3. [Amendment I]

Congress shall make no law respecting an establishment of religion, or prohibiting the free exercise thereof; or abridging the freedom of speech, or of the press; or the right of the people peaceably to assemble, and to petition the Government for a redress of grievances.

Article 4. [Amendment II]

A well regulated Militia, being necessary to the security of a free State, the right of the people to keep and bear Arms, shall not be infringed.

Article 5. [Amendment III]

No Soldier shall, in time of peace be quartered in any house, without the consent of the Owner, nor in time of war, but in a manner to be prescribed by law.

Article 6. [Amendment IV]

The right of the people to be secure in their persons, houses, papers, and effects, against unreasonable searches and seizures, shall not be violated, and no Warrants shall issue, but upon probable cause, supported by Oath or affirmation, and particularly describing the place to be searched, and the persons or things to be seized.

Article 7. [Amendment V]

No person shall be held to answer for a capital, or otherwise infamous crime, unless on a presentment or indictment of a Grand Jury, except in cases arising in the land or naval forces, or in the Militia, when in actual service in time of War or public danger; nor shall any person be subject for the same offence to be twice put in jeopardy of life or limb; nor shall be compelled in any criminal case to be a witness against himself, nor be deprived of life, liberty, or property, without due process of law; nor shall private property be taken for public use, without just compensation.

Article 8. [Amendment VI]

In all criminal prosecutions, the accused shall enjoy the right to a speedy and public trial, by an impartial jury of the State and district wherein the crime shall have been committed, which district shall have been previously ascertained by law, and to be informed of the nature and cause of the accusation; to be confronted with the witnesses against him; to have compulsory process for obtaining witnesses in his favor, and to have the Assistance of Counsel for his defence.

Article 9. [Amendment VII]

In Suits at common law, where the value in controversy shall exceed twenty dollars, the right of trial by jury shall be preserved, and no fact tried by a jury, shall be otherwise re-examined in any Court of the United States, than according to the rules of the common law.

Article 10. [Amendment VIII]

Excessive bail shall not be required, nor excessive fines imposed, nor cruel and unusual punishments inflicted.

Article 11. [Amendment IX]

The enumeration in the Constitution, of certain rights, shall not be construed to deny or disparage others retained by the people.

Article 12 [Amendment X]

The powers not delegated to the United States by the Constitution, nor prohibited by it to the States, are reserved to the States respectively, or to the people.

The Error of Limitations

There is a tendency in society to seek to place legal prohibitions on certain aspects of a right because someone might breach the duty/responsibility aspect of that right, thus interfering with someone else's rights. That is, society tends to want to prevent licentiousness by individuals. Or, put another way, society as a whole is generally willing to penalize the whole of the people for the licentiousness of a few. The premise behind this tendency is flawed in that any right that can be limited because someone might use it improperly is not a right. If a civil authority controls the utility of a "right," then it is only a privilege. The Bill of Rights does not grant privileges; it does not even grant rights. The Bill of Rights recognizes and protects a set of natural, unalienable, rights[71] from interference by civil authorities.

The duty aspect of natural rights, or any right, often takes on a strange character when a right is closely coupled to pending legislation or a court challenge to an existing law. What so many, including great minds of law, seem to forget is the absolute nature of unalienable rights. An individual is permitted to lend natural rights to civil authorities for execution as part of the social compact, but the individual can never surrender an absolute

---

[71] Some rights, such as freedom of the press or trial by jury are not natural rights, but are so closely derived from natural rights, like freedom of speech, that they are treated accordingly, as noted by Madison (Gales, 453).

right, nor have it taken by society at large or by the civil authority.[72] Yet, in many court opinions and legal commentaries, unalienable rights that exist in the Bill of Rights are portrayed as having legal limitations. These "limitations" are based on one of two logical errors. The first is a misunderstanding of what rights are actually being infringed by a breach of duty. The second is that the limitations are incorrectly based in what appear as societal norms because of shortsighted thinking or political calculation, but which are actually transient popular culture.

A simple example of misunderstanding and incorrectly limiting one right to stop licentiousness in another is treating the prohibition of slander as a legal limitation on free speech. Slander is actually an attack on the property of a person by means of verbal defamation, leading to possible loss of income or real property. There is no justifiable way to prohibit and prevent slander as a limitation to free speech, there is only the opportunity to punish slander as an abridgement of another person's right to property in their reputation and livelihood. Furthermore, there is no legally addressable issue if the slandered party does not take issue with the defamation or cannot prove that the speech amounted to defamation. This may seem like a semantic or philosophical difference between a limitation on rights and punishing a breach of someone else's rights, but it is eminently important as a principle to ensure that natural rights are not limited out of faulty good intentions. To set limitations on a natural right is to begin the practical forfeiture of that right.

The second type of limitation based in popular culture is evident in the popular notion of "hate speech." Hate speech is an undefinable, subjective sentiment, labeling speech, or even an idea espoused, by an individual as being hateful to one or more people, therefore proclaiming such speech to be unprotected by the First Amendment of the U.S. Constitution. While civility, courtesy and current popular culture may agree with such sentiment, there is no such limitation in the right of free speech because

---

[72] Unless one breaks the social compact, such as by committing murder.

no right is violated simply in the speaking or thinking of that which might be considered hatred. As is commonly noted by those understanding constitutional rights, the only reason the First Amendment is required is to protect speech which is unpopular.

Case Study in Limitations – The Alien and Sedition Acts

In 1798, a Federalist Congress and President John Adams passed a series of laws collectively known as the Alien and Sedition Acts. These laws created criminal penalties for criticism of the government, limited the free press, and tightened controls on immigration and naturalization. To provide a taste of the incredible nature of these acts, part of the Sedition Act read,

> And be it further enacted, that if any shall write, print, utter, or publish, or shall cause or procure to be written, printed, uttered, or published, or shall knowingly and willingly assist or aid in writing, printing, uttering, or publishing, any false, scandalous, and malicious writing or writings against the government of the United States, or either house of the Congress of the United States, with an intent to defame the said government, or either house of the said Congress, or the President, or to bring them or either of them into contempt or disrepute, or to excite against them, or either or any of them, the hatred of the good people of the United States, &c., — then such persons, being thereof convicted before any court of the United States having jurisdiction thereof, shall be punished by a fine not exceeding two thousand dollars, and by imprisonment not exceeding two years. (Elliot, *Debates*, vol.4, 573-574)

In response to these acts, the legislatures of Virginia and Kentucky passed resolutions declaring the acts null and void within their territory. Virginia sent the resolutions to the governors and legislatures of the other states as a call to have the states drive to rescind the Alien and Sedition Acts.

For this, Virginia received much attention and significant criticism from other states, to which the 1799-1800 session of the Virginia House of

Delegates responded with a report authored by none other than the "Father of the federal Bill of Rights," James Madison. The report is extensive, but elements of it provide a case study in the sanctity of natural rights, and positive rights based in social compact (for example the right to a free press or trial by jury), from government encroachment, even with one of the most respected and liberty-minded founding fathers sitting as President.

The most relevant of the Virginia Resolutions reads,

> That the General Assembly doth particularly protest against the palpable and alarming infractions of the Constitution, in the two late cases of the 'Alien and Sedition Acts,' passed at the last session of Congress; **the first of which exercises a power nowhere delegated to the federal government**; and which, by uniting legislative and judicial powers to those of the executive, subverts the general principles of free government, as well as the particular organization and positive provisions of the Federal Constitution; and **the other of which acts exercises, in like manner, a power not delegated by the Constitution, but, on the contrary, expressly and positively forbidden by one of the amendments thereto** — a power which, more than any other, ought to produce universal alarm, because it is levelled against the right of freely examining public characters and measures, and of free communication among the people thereon, which has ever been justly deemed the only effectual guardian of every other right. (Elliot, *Debates*, vol.4, 554, emphasis added)

The emphasized phrases highlight the two greatest concerns when judging the constitutionality of any law that may infringe on an individual's rights, and Madison expressed the process for judging constitutionality in a straightforward manner in the report,

> Whenever, therefore, a question arises concerning the constitutionality of a particular power, the first question is, whether the power be expressed in the Constitution. If it be,

the question is decided. If it be not expressed, the next inquiry must be, whether it is **properly an incident to an express power, and necessary to its execution**. If it be, it may be exercised by Congress. If it be not, Congress cannot exercise it. (Elliot, *Debates*, vol. 4, 567-568, emphasis added)

To the first point, Madison writes about the context and spirit by which the Constitution was written to make it clear that it granted enumerated limited powers to the Federal Government.

in all the contemporary discussions and comments which the Constitution underwent, it was constantly justified and recommended on the ground that the powers not given to the government were withheld from it; and that, if any doubt could have existed on this subject, under the original text of the Constitution, it is removed, as far as words could remove it, by the 12th amendment[73], now a part of the Constitution, which expressly declares, "that the powers not delegated to the United States by the Constitution, nor prohibited by it to the states, are reserved to the states respectively, or to the people." (Elliot, *Debates*, vol. 4, 547)

If the powers granted be valid, it is solely because they are granted; and if the granted powers are valid because granted, all other powers not granted must not be valid. (Elliot, *Debates*, vol. 4, 548)

There is no enumerated power in the Constitution for the measures contained in the Alien and Sedition Acts.

To the second criterion, that the particular power must be incident to an express power and necessary to its execution, Madison noted that there was a growing overextension of the clause in Article 1, Section 8 of the Constitution which empowers Congress "To make all Laws which shall be necessary and proper for carrying into Execution the foregoing Powers, and all other Powers vested by this Constitution in the Government of the

---

[73] Today, the original 12th amendment is known as the Tenth Amendment.

United States, or in any Department or Officer thereof." He makes the point that this clause, residing after the list of enumerated powers in Article 1, Section 8, is not a grant of new powers to Congress, but merely a declaration to remove any uncertainty that Congress has the authority to exercise the express powers it listed (Elliot, *Debates*, vol. 4, 567).

Yet the chicanery of the Alien and Sedition Acts attempted to use this clause to misapply the express power to "suppress insurrections." Madison, noting the requirement that the supporting law be "necessary and proper," squarely refuted the argument saying,

> But it surely cannot, with the least plausibility, be said, that the regulation of the press, and punishment of libels, are exercises of a power to suppress insurrections.

He went on to show that if a case were made to do so, it would create,

> unlimited means of carrying into execution limited powers. (Elliot, *Debates*, vol. 4, 568)

With regard to the third criterion of whether the power is expressly and positively forbidden by one of the amendments to the Constitution, Madison cited the preamble to the Bill of Rights and wrote,

> Here is the most satisfactory and authentic proof that the several amendments proposed were to be considered as either declaratory or restrictive, and, whether the one or the other, as corresponding with the desire expressed by a number of the states, and as extending the ground of public confidence in the government.

> Under any other construction of the amendment relating to the press, than that it declared the press to be wholly exempt from the power of Congress, the amendment could neither be said to correspond with the desire expressed by a number of the states, nor be calculated to extend the ground of public confidence in the government.

> Nay, more; the construction employed to justify the Sedition Act would exhibit a phenomenon without a parallel in the political world. It would exhibit a number of respectable states, as denying, first, that any power over the press was delegated by the Constitution; as proposing, next, that an amendment to it should explicitly declare that no such power was delegated; and, finally, as concurring in an amendment actually recognizing or delegating such a power. (Elliot, *Debates*, vol. 4, 572)

Madison concluded the segment with,

> If no such power be expressly delegated, and if it be not both necessary and proper to carry into execution an express power; above all, if it be expressly forbidden, by a declaratory amendment to the Constitution, — the answer must be, that the federal government is destitute of all such authority. (Elliot, *Debates*, vol. 4, 573)

As a case study in demonstrating the constitutionality of laws, particularly those directly abridging rights expressed in the Bill of Rights, Madison's report on the Virginia Resolutions has no peer. Not only is the unconstitutionality of the Alien and Sedition Acts demonstrated from all angles, not only was the proper criteria for evaluating constitutionality expressed, but Madison also demonstrated the potential for the abridgement of one right to lay the groundwork for abridgement of other rights by showing that the attacks on freedom of the press in the Alien and Seditions Acts would eventually threaten freedom of religion (Elliot, *Debates*, vol. 4, 576-577) and cascade into other First Amendment rights and beyond.

Preventative Justice

The topic of "preventative justice" is also mentioned in James Madison's report on Virginia's resolutions on the Alien and Sedition Acts and requires some review as a type of limitation on rights. Much like the unconstitutional concept of considering prohibitions of the free press as a preventative measure to potential insurrection, "preventative justice," other than after a just and legal arrest for a crime, attempts to presume an action will be taken which necessarily leads to a criminally licentious result.

Madison described the sacred principles necessary to support a preventative justice measure:

> In the administration of preventive justice, the following principles have been held sacred: that some probable ground of suspicion be exhibited before some judicial authority; that it be supported by oath or affirmation; that the party may avoid being thrown into confinement, by finding pledges or sureties for his legal conduct sufficient in the judgment of some judicial authority; that he may have the benefit of a writ of habeas corpus, and thus obtain his release if wrongfully confined; and that he may at any time be discharged from his recognizance, or his confinement, and restored to his former liberty and rights, on the order of the proper judicial authority, if it shall see sufficient cause. (Elliot, *Debates*, vol. 4, 555)

What is most noteworthy is what is implied, but not written, in Madison's principles. Preventative justice refers to action taken regarding an individual for a specific cause, which also implies contemporaneousness. It is, for example, clearly unjust to take action against an individual for an action they might take in five years, or even that they would certainly take in five years if such were possible to know. Nor does Madison cite confiscation of property as a means of preventative justice, only the confinement of the individual, in accord with Lockean principles. Preventative justice cannot be a general limitation on any right. At most, it can only be a limitation on the right of an individual in a particular circumstance where that individual breaches a legal obligation.

Overall, the principles and process described by Madison are that of the arrest process. And that makes perfect sense in America where one is presumed innocent until proven guilty. Even a person caught in the act of a crime is presumed innocent, and the incarceration of that person is preventative of them committing another crime until they are charged and face trial.

The only other form of preventative justice that seems common today is a protection order, or temporary restraining order, issued by a judge using a sworn statement by a complainant seeking protection from life-threatening behavior of an accused, and requiring the accused to appear in court for the order to be removed or modified. This type of preventative justice must be in response to licentiousness – the invasion of the general rights to life, liberty and the pursuit of happiness of another person, rather than a crime for which an arrest can be made. As opposed to incarceration, this type of preventative justice is a mild encroachment on the rights of the accused, typically targeting only that person's right to be within a prescribed distance from the complainant. Potentially there are effects on the use of property between people in the same domicile, but the order does not affect ownership or other individual property rights.

Such judicial orders have been accepted in America because of the narrow limitations imposed on the rights of one person to ensure that person, after some serious demonstration of licentious behavior threatening life, liberty or property, does not again abridge the rights of one or several other people with their personal behavior.

Cultural Limitations on Natural Rights

Beyond the extremes of preventative justice, society uses its culture to "limit" rights to reduce abuse of the duty aspect of natural rights and licentiousness in general. For America this practice goes directly back to the foundation of equality of man and the Law of Nature and Nature's God in the Declaration of Independence. When society is strong in these base truths as part of culture, promoted through religion and good civics, there is less abuse of rights, coincident with more liberty.

Both religion and good civics, in the practice of society, should seek quiet, polite correction of licentiousness. In greater extremes, society may create acceptable "peer pressure" on individuals to justly exercise their rights.

Such peer pressure comes in the form of social (not organized by civil authority) stigma or ostracism from societal groups that do not exceed the bounds of civil authority,[74] and which should be viewed by society as corrective rather than punitive.

Over time, the bounds of such peer pressure tend to expand, creating a hedge protecting against licentiousness. So, where a duty aspect of free speech may be to not slander someone, the societal hedge may grow to become, "do not publicly speak ill of someone under any circumstances." This expansion may be acceptable in society, with tacit understanding that it can be broken by anyone under certain conditions at the expense of feeling societal pressure, but societal pressure may not go to the extent of violating natural rights. Such a behavioral hedge is commonly known as civility. Unfortunately, with time, the respectful restraint on the exercise of natural rights tends to be viewed as permanent concession of rights by the public.

Nineteenth century philosopher, John Stuart Mill[75] explained the human need to address licentiousness:

> All that makes existence valuable to any one, depends on the
> enforcement of restraints upon the actions of other people.
> Some rules of conduct, therefore, must be imposed, by law in
> the first place, and by opinion on many things which are not
> fit subjects for the operation of law. What these rules should
> be, is the principal question in human affairs; (Mill, 14)

Unfortunately, there are always some who do not hold to culture and when an exceptional breach of civility occurs, society, in anger, fear, or indignation, rises up and calls for the rights of all to be limited to "ensure" that such a breach never again occurs. Consequently, a civic expectation

---

[74] For example, imprisonment would be beyond the scope of proper societal penalty apart from civil authority.

[75] Mill departs from the philosophy of Natural Law in a number of ways, but aligns on the foundational understanding of transient culture, as "custom," in its effect on liberty.

to not publicly speak ill of someone under any circumstances might become a prohibition on "hate speech," with attempts to criminalize such speech as a "legitimately" disallowed exception to the unalienable right of free speech.

Alternatively, as James Madison explained in the arguments for a bill of rights, society at large seeks, via mob rule, to unjustly impose its will to counter an offense. Just as there are those who will not hold to a foundational culture, there are always some who are focused on controlling others via changes in culture. These seek to expand the cultural hedge to become so broad it becomes the infringer of rights and usurps power from the civil authority, and ultimately from the body of the people. In such a case, the definition of "hate speech" might be used to identify and label an entire class of people, expanding the definition to include various sets of religious values, or political and social beliefs. Once labeled, that segment of society may be denied services, boycotted in their businesses, and excoriated in public at the whims of members of the self-justified majority.

Popular Culture is a Bane to Rights

These departures from core culture that usurp rights via the body of the people are the excesses of popular culture.[76] Popular culture is transient style or opinion that strays from timeless or long-standing cultural norms and customs. Popular culture, insofar as it relates to anyone's rights, tends to run counter to historical truth, developing a lexicon based on faulty concepts and half-truths. "Hate speech" is a great example. It has no historical legal basis, is impossible to accurately define, yet is easy for anyone to define in their own way, all of which tends to establish the concept without ever deeply evaluating it. The further popular culture strays from timeless norms of morality and virtue, the more egregious and inexcusable the violations of rights become as social retribution and legal

---

[76] Exemplified by Occupy ICE protestors driving a nearby business to close (KGW Staff).

limitations are placed on liberty and natural rights. This is because truth and the context of history generally do not matter in popular culture, becoming abandoned, along with the cultural foundation from which the popular culture strayed. Like traditions, which through time and inattention tend to replace the remembrance and protection of sacred ideas with hollow actions, popular culture seeks to "protect" certain rights by placing limitations on other rights to hedge against licentiousness. But in the end, liberty is damaged for all.

John Stuart Mill was British, and wrote *On Liberty* some eighty years after America's founding, but his views on customs and culture expand upon the same understanding expressed by Madison, that the Majority is often a greater threat to liberty than the magistrate:

> when society is itself the tyrant — society collectively, over the separate individuals who compose it—its means of tyrannizing are not restricted to the acts which it may do by the hands of its political functionaries. Society can and does execute its own mandates: and if it issues wrong mandates instead of right, or any mandates at all in things with which it ought not to meddle, it practises a social tyranny more formidable than many kinds of political oppression, since, though not usually upheld by such extreme penalties, it leaves fewer means of escape, penetrating much more deeply into the details of life, and enslaving the soul itself. (Mill, 13)

> There is a limit to the legitimate interference of collective opinion with individual independence: and to find that limit, and maintain it against encroachment, is as indispensable to a good condition of human affairs, as protection against political despotism. (Mill, 14)

Mills' comments jibe with the rationale of a Declaration of Independence expressing the just vision for America, and limited government by a Constitution of enumerated powers and checks and balances prescribed by the founders, and the Bill of Rights. The Declaration sets the baseline expectations of society in culture and the Constitution, with the Bill of

Rights, limits the deviation from that culture by both civil authorities and society. In practice, however, the need for patriots of the American Mind is required as part of that just and moral society expressed by John Adams for America's values to rise above the noise of popular culture.

On the practice of mob rule retribution beyond a light hedge against licentiousness, Mill continued to highlight the closed and selfish mindset, antithetical to the Declaration of Independence, which defines the purveyors of popular culture and the premises used for the social domination of the individual,

> Yet the people of any given age and country no more suspect any difficulty in it [deciding the proper rules of conduct in society], than if it were a subject on which mankind had always been agreed. The rules which obtain among themselves appear to them self-evident and self-justifying. This all but universal illusion is one of the examples of the magical influence of custom,[77] which is not only, as the proverb says, a second nature, but is continually mistaken for the first. (Mill, 14-15)

> Men's opinions, accordingly, on what is laudable or blameable, are affected by all the multifarious causes which influence their wishes in regard to the conduct of others, and which are as numerous as those which determine their wishes on any other subject. Sometimes their reason—at other times their prejudices or superstitions: often their social affections, not seldom their antisocial ones, their envy or jealousy, their arrogance or contemptuousness: but most commonly, their desires or fears for themselves— their legitimate or illegitimate self-interest. (Mill, 16)

In essence, Mill has established the components of popular culture as the rationale by which men seek to limit the rights of others and control them. Yet these same components drive men to seek liberty for themselves. The

---

[77] "Custom" may be considered here to be popular culture.

only difference between the seekers of liberty and the seekers of control is acceptance and regard for the equality of mankind in the Law of Nature and Nature's God.

Mill further exposes those lacking regard for the culture of the American Mind when he says,

> They have occupied themselves rather in inquiring what things society ought to like or dislike, than in questioning whether its likings or dislikings should be a law to individuals. They preferred endeavouring to alter the feelings of mankind on the particular points on which they were themselves heretical, rather than make common cause in defence of freedom, with heretics generally. (Mill, 17-18)

This threat to natural rights from popular culture is compounded by unsound legislation and citation of prior court opinions as precedent for new law and court opinion. In contrast to basing law and court opinion on the foundational vision and culture defined by the Declaration of Independence and the law of the Constitution, law and opinion based on precedents will compound any error made. If that error is due to a misreading of popular culture as being part of foundational culture, the error can negatively affect liberty for decades or longer.

Popular culture never goes away and it cannot be corralled or controlled. It is fine as a guide for people exercising their rights, when it is only a guide against which people individually choose to act. However, coercing adherence to popular culture or codifying it into law, be it legislatively or by judicial fiat, is the same as mob rule – the tacit majority as represented by prevailing transient culture, overruling the Law of Nature and Nature's God. In the enjoyment of popular culture and establishment of social pressures which establish it in its time, society must always guard the foundational culture of the American Mind as the basis for law and the touchstone for evaluating cultural phenomena.

An example of the misuse of court precedent can be found in the common nineteenth century prohibition of carrying concealed firearms for self-defense. At the time, openly carrying a firearm for self-defense was deemed appropriate by society. Picture the cowboy with his six-gun in the wild West; everyone had them and many wore them at all times. At the same time, carrying a concealed firearm was considered to be the unmanly action of an assassin.[78] Society used its peer pressure in this popular culture to reduce the carrying of concealed weapons by labeling the practice as evil.[79] However, rather than remaining a tool of societal pressure, legislatures codified, and judges upheld, prohibition of the concealed carry of firearms despite it being based only in the transient culture of the day, contrary to the natural right of self-defense as expressed in the Second Amendment to the Constitution.[80]

Fast forward to the present. The open carrying of firearms is now largely shunned by society as being menacing, while the concealed carrying of firearms is preferred as being non-threatening and providing a better defensive scenario in terms of firearm security and element of surprise in a self-defense encounter. This is a complete reversal of popular culture regarding the carrying of firearms over the past century or so. But neither the present popular firearms culture nor that of the nineteenth century has anything to do with justly limiting the right to self-defense via the Second Amendment of the Constitution. Despite this, the nineteenth century prohibitions on concealed carry are still cited in dictum, even in the acclaimed *District of Columbia v. Heller* case (United States Supreme Court, Heller, hereafter denoted as *Heller*), as being a legitimate limitation of Second Amendment rights because the prohibition was deemed acceptable long ago.

Basing a court opinion on popular culture is like saying that leisure suits are high fashion because they were popular in the late 1970s. It isn't true

---

[78] Louisiana Supreme Court: *State v. Chandler, 5 La. Ann. 489, 52 Am. Dec. 599 (1850).*
[79] Georgia Supreme Court: *Nunn v. State, 1 Ga. (1 Kel.) 243 (1846).*
[80] Thomas Cooley is cited in the dictionary in 1911: "and the secret carrying of those suited merely to deadly individual encounters may be prohibited" (Webster, *Webster's International*, 126).

now, and it wasn't true even during the time it was generally accepted. In similar contrast, prohibition of concealed carrying of firearms was always counter to the principles of self-defense in the Law of Nature and Nature's God of the Declaration, and counter to the Second Amendment in the Bill of Rights.

The culture of America that has always existed, sometimes as an undercurrent to popular culture, sometimes as the mainstream culture – individual liberty, truth, equality and duty – these are the only bases for just court precedent, and even then, they must comport with "the law of God, and the law of nature; so that laws human must be made according to the general laws of nature, and without contradiction to any positive law of scripture" (Locke, 270).

In summary, a natural right belongs to the individual to exercise as he pleases, as long as he does not abridge the rights of others in the course of exercising it (Locke, 170). Beyond this duty, society may encourage an individual to forgo exercising aspects of their rights as part of good citizenship and civility based in the foundational American culture, and in deference to popular culture, but such societal pressures cannot be applied as legal or punitive limitations to the right.

Closing in on the Amendments to the Constitution

The Bill of Rights enhances the ties between the Constitution and Declaration, effectively demonstrating the rights of the people to be the paramount objective of government. The Constitution has so long contained the first ten amendments that John Quincy Adams' sentiments about the necessity of the Bill of Rights seem a long-foregone conclusion in today's world. However, there are modern situations in which the express rights of the people are used in attempt to infringe on the natural rights of the people. Madison's insight is worth repeating once more,

> The prescriptions in favor of liberty ought to be levelled against that quarter where the greatest danger lies, namely, …

in the body of the people, operating by the majority against the minority.

It is incumbent upon all Americans to understand "that they are endowed by their Creator with certain unalienable Rights" and that all must stand against usurpation of those rights not just by government, but by the body of the people, "the mob," who purposefully, or ignorantly, misconstrue and misconstruct them to wrest power from their fellow man who may choose to justly exercise rights outside of the culture *du jour*.

Full exposition of all the amendments of the Bill of Rights is beyond the scope of this book, but Joseph Story, who was appointed as Supreme Court Justice under President James Madison, the principal author of the Bill of Rights, provides excellent commentary on the Constitution and its Amendments (Story, *Commentaries*, vol. 3, 722-755). The beauty of Story's *Commentaries on the Constitution* is that it is not plagued with discussion of court precedent. Story's comments, rather, look back at the debates, the historical context, and the philosophies that drove the creation of the Constitution and Bill of Rights.

However, it is necessary to delve into especially relevant amendments from the Bill of Rights and issues that reflect what has happened to the American Mind over time. Those discussions may be found in Part 2 – Digging Deeper into the Nature of Rights.

Chapter 5 –
Thinking with the American Mind

America arose from a plan of Divine Providence, in the fullness of time, at the hand of Nature's God, the God of the Bible. The American founders believed this, and the evidence is strong for those willing to honestly consider it. The case for America as a divinely inspired and blessed nation can be seen in the time before America's founding, throughout the struggle for independence, in the considered, careful and deliberate debates on the rights of mankind and the role for government, and in the fruit America has produced in the world in the more than 240 years since independence was proclaimed.

America is the greatest nation that mankind has ever experienced; the freest, the most generous, the most industrious, and the greatest economic engine in history. Yes, America remains imperfect, and as an institution of fallen mankind, America never will be perfect. Nor will America's People be perfect. But the fact that the tools have imperfections does not mean that the craftsman cannot use them to create a masterpiece. America can still be the blessing that Divine Providence designed.

This is the idea of Jefferson's "American Mind." Most Americans venerate the Constitution as America's crowning achievement, seldom considering that the Declaration is the true guiding light for America. The Constitution is certainly worthy of praise, nothing like it has been created in the world as a foundation for government, before or since, or brought so many people liberty and prosperity. But the Constitution remains imperfect and subject to the buttress of a moral and religious people to remain standing.

It is the Declaration of Independence that is as pure an instrument of government as possible for a society of diverse views and opinions. The Declaration of Independence is the American Mind and its culture; individual liberty, truth, equality and duty, must be written on the hearts of its people or it too can topple. As expressed by John Quincy Adams,

> But the indissoluble link of union between the people of the several states of this confederated nation, is after all, not in the right [of separation], but in the heart. If the day should ever come, (may Heaven avert it,) when the affections of the people of these states shall be alienated from each other; when the fraternal spirit shall give away to cold indifference, or collisions of interest shall fester into hatred, the bands of political association will not long hold together parties no longer attracted by the magnetism of conciliated interests and kindly sympathies; (Adams, J. Q., 69)

The first thing many people will say when hearing about the "American Mind" is, "that's not who we are any more." The truth is that "we" may not be a people of that American Mind at the present time, but the American Mind is who "We the People" will always be in America. America's foundational culture has always been rejected by some of the people and forsaken by others for transient popular culture, but it has never been fully erased. Although men declared the American Mind, they did not create it. God created the American Mind; therefore, it can be strengthened and expanded.

Benjamin Rush made a great distinction in 1787 regarding this very point about the American Revolution and the war with the British.

> There is nothing more common than to confound the terms of *American Revolution* with those of *the late American War*. The American war is over: but this is far from being the case with the American revolution. On the contrary, nothing but the first act of the great drama is closed. It remains yet to

establish and perfect our new forms of government; and to prepare the principles, morals, and manners of our citizens for these forms of government, after they are established and brought to perfection. (Rush, *Defects*, 147)

The war is long over, and the Constitution and government established under George Washington completed the revolution, but even today the drive of the American Revolution is alive; not to overturn the foundation of the American Mind, but to fulfill it. To do so only requires thinking with the "principles, morals, and manners" of the American Mind.

Chapter 6 –
Living the American Mind

The Culture Bearers

It may seem contradictory to suggest that there remains a foundational American culture and that it still needs to be cultivated and expanded. But, pause to consider the change of tone that occurs in news, social media and general interaction between Americans on patriotic days in America like Independence Day and Veteran's Day. People tend to become more civil, perhaps even more friendly. Ideological adversaries temporarily set aside their differences as they focus on a common history and purpose. The phrases, "life, liberty and the pursuit of happiness," and "We the People" are freely expressed with joy and hope. These are all expressions of the culture of the American Mind that continues today. To cultivate that culture within the popular culture means to increase its daily expression and deepen its understanding in America.

It is widely said that only one-third of colonial America actively supported the Revolutionary War, a third were for the British and a third were neutral.[81] Whatever the actual case, the concept applies that a free culture is held firm by the convictions and actions of a dedicated few while subscribed, and appreciated, by the bulk of society.

---

[81] The origin of this apocrypha seems to be from a letter written by John Adams which was actually in relation to American opinion on the French Revolution, not the American Revolution (Adams, C. F., *Works*, vol. 10, 110).

Just as many people knowing little about Christianity call themselves Christians, or many believing in a healthful lifestyle never exercise, or people knowing nothing of patriotism beyond flag-waving call themselves patriots, an American culture remains across society through the many identifying themselves with the culture while a smaller segment of society puts the culture's best elements into actual practice. These practitioners are the culture-bearers. They existed at America's founding – they were the founders – and they exist now. The more numerous the culture-bearers, the more everyday popular culture equates to foundational American culture.

While the culture-bearers hold to the culture of the American Mind, American society and government will stand. But as John Locke said,

> Whenever the society is dissolved, it is certain the government of that society cannot remain. (Locke, 330)

Therefore, the words of John Adams cannot be repeated enough when it comes to reestablishing the foundational American culture in everyday society.

> Because We have no Government armed with Power capable of contending with human Passions unbridled by morality and Religion. Avarice, Ambition, Revenge or Galantry, would break the strongest Cords of our Constitution as a Whale goes through a Net. **Our Constitution was made only for a moral and religious People. It is wholly inadequate to the government of any other**. (Adams, C. F., *Works*, vol. 9, 229, emphasis added)

French sociologist, historian and political theorist, Alexis de Tocqueville, established a corollary to Adams' statement in his book, *On Democracy in America,*[82] describing the likely fate of an America without a moral and religious people,

---

[82] Written as a guide for French democracy but long cited as the ultimate outsider's evaluation of the early American Republic.

I believe that it is easier to establish an absolute and despotic government amongst a people in which the conditions of society are equal, than amongst any other; and I think that, if such a government were once established amongst such a people, it would not only oppress men, but would eventually strip each of them of several of the highest qualities of humanity. **Despotism, therefore, appears to me peculiarly to be dreaded in democratic times**. (Tocqueville, vol. 2, 397, emphasis added)

It should be clear then, that maintaining foundational American culture is an existential challenge for the people under any form of government based in democratic principles.[83] It should also be clear that Americans allied in virtue, those faithful to the God of the Bible and those who subscribe to the morality of the Law of Nature and Nature's God, must be the culture-bearers of the American Mind for the benefit of all.

This is neither a bold nor exclusionary claim. While all are welcome to join in the sustenance and expansion of the American culture, the American culture already exists, it is not still being defined, and its foundation is set in the Law of Nature and Nature's God expressed in the Declaration of Independence which is based on the biblical morality that underpinned the rise of Western Civilization. To strive for something else by the same name, but not wrought by Divine Providence, and untested by time, is to take another path altogether. Therefore, the right path is through that same wisdom, virtue and morality, and trust in Divine Providence that abounded at the American founding. Recalling Benjamin Franklin's call for prayer at the Constitutional Convention, the future of the American government and culture rests on it.

I also believe, that without his [God's] concurring aid, we shall succeed in this political building no better than the builders of Babel: we shall be divided by our little, partial, local interests; our projects will be confounded; and we

---

[83] See *Left, Center, Right – Framing Political Philosophies* in the Appendix.

ourselves shall become a reproach and a bye-word down to future ages. (Madison, *Debates*, 254)

Review of Foundational American Culture

The foundational American culture was derived from the Declaration of Independence in Chapter 2 – *The Declaration of Independence is the American Mind*:

1. Basic truths are self-evident and eternal, not created by man or government.
2. Men have unalienable rights that come from God, not from man or government.
3. All men are created equal by God.
4. Rights have a duty aspect; respect others and offer rationale for actions that rightly concern others.
5. Seek what is righteous according to God.
6. Sacrifice all for right principles.
7. Cover over the inconsequential mild transgressions of others.
8. Governments are tools to secure God-given rights.
9. Government power is only valid when just.
10. Governments are temporary, whereas people's rights are permanent.
11. People tend to, and should, be patient with the failings of government.
12. Tyrannical government must be replaced.
13. Anarchy is not an alternative to government.

These thirteen points may be summarized further to simple biblical principles:

> He has told you, O man, what is good; And what does the Lord require of you But to do justice, to love kindness, And to walk humbly with your God?[84] (Micah 6:8)

---

[84] Culture points 1, 2, 3, 4, 5, 6, 7, 10, 11.

You shall love the Lord your God with all your heart, and with all your soul, and with all your strength, and with all your mind; and your neighbor as yourself.[85] (Luke 10:25)

Finally, brethren, whatever is true, whatever is honorable, whatever is right, whatever is pure, whatever is lovely, whatever is of good repute, if there is any excellence and if anything worthy of praise, dwell on these things.[86] (Philippians 4:8)

This biblical morality led to the establishment of the American Mind which, in turn, must now seek out its preservation in that original morality. The calling into existence of America was an act of Divine Providence to revive individual freedom for a relationship with the Almighty and in so doing, bring blessings to the world. If God's promise to Abraham may be borrowed to highlight the concept,

And I will make you a great nation, and I will bless you, and make your name great; and so you shall be a blessing;

And I will bless those who bless you, and the one who curses you I will curse.[87] And in you all the families of the earth will be blessed. (Genesis 12:2-3)

America's culture-bearers continue to bless the American Mind established by the founders. And there are those who curse the vision of the American Mind – some through hatred and selfish ambition, but most in ignorance. Still, God has already blessed America for over 240 years. Perhaps by expanding recognition of the culture that Nature's God, the Creator, established through the American founders, these blessings will continue for another 240 years.

---

[85] Culture points 3, 4, 5, 6, 7, 11. Also expressed in Deuteronomy 6:5 and Leviticus 19:18.
[86] Culture point 5.
[87] The curse is not God acting evilly to those who curse, but God abandoning the blessing and leaving the one cursing to live apart from God as they choose.

Live the American Mind

For America's culture-bearers, sustaining the American Mind is as straightforward as daily upholding the Law of Nature and Nature's God through the basic biblical tenets just described.[88] But it is said we live in post-Christian America, so how can these basic biblical tenets of moral society cultivate foundational American culture? Living the American Mind of the Law of Nature and Nature's God with biblical morality makes life better for everyone, and the seeking of betterment for all is contagious to popular culture and naturally, implicitly, exposes elements of unsound popular culture that is in existential opposition to foundational American culture.

In his great work published in 1644, *The Bloody Tenent*,[89] Roger Williams wrote a preface to the British Parliament (Williams, 3):

RIGHT HONOURABLE AND RENOWNED PATRIOTS,

Next to the saving of your own souls in the lamentable shipwreck of mankind, your task as Christians is to save the souls, but as magistrates the bodies and goods, of others.

So, for Christians, the time has passed, and never really was, to keep Christianity in church while being secular humanists in public life. The very foundation of America is built upon recognition of God, not as a justification for theocratic rule, but as an active and benevolent provider offering freedom and abundant life to all. Christians in the American citizenry of "We the People" share the duty expressed by Roger Williams; seek to save souls as Christians, and save bodies and goods as citizens, noting that the latter also serves the former.

And that duty of saving the bodies and goods of one's fellow man – their life, liberty and property – all of America's culture-bearers are obligated

---

[88] Not to be confused with religiosity, theocracy, or party spirit of religious doctrine.

[89] Discussed in Part Two covering the First Amendment right to freedom of religion.

to perform. But what else shall America's culture-bearers do to represent foundational American culture?

Live a Life of Virtue

Considering the words of John Adams and Alexis de Tocqueville, recall John Quincy Adams' summary of the need for virtue to maintain America's Constitution in alignment with the Declaration of Independence:

> This was the platform upon which the Constitution of the United States had been erected. Its VIRTUES, its republican character, consisted in its conformity to the principles proclaimed in the Declaration of Independence, and as its administration must necessarily be always pliable to the fluctuating varieties of public opinion; its stability and duration by a like overruling and irresistible necessity, was to depend upon the stability and duration in the hearts and minds of the people of that virtue, or in other words, of those principles, proclaimed in the Declaration of Independence, and embodied in the Constitution of the United States. (Adams, J. Q., 54)

Benjamin Franklin put it plainly in a letter to friends in 1787,

> only a virtuous people are capable of freedom. (Franklin, *Memoirs*, 100)

Virtues are those things espoused in Philippians 4:8 as used to summarize foundational American culture: whatever is true, whatever is honorable, whatever is right, whatever is pure, whatever is lovely, whatever is of good repute; things of excellence and worthy of praise in the eyes of the Almighty. Virtue is recognizing the God-given equality of mankind and loving one's neighbor as one's self, in liberty. While virtue is largely synonymous with morality, it is much more characterized by active behavior, the outward, unselfish, loving expression of morality. Virtue is to be sought daily. It is not a self-ascribed characteristic. One seeks virtue, but only others can credit virtue as having been attained, and then only for the moment.

Behave as a Citizen

One can live a life of virtue yet remain distant from society. For the amplification of the foundational American culture, culture-bearers must also behave as citizens, living virtuously in connection with society and government.

In the Bible, writing to the same church to whom he encouraged virtue, Paul exhorts Christians to live in the world and act with virtue according to the good news of Jesus Christ. Philippians 1:27 says,

> Only conduct yourselves in a manner worthy of the gospel of
> Christ, so that whether I come and see you or remain absent,
> I will hear of you that you are standing firm in one spirit, with
> one mind striving together for the faith of the gospel.

In this passage, the word, "conduct," is *politeuesthe*, which according to *Strong's Greek Concordance* (Greek, 4176) means to "live as a citizen." Like the calls for good conduct in Romans and 1 Peter,[90] Christians are called to live within the world, behaving as citizens even though true Christian citizenship is in heaven (Philippians 3:20).

For all culture-bearers, the same admonition applies. To behave as a citizen, at a minimum being civil in behavior and just in dealings, and even more so considerate of the needs of others. Recalling that patriotism requires reasoned, moral, and principled sacrifice for one's countrymen, to behave as a citizen within the culture of the American mind is to live daily as a patriot.

---

[90] Discussed fully in the Appendix, *The Christian's Relationship to Government*.

Live Beyond Rights – Civility and Courtesy

Declaration of the American Mind has examined natural rights as understood by the founders, and "limitations" to unalienable rights are only to be found in the countervailing rights of others. As commonly expressed, "Your right to swing your arms ends just where the other man's nose begins." This quotation is attributed to many sources but seems to have originated back in the 1880s and the early Prohibition movement which used it, wrongly,[91] to call for limitations on rights rather than punishment for infraction of obligations (Finch, 165-166). It does, however, express the truth of obligations associated with natural rights and highlights a further option in the exercise of natural rights: civility.

Civility is, using the example of the quotation, stopping the swinging of one's arms before even approaching another's nose. Civility may also be considered as stepping back from the person swinging their arms so that one's own nose cannot be hit. Civility has the same effect as that hedge placed on rights by popular culture, but it is exercised willingly, even purposefully, by the individual regardless of the popular culture. Civility is often defined simply as manners, politeness, or courtesy. Politeness and manners seem to fit. There seems to be more to courtesy.

Courtesy, as applied to the saying, would be recognition that the swinging of one's arms will soon affect the rights, or perhaps just the feelings, of another, leading to the choice to not swing one's arms, or to swing them elsewhere. Courtesy stems not from the obligation of rights or even from a social duty. Courtesy stems from viewing others with equality of value, with love for one's neighbor.

For Christians, the call for courtesy goes even further to say,

---

[91] The author of the speech from which the saying derives eschews the negative rights of the Declaration of Independence and pronounces that liberty derives from government as "civil liberty" which the author defines as a restriction on natural liberty developed by intellectual men (Finch, 162-163).

with humility of mind regard one another as more important than yourselves; ... (Philippians 2:3b)

and to live with the ever-present consideration that

liberty of yours does not somehow become a stumbling block ... (1 Corinthians 8:9)

to one who may not comprehend the right or rationale for using it. These biblical imperatives are just courtesy delivered in love, which is something that anyone can practice.

Unlike the hedge around rights built by popular culture which results in limitations on rights and punishment for offenses that do not exceed one's rights, civility and courtesy do not change or lessen the right of the individual practicing them. While it may be true that rights should be regularly practiced to retain public acknowledgement that they exist, the willingness to not fully assert one's rights in every situation is an equally sound practice which is likely to make the full exercise of rights more palatable to those who disdain them.

Avoid Party Spirit

Defined in *The Christian Observer* quite contemporaneously to the American founding, party-spirit is described this way,

In what, then, does party-spirit properly consist? It consists, I imagine, in *a love of party rather than a love of truth*; in such an attachment and adherence to one system of opinions, and to one set of associates, as will lead men to sacrifice conscience, truth, and charity to their connexions, of whatsoever description those connexions may be. Party-spirit in short, is the love of power, exerting itself to maintain a stand, or to compass an object of ambition, too often regardless of every thing but the end to be accomplished. (Members, 570)

Thus, party spirit is contentious, ends-justify-the-means, self-seeking ambition. This description of the sinful behavior engendered in party spirit is backed up by biblical scripture. Just before proclaiming the fruit of the Spirit, the Apostle Paul lists "deeds of the flesh" (Galatians 5:19-21), meaning behavior outside of spiritual behavior which is the opposite of the fruit, or virtuous behaviors, of godly living:

> Now the deeds of the flesh are evident, which are: immorality, impurity, sensuality, idolatry, sorcery, enmities, strife, jealousy, outbursts of anger, disputes, dissensions, factions, envying, drunkenness, carousing, and things like these, of which I forewarn you, just as I have forewarned you, that those who practice such things will not inherit the kingdom of God.[92] (Galatians 5:19-21)

Disputes, in this passage, is the Greek word, *eritheia* (Strong, Greek 2052). Strong describes the term as deriving from a group of words that also translate as *wrangling* and *provoke*, directly implying faction, contention and strife which, all together, meet the definition of party spirit. Therefore, party spirit is a deed of the flesh, in opposition to the fruits of the Holy Spirit of God.

Paul similarly states in Philippians 2:2-3,

> fulfill my joy, that you think the same, having the same love, one in soul, minding the one thing, doing nothing according to party spirit or self-glory ... (Philippians 2:2-3 LITV)

Here the Literal Version of the Bible translates the Greek, *erithea*, directly as party spirit and associates it with selfishness.

And James, the half-brother of Jesus, proclaims that same connection to express selfish ambition,

---

[92] This verse is not listing acts which define damnation. Salvation in Christianity is a free gift of grace from Jesus Christ (see *Who Christians are in Christ* in the Appendix). Rather, the one in regular practice of these actions is living apart from the blessings of the kingdom of God and is also denying such to those living around them.

For where jealousy and selfish ambition exist, there is disorder and every evil thing. (James 3:16)

That party spirit equally translates to strife, selfishness, ambition, disputes, contentions and rivalry across Bible verses and versions aligns perfectly with the malevolent effects of party spirit described by Washington, Hamilton and Madison in their discussion of the Constitution.[93] Party spirit is not American in the sense of the Declaration of Independence, and not godly in any sense. Avoiding party spirit should be a targeted and intentional act by Americans to prevent the "formal and permanent despotism" of which George Washington forewarned in his *Farewell Address* (Washington, *Farewell*, 20-21).

Overcoming party spirit may be the single greatest challenge in promotion of the American Mind. So great is the human fear of losing political power, which causes the "disorders and miseries" described by Washington, that even the most ardent patriot may suffer temptation to set aside virtue, behaving as a citizen, and the promise of liberty to posterity for fleeting comfort in the herd mentality of party spirit.

For the Christian, when party spirit seems to be the "only way to secure the future," the Bible offers this prescription:

Trust in the LORD with all your heart, and do not lean on your own understanding. In all your ways acknowledge Him, and He will make your paths straight. (Proverbs 3:5-6)

And for all culture-bearers, the virtue and citizenship of the culture of the American Mind – the love of liberty, truth, and justice – with the duty required for equality in liberty, must remain the guide and guard against party spirit and the despotism to which it leads.

---

[93] Refer to Party Spirit in Chapter 3 – *The Constitution Frames the Vision of the American Mind.*

Don't Accept the Lesser of Two Evils

The foundational American culture of the Declaration of Independence includes the admonition from the Law of Nature and Nature's God to seek what is righteous according to God, and the fundamental proposition of representative government is to have qualified and virtuous leaders. As Hamilton[94] wrote in *Federalist 57*,

> The aim of every political constitution is, or ought to be, first, obtain for rulers men who possess most wisdom to discern, and most virtue to pursue, the common good of the society; and in the next place, to take the most effectual precautions for keeping them virtuous, whilst they continue to hold their public trust. (Hamilton, *Federalist*, 309)

While the phrase, "vote for the lesser of two evils" may, to many, simply be an idiom used when voting for weak candidates, its very use, as opposed to saying something like, "vote for the better candidate," should be a red flag for culture-bearers to check their party spirit and to behave as citizens and patriots. Christians, in particular, must remind themselves that they are living in the world, but striving for the Gospel of Jesus Christ by only choosing a candidate that does not represent evil.

For Christians, it should also be clear that there is no call to "strive in one mind" to win elections at all cost by voting for the "lesser of two evils." Anything evil, whether "lesser" than another evil or not, is of the devil (1 John 3:8), and Christians are called to "resist the devil" (James 4:7) and to "put on the full armor of God" against him (Ephesians 6:11).

In his call for the Philippians to behave like citizens, Paul reminded them to stand firm, "in no way alarmed by your opponents" (Philippians 1:28). In this same way, all culture-bearers today ought not to succumb to the call of party spirit to vote for the lesser of two evils against a candidate or legislation one knows, or even suspects, might be in opposition to the Law

---

[94] Or Madison.

of Nature and Nature's God or devoid of wisdom and virtue. To do otherwise is, according to party spirit, selfishness and vain ambition in the world, and is not striving in one spirit, with one mind, for "the Blessings of Liberty to ourselves and our Posterity."

Believe in the Long-term

With the recognition that many of America's problems stem from mistaking popular culture for permanent foundational culture, the importance of discerning longer-term solutions to problems becomes clearer. Although the desire is to reclaim liberty in the present generation, the absolute need, as expressed in the Declaration, is to preserve liberty, or restore it if need be, for posterity. There need be no desperation in seeking to return the popular to the foundational, as desperation tends to lead to unprincipled and ineffective solutions. With an eye to posterity and a hope for the present, the long-term culture of the Declaration of Independence and the Law of Nature and Nature's God can redirect society to the liberty on which it was founded and which people deserve by those timeless laws.

Abraham Lincoln expressed the long-term view on the Civil War battlefield at Gettysburg, Pennsylvania in 1863 with his famous address:

> Four score and seven years ago our fathers brought forth on this continent, a new nation, conceived in Liberty, and dedicated to the proposition that all men are created equal.

> Now we are engaged in a great civil war, testing whether that nation, or any nation so conceived and so dedicated, can long endure. We are met on a great battle-field of that war. We have come to dedicate a portion of that field, as a final resting place for those who here gave their lives that that nation might live. It is altogether fitting and proper that we should do this.

> But, in a larger sense, we can not dedicate – we can not consecrate – we can not hallow – this ground. The brave men, living and dead, who struggled here have consecrated it far

above our poor power to add or detract. The world will little note, nor long remember what we say here, but it can never forget what they did here. **It is for us the living, rather, to be dedicated here to the unfinished work which they who fought here have thus far so nobly advanced. It is rather for us to be here dedicated to the great task remaining before us – that from these honored dead we take increased devotion to that cause for which they gave the last full measure of devotion – that we here highly resolve that these dead shall not have died in vain – that this nation, under God, shall have a new birth of freedom – and that government of the people, by the people, for the people, shall not perish from the earth.** (Nicolay, 602-603, emphasis added)

Each generation can bring new birth, or an end, to the foundational American culture. For those culture-bearers seeking to keep the American Mind from perishing from the earth, the long-term view must be part of one's outlook. Without belief in the long-term, it becomes too easy to operate with an end-justifies-the-means, lesser-of-two-evils mentality, leading to abandonment of the culture of the Declaration of Independence.

Americans of faith are called to "trust in the Lord" (Proverbs 3:5) and understand that God is timeless (Exodus 3:14, Revelation 1:8), which makes the case for believing in the long-term and not fearing short-term challenges. The very concept of faith in one's eternal salvation, believed, but not yet seen, is based in long-term belief.[95]

Think Critically and Gain Wisdom

Wisdom is the antidote for party spirit, and American culture-bearers are called to seek wisdom and confirm instruction like the ancient Bereans.

Now these [the Bereans] were more noble-minded than those in Thessalonica, for they received the word with great

---

[95] See *Who Christians are in Christ* in the Appendix.

> eagerness, examining the Scriptures daily to see whether these
> things were so. (Acts 17:10)

Wisdom always seeks the truth. Wise culture-bearers learn history using multiple validated and, preferably, contemporaneous sources. Critical thinking implies that news and social media stories be validated, not against one's preferred narrative or party line, but against the facts and context. To forfeit critical thinking and wisdom is to become captive to the deceit and machinations of others.

Seek to Encourage Others

Part of wisdom is the willingness and ability to share it. Christians are called to,

> Conduct yourselves with wisdom toward outsiders, making
> the most of the opportunity. Let your speech always be with
> grace, as though seasoned with salt, so that you will know
> how you should respond to each person. (Colossians 4:5-6)

And,

> Let no unwholesome word proceed from your mouth, but only
> such a word as is good for edification according to the need
> of the moment, so that it will give grace to those who hear.
> (Ephesians 4:29)

These are universal principles to "win friends and influence people"[96] with lasting effect.

Overcome Public and Legal Secularism

Labeling America as "post-Christian" does not imply the nation has become an America of some other theistic religion. Rather, America has become a nation with the public and legal religion of secularism in which the Creator of the founders has been prohibited from entering government

---

[96] A phrase made famous from the book by Dale Carnegie.

or the public square. America was founded in the Law of Nature and Nature's God which prescribes liberty in exercising one's conscience and religion.[97] And to bring America's religious foundation in both government and society into perspective, review what Justice Joseph Story wrote in his *Commentaries on the Constitution of the United States*,

> The promulgation of the great doctrines of religion, the being, and attributes, and providence of one Almighty God; the responsibility to him for all our actions, founded upon moral freedom and accountability; a future state of rewards and punishments; the cultivation of all the personal, social, and benevolent virtues; – these never can be a matter of indifference in any well ordered community. It is, indeed, difficult to conceive, how any civilized society can well exist without them. And at all events, it is impossible for those, who believe in the truth of Christianity, as a divine revelation, to doubt, that it is the especial duty of government to foster, and encourage it among all the citizens and subjects. (Story, vol. 3, 722-723)

Christians are not called to live secular lives outside of church, and America was not founded to keep religion out of the public sphere or to abandon religious virtue in law.[98] Just the opposite is true. America's culture-bearers must protect religious freedom under the liberty and duty of the Law of Nature and Nature's God to enable both the religious and secular to exist in peace.

Overcome Abortion

It can easily be said that the American founders did not do enough, soon enough, to end slavery. It can likewise easily be said that founders like

---

[97] The background and basis for freedom of religion is expanded in Part Two under *The First Amendment*.
[98] Refer to Blackstone's "Nature of Laws in General" (Blackstone, *Analysis*, 2).

Washington and Jefferson, who held slaves, were hypocritical, not leveraging every nuance of law to free their slaves, even if one by one.

There exists an analog to slavery in today's American society. That is the sin of abortion of unborn children in direct opposition to the guarantee of life in the Declaration of Independence, and the duty of a pregnant woman to the child while exercising her own right to the pursuit of happiness under the Law of Nature and Nature's God. The same criticism of society and individuals at the founding regarding their inability or unwillingness to end slavery while promoting rights will one day be laid on today's society and individuals regarding abortion.

The argument that abortion is a "woman's right to choose what to do with her own body" when terminating the life growing inside her will sound as wicked in the future as the false arguments made by slaveholders that slavery is supported in the Bible,[99] or that slavery was good for the black race because they were better off in America than their former countries (Elliot, *Debates*, vol. 4, 272). In today's future, they will say that those who did not rise up against the killing of unborn children were weak, didn't care, and perhaps were all secretly in favor of the practice. Yet, it is not easy in a Republic based on the democracy of the public ballot to eliminate the sin of abortion. Where a significant portion of society accepts the practice, even a majority of society is challenged to halt it. And where budgets are built with omnibus legislation, even foes of abortion often end up voting to support the practice, funding providers of abortion simply to keep the rest of government functioning. Future historians will say that today's anti-abortion legislators did not do enough to end the practice. They will say that government should have gone unfunded given such legislation in spending bills. The future will hold the courts accountable, despising the injustice and misapplication of rights, just as we now despise

---

[99] Several scripture verses exhort "slaves obey your masters," (e.g. Colossians 3:22) but the context is one of "slaves, you are in a bad situation so bear it as Christ would" rather than being a sanction for slavery itself. See *The Christian's Relationship to Government* in the Appendix.

the *Dred Scott* Supreme Court opinion for upholding racism and slavery (Howard, 393). Perhaps they will be right in all of these future indictments. Perhaps it is true what is said about Washington and Jefferson. Surely, if it is true of them, it is true of all "We the people," then and now. There is room for understanding human failings in complex situations, but there is no room for moral superiority while working in half measures against the sanctioned killing of innocent human lives.

America paid a terrible price for the sin of slavery. That cost is still being paid by the posterity of those who engaged in it, suffered under it, and of those who failed to eliminate it. While considering the fault of America's founding population for their failure to end slavery, no one should escape the hypocrisy and shame that the future will lay upon America's present citizenry for killing unborn Americans. Be on the record and act to end abortion as being culturally unacceptable – against the Declaration of Independence – and unlawful, being against right reason in the Law of Nature, and against Nature's God.

Practicing the American Mind

If America is to hold on to the American Mind and not succumb to the wanderlust of utopian societies which have never existed nor can exist under the auspices of man, then each one who believes in the reality of the American Mind of the Declaration as the manifestation of Divine Providence, or at least as the highest moral achievement in government that mankind has produced, must purposefully seek it. Those who are equipped to seek and cultivate the foundational American culture of the American Mind are the culture-bearers in accord with the Law of Nature and Nature's God in individual liberty and for equality in the inherent value of each person.

Culture-bearers will often have vastly different ideals and ideas, but they will always meet at natural rights and the obligation to respect the rights of others, enabling the American people to live in a free society with a government that seems most likely "to effect their Safety and Happiness."

No single person can reestablish the American Mind. No grass-roots movement can force a restoration of foundational American culture. But "We the People," thinking and acting individually with the American Mind; behaving as citizens, living liberty with duty, practicing equality and justice founded in the Law of Nature and Nature's God, can expand and invigorate the foundational American culture of the Declaration of Independence to secure the Blessings of Liberty to ourselves and our Posterity.

Seeking to live in the American Mind is little different from the hopes, aspirations and expectations at the beginning of the nation as expressed by George Washington in his first inaugural address:

> Such being the impressions under which I have, in obedience to the public summons, repaired to the present station, it would be peculiarly improper to omit, in this first official act, my fervent supplications to that Almighty Being who rules over the universe—who presides in the councils of nations— and whose providential aids can supply every human defect, that his benediction may consecrate to the liberties and happiness of the people of the United States, a government instituted by themselves for these essential purposes: and may enable every instrument employed in its administration to execute with success, the functions allotted to his charge. In tendering this homage to the Great Author of every public and private good, I assure myself that it expresses your sentiments not less than my own; nor those of my fellow citizens at large, less than either. No people can be bound to acknowledge and adore the invisible hand, which conducts the affairs of men, more than the people of the United States. Every step by which they have advanced to the character of an independent nation, seems to have been distinguished by some token of providential agency; and in the important revolution just accomplished in the system of their united government, the tranquil deliberations and voluntary consent of so many distinct communities, from which the event has resulted, cannot be compared with the means by which most

governments have been established, without some return of pious gratitude, along with an humble anticipation of the future blessings which the past seem to presage.

... I behold the surest pledges, that, as on one side, no local prejudices or attachments, no separate views, nor party animosities, will misdirect the comprehensive and equal eye which ought to watch over this great assemblage of communities and interests; so, on another, that **the foundations of our national policy will be laid in the pure and immutable principles of private morality**; and the pre-eminence of free government be exemplified by all the attributes which can win the affections of its citizens, and command the respect of the world. I dwell on this prospect with every satisfaction which an ardent love for my country can inspire: since there is no truth more thoroughly established, than that **there exists in the economy and course of nature, an indissoluble union between virtue and happiness; between duty and advantage; between the genuine maxims of an honest and magnanimous policy, and the solid rewards of public prosperity and felicity**: since we ought to be no less persuaded that the propitious smiles of Heaven can never be expected on a nation that disregards the eternal rules of order and right, which Heaven itself has ordained: and since the preservation of the sacred fire of liberty, and the destiny of the republican model of government, are justly considered as deeply, perhaps as finally staked, on the experiment entrusted to the hands of the American people. (Washington, *First Inaugural*, 19-20, emphasis added)

George Washington expressed these hopes for a young nation with a finally-matured government. But fulfillment of this hope in human institutions requires action taken with the "pure and immutable principles of private morality." Living and practicing the American Mind has always been a necessity for Americans. In 1834 the "Bank Wars"[100] of the Jacksonian era were at a head and a delegation from Pennsylvania sent a *Memorial* to Congress stating their position on the issues. Congressman Daniel Webster of Massachusetts rose in Congress to state that he believed the citizens of Pennsylvania were "awakening to a just sense of the condition of the country." He went on to express trust in Pennsylvania and extolled the sacrifices and glories that "she" had sustained in acquiring liberty. If one considers the citizenry of Pennsylvania – "Keystone State" of the Union (Morton) – as a proxy for all Americans, and replaces "she" with "The American Mind," Daniel Webster's words stand as a final statement on living and practicing the American Mind.

> I doubt not, sir, she [The American Mind] will examine the conduct of Government, and take counsel with her own thoughts, about the security of the constitution, and the preservation of the authority of the laws. I doubt not that she will well consider the present: and look to the future; and if she finds all well, and all safe, if she feels no evil, and perceives no danger, she will repose in her accustomed tranquillity. But if she feels that evil, and great evil does exist, and if she sees that danger is before the country, it is not to be doubted that she will bring to the crisis her intelligence, her patriotism, and her power.
>
> In acquiring the liberty which we enjoy, she [The American Mind] had her full share, both of the sacrifice and the glory; and she knows that that rich possession is holden only on the condition of watchfulness and vigilance—God grants liberty only to those who love it, and are always ready to guard and defend it. (Congress, *Register of Debates in Congress*, 1864-1865)

---

[100] The politics of the Bank Wars are out of scope for this book.

PART TWO –
DIGGING DEEPER
INTO THE NATURE
OF RIGHTS

Chapter 7 –
The First Amendment

Amendment I

> Congress shall make no law respecting an establishment of religion, or prohibiting the free exercise thereof; or abridging the freedom of speech, or of the press; or the right of the people peaceably to assemble, and to petition the Government for a redress of grievances.

Five Rights Protected in the First Amendment

The First Amendment to the Constitution confirms five unalienable rights as being beyond the reach of any powers granted to the Federal Government elsewhere in the Constitution. These five rights are:

1. Freedom of religion
2. Freedom of speech
3. Freedom of the press
4. Freedom of peaceable assembly
5. Freedom to petition government for the redress of grievances

At present in America there is considerable misunderstanding and misapplication of the first three of these natural rights that is deserving of review.

Freedom of Religion, Not Freedom from Religion

> Before any man can be considered as a member of civil
> society, he must be considered as a subject of the Governor of
> the Universe. And if a member of civil society, who enters
> into any subordinate association, must always do it with a
> reservation of his duty to the general authority; much more
> must every man, who becomes a member of any particular
> civil society, do it with a saving of his allegiance to the
> Universal Sovereign. We maintain, therefore, that in matters
> of religion, no man's right is abridged by the institution of
> civil society; and that religion is wholly exempt from its
> cognizance. (Madison, *Memorial*, 6)
>
> James Madison, writing for the Virginia Legislature, 1819

Freedom of religion comprises both the free exercise of religion and
freedom from the establishment of a State religion. Joseph Story, in his
Commentaries on the Constitution, fully explained the freedom of religion
clauses of the First Amendment to the Constitution. His coverage of this
often-misunderstood topic (Story, *Commentaries*, vol. 3, 722-731) boils
down to a few key concepts:

1. The promulgation of great moral doctrines of religion founded on
    freedom, accountability, and cultivation of virtue, are important
    for any well-ordered community.

2. When the Constitution was written, America was of the mind to
    promote Christianity while supporting freedom of conscience and
    religious worship for all religions. America was not of a mind to
    make all religions equal in the eyes of government.

3. It may be impossible for free government to survive without the
    promotion of religion, but such promotion is not the same as
    forcing beliefs on the consciences of men.

4. The rights of conscience are given by God and cannot be
    encroached upon by human authority without disobedience to the
    Law of Nature and Nature's God.

5. The object of the First Amendment was to exclude all rivalry among Christian sects in the States with respect to establishing one sect with advantage in the Federal Government.

6. The power over the subject of religion was left to the States, leaving all religions the opportunity to participate in Federal Government.

Joseph Story's summary aligns with Madison's assertion that the allegiance of man is first to the Universal Sovereign and subordinately to civil society. The Declaration of Independence acknowledges a Creator and there can be no higher allegiance for man. Further, as Madison said, religion is exempt from the cognizance of government, therefore government cannot force equality of religion on anyone or violate acts of religious conscience, yet if man must be considered as a subject of the Governor of the Universe as Madison says, then government's function is entirely right and aligned with the American Mind to promote religion that seeks equality and liberty in alignment with the Law of Nature and Nature's God. In short, government promotion of religion that supports the great moral doctrines of freedom, accountability, virtue and equality is nothing more than government promoting the culture of the American Mind.

This view of the freedom of religion is likely surprising to many Americans today. So twisted has the understanding of "freedom of religion" become that the prevailing belief in American society is that all government must be completely secular, free from any consideration of religion, much less promotion of it, and that a religious person serving in any public capacity must abandon all beliefs and conscience in order to serve the public. Nothing could be further from the truth of the First Amendment.

America was founded on the Law of Nature and Nature's God as explicitly written in the Declaration of Independence. How then can forced secularism, a form of religious persecution and attack upon the conscience of all religion, be a requirement of the First Amendment? It cannot be. As

James Madison stated, the first duty of mankind is to the "Governor of the Universe," the "Universal Sovereign."

The religion clauses of the First Amendment are like two sides of the same coin, one side relating to government's position and responsibilities in relation to religion, and the other side to individual conscience and belief. This view is analogous to the two tablets of the Ten Commandments (Exodus 20:1-17) of the Bible. Many reformation-era theologians (Williams, Roger, 124-126) characterized the first tablet, or table, as being the laws of Nature's God relating to individual conscience and exercise of religion; untouchable by government. The second table contained the revealed law for relating to one's neighbor which is subject to both individual conscience and civil authority (Noble, 296).

The "first table" comprises duties for the individual worship of God, which is exercise of religion and conscience, that is not subject to civil law (Noble, 296):

> You shall have no other gods before Me.
>
> You shall not make idols.
>
> You shall not take the name of the LORD your God in vain.
>
> Remember the Sabbath day, to keep it holy.

These duties are summarized by a single verse of scripture, Deuteronomy 6:5, which is also repeated in the New Testament Gospels of Matthew, Mark and Luke:[101]

> You shall love the LORD your God with all your heart and with all your soul and with all your might. (Deuteronomy 6:5)

The "second table" comprises civil duties of the individual in relationship to others, which may also come under civil authority.

---

[101] Matt 22:37, Luke 10:27, Mark 12:30.

Honor your father and your mother.

You shall not murder.

You shall not commit adultery.

You shall not steal.

You shall not bear false witness against your neighbor.

You shall not covet.

The duties of the second table are summarized by Leviticus 19:18, also repeated across the New Testament.[102]

> you shall love your neighbor as yourself. (Leviticus 19:18)

These are the very same scriptural precepts that were recognized as a summary of the American Mind in Chapter 6 – *Living the American Mind*.

Except for honoring parents and covetousness, these second table obligations are all physical actions involving other people. Honoring parents and covetousness, if only in thought, would not be touchable by civil authority. But breaches of these obligations often manifest in a physical sense which could be actionable by civil authority or accountable to society.

Adultery, today, may be viewed as permissible consenting activity between two adults, but in a moral society holding the bond of marriage as a contract, if not a sacred religious institution, adultery is a direct assault on the life and liberty, even property held jointly, of the injured party. All breaches of the second table, then, are destructive of the bonds which hold society together, making them in some way subject to civil accountability.

The consideration for society here is what constitutes the basis for civil law. Under the Law of Nature and Nature's God of the Declaration of

---

[102] James 2:8, Galatians 5:14, Matthew 19:19, Mark 12:31, Matthew 22:39, Romans 13:9, Luke 10:27.

Independence the first table is honored, if not practiced, by a moral society, but not enforced by society or civil authority. This creates a strong foundation supporting the civil relationship to the second table. A moral people will not condone or practice murder, so the duty of the first table is reflected in the need for minimal civil authority to enforce the second table. To the contrary, when a society is immoral and does not respect or practice the first table, there is little option other than coercive civil authority to enforce behavior to the duties required of the second table. Because a coercive civil state, by nature, will always breach liberty, no liberty will long stand where there is no honor and practice of moral, principled, religion. Justice Joseph Story wrote,

> It yet remains a problem to be solved in human affairs, whether any free government can be permanent, where the public worship of God, and the support of religion, constitute no part of the policy or duty of the state in any assignable shape. (Story, *Commentaries* vol. 3,727)

Put simply, freedom of religion is freedom of conscience and belief, which is a natural right. To attempt to force someone into another set of beliefs violates that natural right. To force someone to act apart from their beliefs, so long as those beliefs are within the right reason of the Law of Nature and Nature's God,[103] also violates that natural right. Therefore, the First Amendment does not create a right to "freedom from the religion of others," which requires government intervention, but only the protection of natural religious rights from interference by a state-established religion.

Free Exercise of Religion

The "free exercise of religion" written in the First Amendment is not equal to "freedom of worship" as some would contend. Much more than religious worship, the free exercise of religion means the free exercise of the dictates of one's conscience in all moral activities. Joseph Story

---

[103] For example, a religion of human sacrifice is not within the right reason of the Law of Nature and Nature's God.

characterized it as, "the private rights of conscience, and the freedom of religious worship" (Story, *Commentaries*, vol. 3, 726). From the perspective of seventeenth-century theologian and religious freedom activist, Roger Williams, freedom of religion prescribed an inability of the government to punish the breach of the first table of the Ten Commandments so long as it does not disturb the civil peace (Williams, Roger, xiv). Williams was fully aligned with the philosophy of natural rights more than one hundred years before the Declaration of Independence. His unalienable right of freedom of religion extended as far as the unalienable rights of those around him, with complete equality.

Establishment of Religion

"Congress shall make no law respecting an establishment of religion" is known today as the *Establishment Clause*. Joseph Story understood the purpose and context of the *Establishment Clause* to exclude all rivalry among Christian sects in the States with respect to establishing one sect with an advantage in the Federal Government (Story, *Commentaries*, vol. 3, 728). It was not a prohibition of government promotion of the virtue and importance of religion (Story, *Commentaries*, vol. 3, 722-723). A plurality, if not a majority, of the people who immigrated to America prior to its founding came seeking religious freedom, very often due to persecution by government and society. The Quakers, had been persecuted by the Church of England, the state-run church (Penn, 17). Others, like the French Huguenots, had been violently persecuted by the Roman Catholic Church. Even the venerated English Bill of Rights of 1671 made allowance only for Protestant Christians to own arms (Ralph, 54). From history, the understanding of the founders was that national religions lead to infringement of rights or outright persecution (Story, *Commentaries*, vol. 3, 728). Therefore, the Federal Government was explicitly disallowed from establishing a national religion. Yet, today, "establishment" has become a term unto itself when speaking of religion and government.

James Madison penned, *Religious Freedom. A Memorial and Remonstrance* , in response to a Virginia law enacting a tax specifically to support teachers of Christianity in public schools, and implicitly to support the Virginia State Episcopal Church. Using Madison's work, the characteristics of "establishment of religion" can be derived,

> Because we hold it for a fundamental and unalienable truth, that religion, or the duty which we owe to the Creator, and the manner of discharging it, can be directed only by reason and conviction, not by force or violence. (Madison, *Memorial*, 5)

This statement highlights the first rule of establishment:

1. Establishment is any law, policy or action that forces or uses violence in directing one to discharge a duty of religion.

Madison then wrote,

> The preservation of a free government requires, not merely that the metes and bounds which separate each department of power, be invariably maintained; but more especially, that neither of them be suffered to overleap the great barrier which defends the rights of the people. The rulers, who are guilty of such an encroachment, exceed the commission from which they derive their authority, and are tyrants. (Madison, *Memorial*, 6)

Defining the second indicator of establishment:

2. Establishment is an encroachment of civil government on religion which exceeds the commission from which they derive their authority.

The next rule of establishment is derived from,

> Because the bill violates that equality which ought to be the basis of every law; and which is more indispensable, in proportion as the validity or expediency of any law is more liable to be impeached. ... As the bill violates equality, by subjecting some to peculiar burdens; so it violates the same principle, by granting to others peculiar exemptions. (Madison, *Memorial*, 7)

Therefore, the third rule of establishment is:

3. Establishment is law that violates equality by subjecting some to peculiar burdens or by granting others peculiar exemptions.

Next, Madison explains,

> Because the bill implies, either that the civil magistrate is a competent judge of religious truths, or that he may employ religion as an engine of civil policy. The first is an arrogant pretension, falsified by the extraordinary opinion of rulers, in all ages, and throughout the world; the second, an unhallowed perversion of the means of salvation. (Madison, *Memorial*, 8)

Showing the last two rules for establishment:

4. Establishment is a law or legal opinion that makes a civil magistrate the judge or arbiter of religious truths.

5. Establishment is any law leveraging religion as an engine of compulsory civil policy.[104]

All these characteristics of establishment of religion are countered in the proper role of government; defense of the liberties of the people, completely in line with that defined for America by the Declaration of Independence. As Madison went on to state,

> A just government … will be best supported by protecting every citizen in the enjoyment of his religion, with the same equal hand which protects his person and property; by neither invading the equal rights of any sect, nor suffering any sect to invade those of another. (Madison, *Memorial*, 9)

To be clear, the guidelines for religious promotion by government are not in conflict with the rules for identifying establishment derived from Madison. It is not establishment to promote virtuous religion as part of foundational culture. Promotion of virtuous religion does not exceed the

---

[104] The context of Madison's Remonstrance was compulsory taxation.

commission of authority based on the Declaration of Independence which promotes such virtue. Promotion of virtuous religion does not establish peculiar burdens or exemptions or force religious action. And promotion of virtuous religion – as done by proclamation of days of prayer and fasting, as highlighted in the Declaration of Independence, and as long expressed on American currency – does not make government officials the arbiters of religious truth or establish religion as an engine of compulsory civil policy.

Nor is it establishment for people to practice religion while serving in government or to pray while holding civil office as judge or arbiter. Such contentions would be outside the context of Madison's essay. To seal this understanding, Madison ended his essay, written in official legislative capacity and subscribed to by many others from the Virginia General Assembly, saying,

> We the subscribers say, that the General Assembly of this Commonwealth have no such authority; and that no effort may be omitted on our part, against so dangerous an usurpation, we oppose to it this Remonstrance, earnestly praying, as we are in duty bound, that the Supreme Lawgiver of the Universe, by illuminating those to whom it is addressed, may, on the one hand, turn their councils from every act, which would affront his holy prerogative, or violate the trust committed to them; and, on the other, guide them into every measure which may be worthy of his blessing, may redound to their own praise, and may establish more firmly the liberties, the property, and the happiness of this Commonwealth. (Madison, *Memorial*, 12)

It is interesting to note that Madison's *Memorial and Remonstrance* was not written about a case involving the federal First Amendment, but a case at the state level, which is why Jefferson and his colleagues made the appeal to the people and legislature of Virginia to stop enactment of the law. In America, many of the states had state-sanctioned religions or religious requirements for state office (Story, *Commentaries*, vol. 3, 731). For example, Pennsylvania, as part of William Penn's "holy experiment" prior to the state's 1776 constitution, required office holders to profess faith in Christianity, but allowed people of any peaceful faith to live and freely exercise religion within the state. The key point being that the First Amendment in the federal Bill of Rights only applied to the Federal Government,[105] preventing it from interfering in the religions of the states. States were free to have state religions (Story, *Commentaries*, vol. 3, 731). While not, in principle, a great example of universal liberty because it often led to unequal treatment of other sects within a state, state religions were generally accepted because states were founded as individual communities largely for the singular purpose of freely practicing a specific religion which was practiced as the foundation of the society by the will of the people under a republican form of government, which could change by the will of the people.

"Separation of Church and State"

The *Establishment Clause* is, today, better known, but not well understood, under the label, "separation of church and state." This phrase has become the rallying cry for a pernicious movement against freedom of religion and religion itself, and is borne out of the very misconstruction and mischaracterization that the Bill of Rights sought to prevent. The history of the phrase derives from the phrase, "wall of separation," used in the positive context of *protecting religion from government*. Through the tumbling torrent of time it has been brutally beaten into the exact opposite; to mean *protecting government from religion*. It is unfortunate that this history must even be discussed. The positive in doing so is that it provides an excellent example of what may happen to liberty without constant vigilance of the people.

Roger Williams and the Origin of "Separation of Church and State"

The origin of the "separation of church and state" comes from Roger Williams in his book, *The Bloudy Tenent of Persecution for Cause of*

---

[105] See Chapter 10 – *The Tenth and Fourteenth Amendments*.

Conscience Discussed, published in 1644. Williams set out the course of this work, in part, to prove:

> All civil states, with their officers of justice, in their respective constitutions and administrations, are proved essentially civil, and therefore not judges, governors, or defenders of the spiritual, or Christian, state and worship. (1)

> God requireth not an uniformity of religion to be enacted and enforced in any civil state; which enforced uniformity, sooner or later, is the greatest occasion of civil war, ravishing of conscience, persecution of Christ Jesus in his servants, and of the hypocrisy and destruction of millions of souls. (2)

> An enforced uniformity of religion throughout a nation or civil state, confounds the civil and religious, denies the principles of Christianity and civility, and that Jesus Christ is come in the flesh. (2)

> The permission of other consciences and worships than a state professeth, only can, according to God, procure a firm and lasting peace; good assurance being taken, according to the wisdom of the civil state, for uniformity of civil obedience from all sorts. (2)

> Lastly, true civility and Christianity may both flourish in a state or kingdom, notwithstanding the permission of divers and contrary consciences, either of Jew or Gentile. (2)

Williams' goals read very much like positive practices to counter church establishment as derived from Madison. And on the very first page of the actual text, Williams, as did Madison, aligned to the truth that government and civil authorities are not to become secular when he addressed the British Parliament with their duty,

> Next to the saving of your own souls in the lamentable shipwreck of mankind, your task as Christians is to save the souls, but as magistrates the bodies and goods, of others. (3)

It is in this context of civil government refraining from being the arbiter of religion or causing uniformity of religion – refraining from establishment of religion; and with understanding that both religion and civil authority can thrive together, with religious people in civil office serving a wise and virtuous civil state – that Williams wrote of a "wall of separation" between the world and the church,

> First, the faithful labours of many witnesses of Jesus Christ, extant to the world, abundantly proving, that the church of the Jews under the Old Testament in the type, and the church of the Christians under the New Testament in the antitype, were both separate from the world; and that when they have opened a gap in the hedge, or **wall of separation**, between the garden of the church and the wilderness of the world, God hath ever broke down the wall itself, removed the candlestick, &c and made his garden a wilderness, as at this day. And that therefore if he will ever please to restore his garden and paradise again, it must of necessity be walled in peculiarly unto himself from the world, and that all that shall be saved out of the world, are to be transplanted out of the wilderness of the world and added unto his church or garden. (435, emphasis added)

Williams' "wall of separation" was one by which the church was "walled in" by God in protection from the world. In a footnote, Williams placed the context as clearly referring to the church being separated from the "world" by the people of the church, out of the reach of, and conformance to, civil government, for the protection of the church to be ready for the purposes of God.

> The world is taken in more ways than one, and so is separation; ... From the world, as taken for civil government of it, we are to separate our church bodies, and the government thereof in frame and constitution. (435)

Nothing described here suggests that people of the church should not participate in government, only that church bodies should be separate from government in frame and constitution. Roger Williams, himself, founded "Providence Plantations" in 1644 which became Rhode Island, and which had complete religious freedom (Charles II, 8). He was politically active as a separatist from the Church of England before coming to America, as well as being active as an abolitionist and in aboriginal affairs in America. Furthermore, in *The Bloudy Tenent*, he stated a very clear understanding of religion under the Law of Nature and Nature's God, expressing the same notion that Madison expressed 140 years later, that the government can have no more power than what is entrusted by the people (Madison, *Memorial*, 6),

> Now what kind of magistrate soever the people shall agree to set up, whether he receive Christianity before he be set in office, or whether he receive Christianity after, he receives no more power of magistracy than a magistrate that hath received no Christianity. For neither of them both can receive more than the commonweal, the body of people and civil state, as men, communicate unto them, and betrust them with. (Williams, Roger, 341)

Thomas Jefferson and the Danbury Baptists

In 1801, in the first year of his presidency, Thomas Jefferson received a letter from the Danbury Baptist Association which comprised Baptist churches principally in Connecticut and a few in New York. The letter expressed concern about the state religion of the Connecticut constitution taking priorities in legislation, leaving the Baptists, who were a small minority in the state, to enjoy religious privileges only as "favors granted." The Baptists asked Jefferson for his help in establishing more religious freedom, knowing him as a proponent of religious rights,

> Sir, we are sensible that the President of the United States is not the National Legislator and also sensible that the national government cannot destroy the laws of each State, but our hopes are strong that the sentiment of our beloved President, which have had such genial effect already, like the radiant beams of the sun, will shine and prevail through all these

States–and all the world–until hierarchy and tyranny be destroyed from the earth. (Rippon, 854)

President Thomas Jefferson, writing in his official capacity, responded with,

> Believing with you that religion is a matter which lies solely between man and his God, that he owes account to none other for his faith or his worship, that the legislative powers of government reach actions only, and not opinions, I contemplate with sovereign reverence that act of the whole American people which declared that their legislature should "make no law respecting an establishment of religion, or prohibiting the free exercise thereof," thus building a **wall of separation between church and State**. Adhering to this expression of the supreme will of the nation in behalf of the rights of conscience, I shall see with sincere satisfaction the progress of those sentiments which tend to restore to man all his natural rights, convinced he has no natural right in opposition to his social duties. (Jefferson, *Writings*, vol. 8, 113, emphasis added)

Jefferson's response reflects not only his understanding of religious freedom and natural rights, but also the history of Roger Williams and the Baptists in New England. Jefferson noted that "governments reach actions only, and not opinions," in subtle reference to Roger Williams' use of the first and second tablets of the Ten Commandments for the relationship between religion and civil authority (Williams, Roger, 124-126). Jefferson also invoked Williams' "wall of separation," knowing that the reference would enhance the understanding of support for religious freedom that he was conveying to the Danbury Baptists. Finally, Jefferson noted that he saw no natural right of man, including the right to free exercise of religion, that was in opposition to his social duties. Everything Jefferson stated was in conformance with the Law of Nature and Nature's God, the First Amendment and with the religious freedom views of Roger Williams.

To further ensure an understanding of Jefferson's position, it is instructive to cite the summation of the 1785 Virginia *Act For Establishing Religious Freedom* which was principally authored by Jefferson in 1776, shepherded through the Virginia legislature by James Madison, and finally signed by Jefferson, as he was then governor, in 1785 (Foote, 325-348). Jefferson's understanding of freedom of religion in 1776 was the same one he held in 1801: one of freedom from compunction of government in conformance with the Law of Nature and Nature's God and a right of conscience that carried into civil capacities.

> We the General Assembly of Virginia do enact that no man shall be compelled to frequent or support any religious worship, place, or ministry whatsoever, nor shall be enforced, restrained, molested, or burthened in his body or goods, nor shall otherwise suffer, on account of his religious opinions or belief; but that all men shall be free to profess, and by argument to maintain, their opinions in matters of religion, and that the same shall in no wise diminish, enlarge, or affect their civil capacities.

> And though we well know that this Assembly, elected by the people for the ordinary purposes of legislation only, have no power to restrain the acts of succeeding Assemblies, constituted with powers equal to our own, and that therefore to declare this act irrevocable would be of no effect in law; yet we are free to declare, and do declare, that the rights hereby asserted are of the natural rights of mankind, and that if any act shall be hereafter passed to repeal the present or to narrow its operation, such act will be an infringement of natural right. (Foote, 347-348)

A Letter Surpasses the Law

In 1878, the United States Supreme Court took up the case of *Reynolds v. United States* regarding the legality of the Mormon practice of polygamy. In its unanimous opinion (Schaff, 119-123), the court cited the paragraph of Jefferson's letter to the Danbury Baptist Association as cited above, and commented,

> Coming as this does from an acknowledged leader of the advocates of the measure, it may be accepted almost as an authoritative declaration of the scope and effect of the amendment thus secured. Congress was deprived of all legislative power over mere opinion, but was left free to reach actions which were in violation of social duties or subversive of good order. (Schaff,121)

The twisting of "wall of separation between church and state" had begun. The Supreme Court decision placed the phrase into the legal lexicon, ever so slightly changing "governments reach actions only, and not opinions," Jefferson's hat-tip to the first and second tables of Roger Williams and others, and made it, "Congress was deprived of all legislative power over mere opinion, but was left free to reach actions ..." The words of Jefferson were focused on the fact that governments were prohibited from legislating on opinions. The court opinion reversed that priority, creating a function of government to be free to legislate on actions deemed to be subversive of good order.

Then, in 1947, the transformation of "wall of separation" into "separation of church and state" was completed. The Supreme Court case of *Everson v. Board of Education of the Township of Ewing* (New Jersey) questioned the legality of the school board reimbursing parents for fares paid for the transportation by public carrier of children attending Catholic schools. In short, the question was if a public-school district should pay to transport children to a religious Catholic school. In his majority opinion, Justice Hugo Black made an historical segue into religious freedom and taxation, creating dictum on what the "establishment of religion" clause of the First Amendment means in his own opinion, but then settled the question of the suit using simple comparisons of everyday public-religious interactions in New Jersey.

Justice Hugo Black wrote,

> The structure of our government has, for the preservation of civil liberty, rescued the temporal institutions from religious

interference. On the other hand, it has secured religious liberty from the invasion of the civil authority.[106]

The "establishment of religion" clause of the First Amendment means at least this: neither a state nor the Federal Government can set up a church. Neither can pass laws which aid one religion, aid all religions, or prefer one religion over another. Neither can force nor influence a person to go to or to remain away from church against his will or force him to profess a belief or disbelief in any religion. No person can be punished for entertaining or professing religious beliefs or disbeliefs, for church attendance or non-attendance. No tax in any amount, large or small, can be levied to support any religious activities or institutions, whatever they may be called, or whatever form they may adopt to teach or practice religion. Neither a state nor the Federal Government can, openly or secretly, participate in the affairs of any religious organizations or groups, and *vice versa*. In the words of Jefferson, the clause against establishment of religion by law was intended to erect "a wall of separation between church and State." (Supreme Court, *Everson*, 15-16)

Black's entire tack was, from the start, laying out a false premise that "our government has ... rescued the temporal institutions from religious interference." Just the opposite is true. To repeat the words of a Supreme Court Justice prior to Hugo Black, Justice Joseph Story wrote on the true premise,

It was under a solemn consciousness of the dangers from ecclesiastical ambition, the bigotry of spiritual pride, and the intolerance of sects, thus exemplified in our domestic, as well as in foreign annals, that it was deemed advisable to exclude from the national government all power to act upon the subject. (Story, *Commentaries*, vol. 3, 730)

---

[106] Used by Black, this statement originated in prior state and Supreme Court cases.

That Black's opinion upheld the payments for busing children to Catholic schools while further eroding the proper meaning of the First Amendment was not lost on other members of the Supreme Court. In a dissent to Black's opinion, Justice Robert Jackson stated,

> In fact, the undertones of the opinion, advocating complete and uncompromising separation of Church from State, seem utterly discordant with its conclusion yielding support to their commingling in educational matters.[107] (Supreme Court, *Everson*, 19)

From there on, Black's usurpation of religious freedom continued as he interspersed unsubstantiated opinion with contextual fundamentals about the First Amendment:

> **Fundamental:** Neither a state nor the Federal Government can set up a church.

> **Fabrication:** Neither a state nor the Federal Government can pass laws which aid one religion, aid all religions, or prefer one religion over another.

Black's assertions are tantamount to a requirement for secular government. No such law or intent was ever considered by the founders. Joseph Story said it was right for government to promulgate religious virtue. And the Declaration of Independence is built on the Law of Nature and Nature's God, appealing to the Supreme Judge of the World, and seeking the blessings of Divine Providence. Government can prefer a religion of virtue aligned with the Law of Nature and Nature's God that underpins the Declaration of Independence to one that promotes, for extreme example, human sacrifice.

---

[107] A cynic, or one understanding the Ku Klux Klan background of Justice Black, might consider his opinion to be a trojan horse for the future of "separation of church and state" via a small gift of superficial deference to religion. This cynical view is borne out by Justice Black's lead opinion just a year later in *McCollum v. Board of Education, 333 U.S. 203 (1948)*.

Fundamental: Neither state nor Federal Government can force nor influence a person to go to or to remain away from church against his will or force him to profess a belief or disbelief in any religion.

Fundamental: No person can be punished for entertaining or professing religious beliefs or disbeliefs, for church attendance or non-attendance.

Fabrication: No tax in any amount, large or small, can be levied to support any religious activities or institutions, whatever they may be called, or whatever form they may adopt to teach or practice religion.

The Continental Congress which gave America the Declaration of Independence also paid for chaplains out of money raised from the colonies. The same was proposed at the Constitutional Convention (Madison, *Debates*, 253-254). Even today, Congress has a chaplain who is paid from taxes collected. At its root, Black's assertion is untrue. Certainly, tax revenue should be spent judiciously, and as outlined in Madison's "rules" on establishment must equally applied without "peculiar" benefit or burden. Anything further would, again, be tantamount to the requirement for a completely secular government, which runs counter to all history of America.

Fabrication: Neither a state nor the Federal Government can, openly or secretly, participate in the affairs of any religious organizations or groups, and vice versa.

This assertion is a gross overstatement of what would characterize an "establishment," as was shown from both Madison and Williams. Were Black's assertion law, it would be illegal for a presidential candidate or member of Congress to visit a church. It would likewise be illegal for the government to work with a group of churches in disaster recovery after an earthquake. It would be illegal to have chaplains in the military. It also means, based on the "vice versa," that churches would be disenfranchised from the same lobbying and seeking of redress for grievances in courts which is available to all other types of organizations. Were this statement true, it would put churches in the same position of religious persecution as if a different religion had been established by the government.

With all of this asserted as actual law, Black then bound it up with the corrupted phrase, "wall of separation between church and state." Essentially, and sadly ironically, Black had established the national church as Secularism.

Secularism Becomes America's Established Church

In 1962, the new national religion of Secularism expanded the height and breadth of its wall of separation of church and state to "protect the state from religion." The legal dismemberment of "the free exercise" of religion was complete in government, only waiting for society to catch up. The Supreme Court case, *Engel v. Vitale,* was brought in opposition to voluntary, non-denominational, non-religion-specific prayer, said along with the Pledge of Allegiance (Supreme Court, *Engel v. Vitale*) at the start of the day in New York public schools. The prayer was fixed, and written by the New York State Board of Regents,

> Almighty God, we acknowledge our dependence upon Thee,
> and we beg Thy blessings upon us, our parents, our teachers
> and our Country. (Supreme Court, *Engel v. Vitale*, 422)

The New York Supreme Court and its Appellate Division upheld the right to voluntary prayer. The complainant then took the case to the United States Supreme Court. In a six to one decision, two justices not participating, the Supreme Court overturned the lower rulings, saying it was unconstitutional to have the voluntary prayer in public schools. The author of the opinion: Justice Hugo Black.

Black's majority opinion reads, in part,

> [The] petitioners argue, the State's use of the Regents' prayer
> in its public-school system breaches the constitutional wall of
> separation between Church and State. We agree with that
> contention, since we think that the constitutional prohibition

against laws respecting an establishment of religion must at least mean that, in this country, it is no part of the business of government to compose official prayers for any group of the American people to recite as a part of a religious program carried on by government. (Supreme Court, *Engel v. Vitale*, 425)

This initial argument presupposes the meaning of "wall of separation between Church and State," leveraging the incorrect usage of that phrase established in Black's 1947 *Everson v. Board of Education* opinion. Also, note that "Church" is now capitalized, implying that the church is a grand monolithic establishment to be reckoned with and challenged by the State for the good of the people. Neither premise is correct or true. Next, for the second time in court opinions on the First Amendment, Black used the phrase, "establishment of religion must at least mean," abandoning an opportunity to set a clear definition as precedent, thus leaving the door wide open to expand "establishment," and as a literary tool, to imply that even more "evidence" could be weighed against it. Regarding the business of the government in composing official prayers, Black uses the word "official" here as a surrogate for "compulsory." A compulsory prayer would be a government act against conscience. An official prayer, much like the pledge of Allegiance as a "secular prayer" or oath, when voluntary, is nothing more than a suggested guide for good civics in a moral society. Black also had his history wrong, which becomes evident upon review of his opinion.

Black continued,

It is a matter of history that this very practice of establishing governmentally composed prayers for religious services was one of the reasons which caused many of our early colonists to leave England and seek religious freedom in America. (Supreme Court, *Engel v. Vitale*, 425)

By the time of the adoption of the Constitution, our history shows that there was a widespread awareness among many Americans of the dangers of a union of Church and State.

These people knew, some of them from bitter personal experience, that one of the greatest dangers to the freedom of the individual to worship in his own way lay in the Government's placing its official stamp of approval upon one particular kind of prayer or one particular form of religious services. They knew the anguish, hardship and bitter strife that could come when zealous religious groups struggled with one another to obtain the Government's stamp of approval from each King, Queen, or Protector that came to temporary power. The Constitution was intended to avert a part of this danger by leaving the government of this country in the hands of the people, rather than in the hands of any monarch. But this safeguard was not enough. Our Founders were no more willing to let the content of their prayers and their privilege of praying whenever they pleased be influenced by the ballot box than they were to let these vital matters of personal conscience depend upon the succession of monarchs. (Supreme Court, *Engel v. Vitale*, 429)

Via Black's opinion, the prayer in the *Engel v. Vitale* case has now become a "union of Church and State," going even beyond what one might consider an establishment of a church by a state. Black further stirred the emotions of "bitter personal experience" and "anguish, hardship and bitter strife" of unnamed people in an uncited history, going beyond even the implied history of the founding of America to all times past under all sorts of powers. Black set up a strawman argument, implying in his nebulous account from history that the New York prayer established "one particular form of religious" service and suggested that by doing so New York was being monarchical and out of the hands of the people. At the root of this tragedy of history, Black is speaking of the *Common Book of Prayer* of the Church of England. By that comparison, however, the branches of Black's argument grew wide from the stem, setting up the New York prayer as being tantamount to the official documents of a state church. But the *Common Book of Prayer* in England was not just official, it was compulsory for use.

A common theme in Black's opinions is reliance on the circumstances of Virginia to the exclusion of all other American history, and obfuscation of the differences between support for religion as a benefit to moral society and a compulsion to religion.

Black further opined,

> The First Amendment was added to the Constitution to stand as a guarantee that neither the power nor the prestige of the Federal Government would be used to control, support or influence the kinds of prayer the American people can say – (Supreme Court, *Engel v. Vitale*, 429)

Black's wording, "control, support or influence the kinds of prayer the American people can say," is more hyperbole. The prayer in the case was neither exhibiting nor influencing what kind of prayers Americans *can or must* say. The Regents' prayer offered a short, non-doctrinal acknowledgement of Almighty God that Americans could say. As to the term, "support," if freedom of religion is a liberty based in natural rights, and the government is a tool to secure the rights of the people, then surely support, apart from all compunction, in seeking blessings from the Almighty God is allowable. The signers of the Declaration of Independence seemed to think so when they approved, "We, therefore, the Representatives of the United States of America, in General Congress, Assembled, appealing to the Supreme Judge of the world for the rectitude of our intentions," and "for the support of this Declaration, with a firm reliance on the protection of divine Providence."

Black then set up his closing with,

> There can be no doubt that New York's state prayer program officially establishes the religious beliefs embodied in the Regents' prayer. (Supreme Court, *Engel v. Vitale*, 430)

> It is true that New York's establishment of its Regents' prayer as an officially approved religious doctrine of that State does not amount to a total establishment of one particular religious sect to the exclusion of all others – that, indeed, the

governmental endorsement of that prayer seems relatively insignificant when compared to the governmental encroachments upon religion which were commonplace 200 years ago. (Supreme Court, *Engel v. Vitale*, 436)

Here Black concedes that New York's actions were not "total establishment," whatever that means, but then he extends his false premise with the untrue phrase, "there can be no doubt" that the prayer establishes a religion. There most certainly can be doubt, as can be seen by the two New York Supreme Court rulings stating that the prayer was not an establishment of religion. But the use of Black's phrase furthers his less than impartial purposes. Justice Black then extended the villainy of a simple non-denominational, non-religion-specific prayer from its prior designation as an "official prayer" to make it into a complete "officially approved religious doctrine of that State." All that remained to complete making his case was to quote a respected American founder out of context. Black did not disappoint:

To those who may subscribe to the view that, because the Regents' official prayer is so brief and general there can be no danger to religious freedom in its governmental establishment, however, it may be appropriate to say in the words of James Madison, the author of the First Amendment:

"It is proper to take alarm at the first experiment on our liberties. ... Who does not see that the same authority which can establish Christianity, in exclusion of all other Religions, may establish with the same ease any particular sect of Christians, in exclusion of all other Sects? That the same authority which can force a citizen to contribute three pence only of his property for the support of any one establishment may force him to conform to any other establishment in all cases whatsoever?" (Supreme Court, *Engel v. Vitale*, 436)

Madison's quote is in regard to the bill Patrick Henry proposed to the Virginia Assembly in 1785 to support "Teachers of the Christian Religion" for the purposes of teaching Christianity specifically, and which was to be paid by a *direct tax on the people* of Virginia. The very text from which the characteristics of establishment were derived earlier in this chapter. This legislation closely followed passage of the Virginia Declaration of Rights for which Madison had fought for years, thus, Madison's designation of "first experiment on our liberties." The bill was widely opposed, including opposition by Christian churches and organizations in Virginia (Madison, Memorial, 3). The bill was considered a compulsion to support the established Church of England in Virginia, the Anglican Church. The sway of broad public opinion, including Madison's *Religious Freedom, a Memorial and Remonstrance*, killed the bill without a vote (Madison, *Memorial*, 4).

Revisiting some of the actual reasons Madison cited in that work for not supporting *A Bill, establishing provision for the Teachers of the Christian Religion*, draws Black's cherry-picked quote back into context,

> Because the bill violates that equality which ought to be the basis of every law; ... As the bill violates equality, by subjecting some to peculiar burdens; so it violates the same principle, by granting to others peculiar exemptions. (Madison, *Memorial*, 7)

Madison's argument was not against government supporting religion as a general principle, it was against unequal application of the law and compulsory support of a specific religion.

> Because the bill implies, either that the civil magistrate is a competent judge of religious truths, or that he may employ religion as an engine of civil policy. The first is an arrogant pretension, falsified by the extraordinary opinion of rulers, in all ages, and throughout the world; the second, an unhallowed perversion of the means of salvation. (Madison, Memorial, 8)

> Because the establishment in question is not necessary for the support of civil government. If it be urged as necessary for the support of civil government, only as it is a means of supporting religion, and it be not necessary for the latter

purpose, it cannot be necessary for the former. (Madison, *Memorial*, 9)

The use of "establishment" by Madison refers to a compulsory and unnecessary tax, whereas Black is referencing a voluntary and non-sectarian prayer.

It is also noteworthy what is missing from under the ellipsis (...) in Black's quote of Madison. There Madison said,

> The freemen of America did not wait till usurped power had strengthened itself by exercise, and entangled the question in precedents. They saw all the consequences in the principle, and they avoided the consequences by denying the principle. (Madison, *Memorial*, 6)

It would seem that Justice Black did not want the principles of a compulsory direct tax for the support of a particular religion to be discussed per the context, only the entanglement in his own precedents and their continued strengthening in exercise of the opinion that America is secular, quite to the contrary of Madison's point.

Promotion of values that support the Laws of Nature and Nature's God is not the same as establishment. Establishment implies enforcement or compunction. Promotion, like many historical proclamations, is a means of encouragement or recommendation, applied equally to all. There is a middle ground on the spectrum from establishment to religious promotion that would be called propaganda, which lacks compulsion but also lacks equality. Propaganda is to be guarded against. So also, a systemic disestablishment of religious promotion, the making of a secular State in violation of the First Amendment, is to be guarded against.

Overall, Black's opinions on the First Amendment read like those of a zealot with a cause far beyond that of someone serving as an impartial arbiter of the Constitution and justice in the full context of American history. Unfortunately, America has either accepted Black's false premises or overlooked them completely, just as was done with his Ku Klux Klan history (Sprigle), and much to the contrary of the founders' vigilance expressed in the part of Madison's quote which Black eliminated from his *Engle v. Vitale* opinion.

The point of reviewing the *Engel v. Vitale* opinion is less about what the outcome was, but rather the manipulation of the opinion to change the meaning of the First Amendment. The opinion is not about state establishment of Christianity. It is not even about establishment of religion. Instead, it is about the presumption of the Law of Nature and Nature's God, accepted in the Declaration of Independence as the source for the equality of all men and the touchstone of all American law. The point of reviewing this opinion is to show the manipulation of the truth contained in the Declaration of Independence, and the First Amendment to the Constitution, in order to achieve an end far removed from the vision of the American Mind.

Again, the importance of revisiting Supreme Court decisions on "separation of church and state" has nothing to do with the outcome of the particular cases. It is, instead, to review the rationale on which those cases were decided. Consider three ways of becoming wealthy: hard work, theft, and sweet-talking little old ladies out of their money. Hard work is virtuous and legal. Stealing is evil and unlawful. Sweet-talking little old ladies out of their money may be legal, but it is immoral; being contrary to both justice and virtue. America is like the little old lady. She has been sweet-talked into giving away her liberty by slick tongues and narrow legalities broadened to consume the truth from which they were derived.

American Promotion of Religion

Having read the discussion of "separation of church and state" and the rationale of Justice Hugo Black"s opinions, consider again the words of Supreme Court Justice Joseph Story from 1845,

> The promulgation of the great doctrines of religion, the being, and attributes, and providence of one Almighty God; the responsibility to him for all our actions, founded upon moral

freedom and accountability; a future state of rewards and punishments; the cultivation of all the personal, social, and benevolent virtues; – these never can be a matter of indifference in any well ordered community. It is, indeed, difficult to conceive, how any civilized society can well exist without them. (Story, *Commentaries*, vol. 3, 722)

And consider the just promotion of such behavior in American government, starting with the call for a fast by the Continental Congress on March 16, 1776 as that body sought guidance on the resolution for Independence,

In times of impending, calamity and distress: when the Liberties of America are imminently endangered by the secret machinations and open assaults of an insidious and vindictive administration, **it becomes the indispensable duty of these, hitherto free and happy Colonies, with true penitence of heart, and the most reverent devotion, publickly to acknowledge the over-ruling providence of God: to confess and deplore our offences against him; and to supplicate his interposition for averting the threatened danger, and prospering our strenuous efforts in the cause of freedom, virtue, and posterity.**

The Congress, therefore, considering the warlike preparations of the British ministry to subvert our invaluable rights and privileges, and to reduce us by fire and sword, by the savages of the wilderness, and our own domestics, to the most abject and ignominious bondage: **desirous, at the same time, to have people of all ranks and degrees, duly impressed with a solemn sense of God's superintending providence, and of their duty, devoutly to rely in all their lawful enterprizes on his aid and direction— do earnestly recommend, that Friday, the 17th day of May next, be observed by the said Colonies as a day of humiliation, fasting, and prayer; that we may with united hearts confess and bewail our manifold sins and transgressions, and by a sincere repentance and amendment of life,**

appease his righteous displeasure, and through the merits and mediation of Jesus Christ, obtain his pardon and forgiveness; humbly imploring his assistance to frustrate the cruel purposes of our unnatural enemies; and by inclining their hearts to justice and benevolence, prevent the further effusion of kindred blood. But if, continuing deaf to the voice of reason and humanity, and inflexibly bent on desolation and war, they constrain us to repel their hostile invasions by open resistance, **that it may please the Lord of Hosts, the God of Armies, to animate our officers and soldiers with invincible fortitude, to guard and protect them in the day of battle, and to crown the continental arms by sea and land with victory and success: earnestly beseeching him to bless our civil rulers, and the representatives of the people, in their several assemblies and conventions; to preserve and strengthen their union, to inspire them with an ardent disinterested love of their country: to give wisdom and stability to their councils; and direct them to the most efficacious measures for establishing the rights of America on the most honourable and permanent basis—that he would be graciously pleased to bless all his people in these Colonies with health and plenty, and grant that a spirit of incorruptible patriotism, and of pure undefiled religion, may universally prevail;** and this continent be speedily restored to the blessings of peace and liberty, and enabled to transmit them inviolate to the latest posterity. **And it is recommended to christians of all denominations to assemble for public worship, and abstain from servile labour on the said day**. (Continental Congress, *Journal*, 155, emphasis added)

Of course, one may choose to overlook the collective soul of the people who made this invocation of Jesus Christ and the Lord of Hosts, the God of Armies; and the recommendation, not requirement, for Christian abstention from labor. It was, technically, made before the Declaration of Independence and America's official birth.

However, if the First Amendment to the Constitution intended a secular government, as implied by Justice Black and modern use of "separation of church and state," it would make no sense for the same Congress, having just released the proposed Bill of Rights to the states for ratification on September 25, 1789, to pass a joint resolution of both houses asking the President to proclaim a day of national Thanksgiving to God. Yet, on September, 28, 1789, Congress requested such a proclamation, and the Chief Executive, George Washington, serving under the Constitution, responded on October 3rd with the first presidential Thanksgiving proclamation, saying,

> By the President of the United States of America. a Proclamation.

> Whereas it is the duty of all Nations to acknowledge the providence of Almighty God, to obey his will, to be grateful for his benefits, and humbly to implore his protection and favor—and whereas both Houses of Congress have by their joint Committee requested me "to recommend to the People of the United States a day of public thanksgiving and prayer to be observed by acknowledging with grateful hearts the many signal favors of Almighty God especially by affording them an opportunity peaceably to establish a form of government for their safety and happiness."

> Now therefore I do recommend and assign Thursday the 26th day of November next to be devoted by the People of these States to the service of that great and glorious Being, who is the beneficent Author of all the good that was, that is, or that will be—That we may then all unite in rendering unto him our sincere and humble thanks—for his kind care and protection of the People of this Country previous to their becoming a Nation—for the signal and manifold mercies, and the favorable interpositions of his Providence which we experienced in the course and conclusion of the late war—for the great degree of tranquillity, union, and plenty, which we have since enjoyed—for the peaceable and rational manner,

in which we have been enabled to establish constitutions of government for our safety and happiness, and particularly the national One now lately instituted—for the civil and religious liberty with which we are blessed; and the means we have of acquiring and diffusing useful knowledge; and in general for all the great and various favors which he hath been pleased to confer upon us.

And, also, that we may then unite in most humbly offering our prayers and supplications to the great Lord and Ruler of Nations and beseech him to pardon our national and other transgressions—to enable us all, whether in public or private stations, to perform our several and relative duties properly and punctually—to render our national government a blessing to all the people, by constantly being a Government of wise, just, and constitutional laws, discreetly and faithfully executed and obeyed—to protect and guide all Sovereigns and Nations (especially such as have shewn kindness unto us) and to bless them with good government, peace, and concord—To promote the knowledge and practice of true religion and virtue, and the encrease of science among them and us—and generally to grant unto all Mankind such a degree of temporal prosperity as he alone knows to be best.

Given under my hand at the City of New-York the third day of October in the year of our Lord 1789.

Go: Washington

(Sparks, *Writings*, vol. 12, 119) (Congress, Executive, 192)

Such proclamations of thanksgiving and appeals to Almighty God have continued in America. From John Adams, to the very James Madison quoted by Hugo Black in his attempt to demonstrate a godless society (Madison, *Thanksgiving*, 17), to Abraham Lincoln (Maltby, 265-266), Ulysses S. Grant, Calvin Coolidge, and many more presidents; to modern day with Presidents Bill Clinton, George W. Bush, Barack Obama (Thanksgiving) and Donald Trump (Trump).

It all harkens back to the American Mind, the soul of America in the Declaration of Independence, by which America was established. America is founded on the Law of Nature and Nature's God, supported by Divine Providence, overshadowed by the Supreme Judge of the World. Religion – relationship to, and reliance on, Almighty God – is bedrock foundation for America. That foundation is carved of virtue and morality from the Law of Nature and Nature's God. America is not a secular nation, unable to utter religious words or promote the virtue of religion. To be so constrained can only be viewed as having a state established religion of Secularism or Atheism. To the contrary, America is the home of freedom of religion for all virtuous and moral religion acknowledging the Law of Nature and Nature's God.

Freedom of Speech

> Congress shall make no law ... abridging the freedom of speech

The First Amendment states quite simply that one is legally free to speak anything they want.[108] Freedom of speech is closely interrelated with the freedom of religion and freedom of the press, these rights becoming greatly diminished if the right to free speech is abridged, particularly the freedom of religion. Viewed as freedom of conscience, if one is unable to speak the dictates of their conscience, they are not truly free to exercise their conscience or religion.

As with all natural rights, there is an obligation to the right of freedom of speech. The right only goes as far as the rights of another. So, while speech is free, the law provides for restraint of a few related conditions. One can say what one wants, but a lie or promotion of false facts about another person in a way that may damage their reputation or cause them a loss of property, makes one subject to a charge of libel or slander and reparation of damages to the aggrieved person. Similarly, if one steals or otherwise

---

[108] The written word is included in the freedom of speech.

misuses the works of another, such as printing a copyrighted work, one is subject to payment of damages. Incitement to violence is another example. One may say what one wants, but if it is intended to incite imminent and lawless action, that intent may be subject to criminal penalties.

Strictly speaking, there is complete freedom of speech in these actions. However, such speech may lead to other consequences, which generally must be pursued by the aggrieved party, or in cases like incitement, by the civil authorities. The authorities cannot arrest someone simply for the words spoken.

Hate Speech

Unfortunately, much of what is construed today as the rights of others, are not natural rights legally subject to consideration in one's speech. There is no unalienable right to not have one's feelings hurt or to keep one from hearing something objectionable. Some speech may be socially insensitive or downright mean, but the condition of the hearer's emotions is not restrictive of the free speech of the speaker. In short, there is no such thing as "hate speech" as a class of speech exempt from the First Amendment to the Constitution. One is unable to infringe the rights of a class of people with racist, bigoted, or biased remarks, nor can one be arrested for speaking an ugly truth, or mean-spirited opinion about another person. Rather, these are breaches of civil behavior which a moral society prevents by sustaining a virtuous culture.

You Can Yell, "Fire!" in a Crowded Theater

"Well, you can't yell 'Fire!' in a crowded theater" is the almost automatic response when someone is challenged about the sanctity of free speech in America. The truth is, you can yell "Fire!" in a crowded theater. Firstly, most people appreciate the exclamation if there indeed is a fire. Secondly, if there isn't a fire, it is not a matter of the speech itself being called into question, it is a matter of what result is incited by that speech. If everyone in the theater ignores the speaker there is no crime, although the management may ask the speaker to leave due to the disruption. If the speaker continues to yell, "Fire!" then he may be subject to a charge of disturbing the peace or disorderly conduct, but not because he uttered the word, "Fire!" Only if the speaker incites actual harm to life, limb or property; a situation in which the natural rights of others are significantly affected, might the speaker be subject to criminal penalty – for the incitement, not for the words spoken.

The history of "you can't yell 'Fire!' in a crowded theater" stems from a 1919 Supreme Court case, *U.S. v. Schenck*. In the majority opinion, Justice Oliver Wendell Holmes wrote,

> The most stringent protection of free speech would not protect
> a man in falsely shouting fire in a theatre and causing a panic.
> (Supreme Court, *Schenck*, 52)

Holmes further suggested that it was the circumstances in which the words were spoken and the *potential* for an undesired outcome that made the speech unprotected. By that criteria, any speech in any place deemed to be subject to an undesired action would be unprotected by the Constitution. In essence, "free speech" would be subject to popular culture and guidelines created by some civil authority. That is not what the founders intended by enshrining free speech as an unalienable right not to be misconstrued or misconstructed in American law.

U.S. v. Schenck was not even about a panic in a theater. It was about the Secretary of the Socialist Party distributing a pamphlet expressing opposition to the draft for World War I, calling for peaceful resistance. For this act, Mr. Schenck was charged under the Espionage Act of 1917, a law tantamount to the Alien and Sedition Acts. The case was wrongly decided, sending Schenck to prison, but overturned fifty years later in *Brandenburg v. Ohio* (Supreme Court, *Brandenburg v. Ohio*). Yet Holmes' strained and misquoted analogy from the opinion has lived on in popular culture as the prime example of a limitation on free speech.

Freedom of the Press

Freedom of the press[109] is closely linked to freedom of speech, essentially extending free speech to an organized sphere for mass distribution and consumption. In today's popular culture, freedom of the press is much more hallowed in the public eye than freedom of speech. If anything, the public is uncritical of the press, the press having become polarized by faction and the public enraptured by party spirit, eager to hear news that validates their particular position. Here, because of the First Amendment, the government can do nothing, and must not be able to do anything. Freedom of the press is legally constrained only by libel and slander, not by veracity or integrity. It is up to the People, really the culture-bearers of the American Mind, to demand these principles in the free market of ideas.

---

[109] For historical perspective on freedom of the press the reader is referred to *An Essay on the Liberty of the Press* by George Hay.

Chapter 8 –
The Second Amendment

Amendment II

> A well regulated Militia, being necessary to the security of a
> free State, the right of the people to keep and bear Arms, shall
> not be infringed.

The Second Amendment is less about arms, and more about the natural
right to defend one's self and one's community from threats of violence to
life, liberty or property. Self-defense is the first right and first law of the
Law of Nature (Peabody, 32-33) on which America is founded in the
Declaration of Independence.

The Right to Self-defense in Natural Law

John Locke provides a foundation for understanding self-defense in the
Law of Nature, but to set the scene, consider two small children alone on
a playground. They meet and begin to play harmoniously. Then one begins
playing with a toy he brought from home. Seeing it, the other child decides
that he wants the toy. Having ownership, the first child may choose to
share it freely, keep it to himself, or exchange it for consideration. The
second child can offer something for it, accept that it is not available, or
steal it by guile or force. More simply, they can work it out peacefully and
equitably, or they can fight over it. This is natural law, and the potential
for a fight is the potential for the need for the right to self-defense by the

child who has the toy. Noting that such situations can't always be worked out peacefully, Locke summarizes:

> And in the case, and upon this ground, every Man hath a Right to punish the Offender, and be Executioner of the Law of Nature. (Locke, 171)

Locke also explains the state of war, be it between individuals, an individual and government, or governments:

> And hence it is, that he who attempts to get another man into his absolute power, does thereby put himself into a state of war with him; it being to be understood as a declaration of a design upon his life: for I have reason to conclude, that he who would get me into his power without my consent, would use me as he pleased when he had got me there, and destroy me too when he had a fancy to it; for no body can desire to have me in his absolute power, unless it be to compel me by force to that which is against the right of my freedom, i.e. make me a slave. To be free from such force is the only security of my preservation; and reason bids me look on him, as an enemy to my preservation, who would take away that freedom which is the fence to it; so that he who makes an attempt to enslave me, thereby puts himself into a state of war with me. (Locke, 177-178)

The right to execute the law of nature and the definition of the state of war, together supply the basis for understanding the individual's right to take the life of another in self-defense:[110]

> This makes it lawful for a man to kill a thief, who has not in the least hurt him, nor declared any design upon his life, any farther than, by the use of force, so to get him in his power, as to take away his money, or what he pleases, from him; because using force, where he has no right, to get me into his power, let his pretence be what it will, I have no reason to

---

[110] The same concept is supported in Exodus 22:2 in the Bible.

suppose, that he, who would take away my liberty, would not, when he had me in his power, take away every thing else. And therefore it is lawful for me to treat him as one who has put himself into a state of war with me, i.e. kill him if I can; for to that hazard does he justly expose himself, whoever introduces a state of war, and is aggressor in it. (Locke, 178-179)

No reasonable person wants to have to kill another in self-defense, or to even be in a position where they have to consider it. The Law of Nature is built upon reason supplied by the Law of Nature's God.

And here we have the plain difference between the state of nature and the state of war, ... Men living together according to reason, without a common superior on earth, with authority to judge between them, is properly the state of nature. (Locke, 179)

Men build communities to live together in peace and support each other. This, too, is comprehended in the Law of Nature from which the American founders derived the Declaration of Independence. Yet it is obvious that civil authorities cannot protect everyone all of the time. Therefore, self-defense is the right of all people.

But force, or a declared design of force upon the Person of another, where there is no common Superior on Earth to appeal to for relief, is the State of War: And 'tis the want of such an appeal gives a Man the Right of War even as gainst an aggressor, though he be in Society and a fellow Subject. ... because the Law which was made for my Preservation, where it cannot interpose to secure my Life from present force, which if lost, is capable of no reparation, permits me my own Defence, and the Right of War, a liberty to kill the aggressor, because the aggressor allows not time to appeal to our common judge, nor the decision of the Law; for remedy in a Case where the mischief may be irreparable. (Locke, 179)

This same right applies to self-defense respecting the potential for the civil authorities, themselves, to breach right reason and place themselves into a state of war with the very people whom they were charged to protect. Such was the case between the American colonies and the British, which lead to the Declaration of Independence. In effect, the Declaration of Independence declared that Britain had abandoned its position as judge and arbiter of just and equal laws, thus putting them in a state of war with, and subject to self-defense by, the new States.

Recognizing the potential for government to again put itself into a state of war with the people, the founders codified the natural right of self-defense into the Bill of Rights as the right to keep and bear arms for the protection of both individuals and society. The use of arms, in particular firearms, just happens to be an effectual means for self-defense.

Brief History of the Right to Bear Arms

In the modern sense, the right to self-defense through the bearing of arms began with the English Bill of Rights in 1689. Under Charles II of England, the first known gun control law had been enacted, leading to the inclusion of the right to keep arms and be reasonably free from standing armies in the English Bill of Rights under William and Mary:

> That the raising and keeping a Standing Army within the Kingdom in time of Peace, unless it be by Consent of Parliament, is against Law.
>
> That the Subjects, being Protestants, may have Arms for their Defence suitable to their Condition, and as allow'd by Law. (Ralph, 54)

That the right to arms had become implicit in English, and thus Colonial American, society for one hundred years by the time of the United States Bill of Rights is emphasized in the words of Sir William Blackstone in his comprehensive *Commentaries on the Laws of England*. By 1765 the natural law philosophy of Locke and the English Bill of Rights had become a "birthright" even to the prominent English jurist:

And we have seen that these rights consist, primarily, in the free enjoyment of personal security, of personal liberty, and of private property. So long as these remain inviolate, the subject is perfectly free; for every species of compulsive tyranny and oppression must act in opposition to one or other of these rights, having no other object upon which it can possibly be employed. To preserve these from violation, it is necessary that the constitution of parliaments be supported in it's full vigor; and limits certainly known, be set to the royal prerogative. And, lastly, to vindicate these rights, when actually violated or attacked, the subjects of England are entitled, in the first place, to the regular administration and free course of justice in the courts of law; next to the right of petitioning the king and parliament for redress of grievances; **and lastly to the right of having and using arms for self preservation and defence. And all these rights and liberties it is our birthright to enjoy entire**; unless where the laws of our country have laid them under necessary restraints. Restraints in themselves so gentle and moderate, as will appear upon farther enquiry, that no man of sense or probity would wish to see them slackened. For all of us have it in our choice to do every thing that a good man would desire to do; and are restrained from nothing, but what would be pernicious either to ourselves or our fellow citizens. (Blackstone, *Commentaries*, vol. 1, 140, emphasis added)

The practice of keeping and bearing arms truly was a birthright at the time of the American founding, and many of the founders expressed as much in their writings:

James Madison

Besides the advantage of being armed, which the Americans possess over the people of almost every other nation, the existence of subordinate governments, to which the people are attached, and by which the militia officers are appointed, forms a barrier against the enterprises of ambition, more insurmountable than any which a simple government of any form can admit of. (Hamilton, *Federalist*, 259)

John Adams

Resistance to sudden violence, for the preservation not only of my person, my limbs and life, but of my property, is an indisputable right of nature which I never surrendered to the public by the compact of society, and which, perhaps, I could not surrender if I would. (Adams, C. F., *Works*, vol. 3, 438)

Richard Henry Lee as "Federal Farmer"

to preserve liberty, it is essential that the whole body of the people always possess arms, and be taught alike, especially when young, how to use them; (Lee, R. H.)

Samuel Adams

Among the natural rights of the colonists are these: First, a right to life. Second, to liberty. Thirdly, to property: together with the right to support and defend them in the best manner they can. These are evident branches of, rather than deductions from, the duty of self-preservation, commonly called the first law of nature. (Peabody, 32-33)

Alexander Hamilton

but if circumstances should at any time oblige the government to form an army of any magnitude, that army can never be formidable to the liberties of the people, while there is a large body of citizens, little, if at all, inferior to them in discipline and the use of arms, who stand ready to defend their own rights and those of their fellow citizens. (Hamilton, *Federalist*, 151)

Thomas Jefferson

A strong body makes the mind strong. As to the species of exercise, I advise the gun. While this gives a moderate exercise to the body, it gives boldness, enterprise, and independence to the mind. Games played with the ball, and others of that nature, are too violent for the body, and stamp no character on the mind. Let your gun therefore be the constant companion of your walks. (Jefferson, *Memoirs*, 287)

Thomas Paine

> The supposed quietude of a good man allures the ruffian; while on the other hand, arms like laws discourage and keep the invader and the plunderer in awe, and preserve order in the world as well as property. (Moncure, 56)

Patrick Henry

> Guard with jealous attention the public liberty. Suspect every one who approaches that jewel. Unfortunately, nothing will preserve it, but downright force. Whenever you give up that force you are inevitably ruined. (Wirt, 194)

Bearing Arms in Self-defense

If self-defense is a natural right, then it is also natural that a man should not be limited in how he defends himself. Otherwise, by definition, his right would not be unalienable. But there is also always the duty aspect of any natural right which implies that one's natural right must be self-attenuated or unexercised when it intersects with the natural right of another. This is the only limiting factor on the natural right to self-defense and the right to keep and bear arms.

The Meaning of "Arms"

Some people, in an attempt to limit the types of arms they feel are permissible to bear, like to say that the founders only intended muskets by the meaning of "arms" in the Second Amendment. The benevolent purveyors of this concept then grant that the right is extended to simple handguns and rifles in "common use" today.

Yet the founders never made such statements or excluded cannon or explosives (e.g. black powder), which were readily available at the time. In fact, English language dictionaries of the time define arms as any kind of weaponry. Dictionary definitions from a 1760 dictionary, while the Colonies were under British rule, and 1789, the very year that the Bill of Rights was completed by the United States Congress, make this clear.

ARMS [S.] in general, all kinds of weapons, offensive and defensive; a state of hostility. Arms denote also the natural weapons of beasts, as claws, spurs, teeth, beaks, &c. (Bellamy, emphasis added)

ARMS, A'rmz. s. Weapons of offence, or armour of defence; a state of hostility; war in general; action, the act of taking arms; (Sheridan, emphasis added)

In 1857, Webster's Dictionary remains consistent, and even provides examples consistent with the broadest meaning of the Second Amendment:

ARMS, 7i. pi. [L. arma; Fr. arme.; Sp. It arma.] 1. Weapons of offense, or armor for defense and protection of the body. 2. War; hostility. 3. The ensigns armorial of a family. Fire-arms are such as may be charged with powder, as cannon, muskets, mortars, &c. A stand of arms consists of a musket bayonet cartridge-box, and belt, with a sword.—In falconry, arms are the legs of a hawk from the thigh to the foot. To be in arms, to be in a state of hostility, or preparation for war. To take arms, to arm, for attack or defense. To bear arms, to be trained to the profession of a soldier. To arms! denotes the taking of arms; or as an exclamation, it is a summons to take arms. (Webster, *American Dictionary*, 60, emphasis added)

Even in 1911, Webster's Dictionary remained consistent on the meaning of arms, although with the Progressive Era of the early 20th century underway it began to show itself as a tool of propaganda to diminish individual liberty by defining "arms," citing it in the Second Amendment, and then constraining that meaning in example use by altering a quotation:

arms (ärmz), n. pl. [ME. armes, F. arme, pl. crmes, fr. L. arma, pl., arms. Cf. ALARM.] 1. Instruments, or weapons of offense or defense; loosely, objects of any kind that may be used as weapons.

Three horses and three goodly suits of arms. *Tennyson.*

The right of the people to keep and bear arms shall not be infringed. *U. S. Const., Amend. II*

The arms intended by the Constitution [of the United States] are such as are suitable for the general defense of the community – and the secret carrying of those suited merely to deadly individual encounters may be prohibited. *T. M. Cooley.*[111] (Webster, *Webster's International*, 126)

The definition of arms as any weapon for offense or defense still makes sense today. If someone says they are an international arms dealer, the natural response is to think of them as dealing in everything from tanks to rocket launchers to rifles and handguns. *Firearms*, as Webster's Dictionary noted, is any arm, large or small, that is charged with powder and fires a projectile by igniting that powder. *Small arms* is a designation within firearms, describing those carried by individuals. And if someone says they are carrying a *sidearm*, one tends to think of a pistol, because "side" denotes a subclass of small arms. There simply is no reasoned way of getting around the broad meaning of arms in the Second Amendment to suggest it is limited to one of the subclasses.

As a case in point, arms at the founding would have included cannon, and private citizens did indeed own cannons, especially ship owners who needed to defend themselves on the high seas. This was not only common, it was government-sanctioned during times of war through letters of marque (U.S. Constitution Article 1, Section 8), permitting private ships – privateers – to act on behalf of the American government in policing the seas, going so far as to attack and seize enemy vessels for profit. In essence, letters of marque call up the "militia" of the seas to use their private arms, normally used for self-defense, in defense of the country. One such privateer vessel was the Prince de Neufchatel, authorized by a letter of marque from President James Madison in the War of 1812

---

[111] Thomas Cooley's actual quote is, "suitable for the general defense of the community from invasion or oppression, ..." (Cooley, 271-272)

(Madison, *Letter of Marque*),[112] the exploits of which were written in 1900 by soon-to-be president, Theodore Roosevelt (Roosevelt, 71-72).

Permissible Arms Under the Second Amendment

Therefore, any arms are permissible under the Second Amendment, but they must be used in such fashion as to not abridge the natural rights[113] of innocent individuals. In practicality, an individual using a nuclear device would be out of the scope of their rights, because its use would indiscriminately endanger the lives of others. Likewise, the use of a hand grenade would likely abridge the rights of others if used in self-defense anywhere except for remote private property. Yet, in a situation in which the civil authorities have breached their responsibility, putting them in a state of war with the people – a case not to be taken lightly or for transient causes as the Declaration of Independence states – even the most sophisticated military arms are within the scope of just use under the Second Amendment. This was, in fact, the mainstay for codifying the Second Amendment. As Thomas Cooley put it in 1880,

> The arms intended by the Constitution are such as are suitable
> for the general defence of the community against invasion or
> oppression … (Cooley, 271)

The proper choice of arms depends on the context of use, with the duty of use lying with the arms-bearer. Even a handgun, when used indiscriminately, may cause one to abridge the rights of another, thus making the shooter subject to penalty. Civil society can have an opinion on choice of arms and context of bearing arms, however, the right being unalienable, and the Second Amendment saying that it shall not be infringed, the choice, and the duty, belongs to the individual. If the individual has shown a neglect for their duty, abridging the rights of

---

[112] The letter is archived in the Public Record Office in Richmond, Surrey, UK; High Court of Admiralty HCA32/1342.

[113] "Natural rights" is explicitly used here to avoid the game of "what if the government gives me the right to be free of people with guns?" and similar frivolous positive rights arguments.

others, only then is it potentially appropriate for society to deal with the person, with just two caveats to be discussed. For the time in which the Bill of Rights was written, the chief mechanism for addressing behavioral issues surrounding the right to keep and bear arms was through the militia.

A well regulated Militia, being necessary to the security of a free State, ...

The small "m" militia is simply the natural body of the people acting together for the protection of the community. It is not something created by government. Joseph Story notes this in his *Commentaries on the Constitution* stating, "The militia is the natural defence of a free country ..." (Story, vol. 3, 746). A well-regulated Militia with capital "M," then, is that natural body of men organized and trained for effectiveness.

While the prefatory clause in the Second Amendment is both maligned and misused today, it was well understood and incredibly important to the American founders. The founders were strongly against keeping large armies during times of peace. They knew the history of England and the prohibition of standing armies in the English Bill of Rights. Despite this, the American colonies under King George III continued to suffer from the practice. Therefore, the grievance against the standing armies of George III in the Declaration of Independence was a strong indictment of the hypocrisy of the King.

With victory over Britain in the Revolutionary War, George Washington, made it clear in his 1783, *Sentiments on a Peace Establishment*, written six years before the Bill of Rights and Second Amendment, that standing armies would continue to be a bane of liberty in America,

> a large standing Army in time of Peace hath ever been considered dangerous to the liberties of a Country ... (Washington, *Writings*, vol. 26, 375)

James Madison commented on the impropriety of standing armies during the debates on the Constitution,

The means of defence against foreign danger have been always the instruments of tyranny at home. Among the Romans it was a standing maxim, to excite a war whenever a revolt was apprehended. Throughout all Europe, the armies kept up under the pretext of defending, have enslaved, the people. It is, perhaps, questionable, whether the best-concerted system of absolute power in Europe could maintain itself, in a situation where no alarms of external danger could tame the people to the domestic yoke. The insular situation of Great Britain was the principal cause of her being an exception to the general fate of Europe. It has rendered less defence necessary, and admitted a kind of defence which could not be used for the purpose of oppression. (Madison, *Debates*, 257)

And Thomas Jefferson stated even more emphatically in March of 1789 as the Bill of Rights loomed on the horizon,

There are instruments so dangerous to the rights of the nation and which place them so totally at the mercy of their governors that those governors, whether legislative or executive, should be restrained from keeping such instruments on foot but in well-defined cases. Such an instrument is a standing army. (Jefferson, *Writings*, vol. 3, 13)

Without standing armies, there needed to be a means of protection from both insurrection and oppression from within, as well as invasion from without. The founders' solution to the ready defense of the United States of America was the organized Militia. George Washington expressed the militia concept as being so natural in America that it should be unnecessary to prove or explain,

Were it not totally unnecessary and superfluous to adduce arguments to prove what is conceded on all hands the Policy and expediency of resting the protection of the Country on a respectable and well established Militia ...

we might see, with admiration, the Freedom and Independence of Switzerland supported for Centuries, in the midst of powerful and jealous neighbours, by means of a hardy and well organized Militia. We might also derive useful lessons of a similar kind from other Nations of Europe, but I believe it will be found, the People of this Continent are too well acquainted with the Merits of the subject to require information or example. (Washington, *Writings*, vol. 26, 388)

George Washington also stated,

The militia of this country must be considered as the palladium of our security and our first effectual resort in case of hostility; It is essential therefore, that the same system should pervade the whole; that the formation and discipline of the Militia of the Continent should be absolutely uniform, and that the same species of Arms, Accoutrements and Military Apparatus, should be introduced in every part of the United States; (Washington, *Writings*, vol. 26, 494)

James Madison combined the founders' disdain for standing armies with the desire for a strong militia when he said,

As the greatest danger to liberty is from large standing armies, it is best to prevent them by an effectual provision for a good militia. (Madison, *Debates*, 466)

Similarly, in 1803, President Thomas Jefferson said,

None but an armed nation can dispense with a standing army; to keep ours armed and disciplined is therefore at all times important. (Jefferson, *Writings*, vol. 4, 469)

Later, in 1808, Jefferson further expressed,

For a people who are free, and who mean to remain so, a well organized and armed militia is their best security. (Congress, Journal, 16)

Jefferson's words convey the understanding that the militia is simply an "armed nation" of "people who are free," organized and disciplined to be able to protect the country. That the nation is armed and free is given. The crux of securing the safety of the nation is how well the people can be organized and disciplined to be a ready and effectual fighting force.

That organization and discipline became broadly known as "well-regulated" in the Bill of Rights as the Second Amendment to the United States Constitution. By 1794, three years after ratification of the Bill of Rights, George Washington aligned his language to that of the amended Constitution, saying,

> The devising and establishing of a well-regulated militia would be a genuine source of legislative honor, and a perfect title to public gratitude. (Williams, Edwin, 59)

This is the meaning of, "A well regulated Militia, being necessary to the security of a free State, ..." The well-regulated Militia of the founders was viewed as a sacrosanct institution for protecting liberty in the United States of America; the "palladium of security" and the best security institution "for a people who are free, and who mean to remain so."

The importance of the Militia to America at the time of its founding is key to understanding the context of the Second Amendment. The prefatory clause of the Second Amendment is derived from the founders' recognition that the declaration of the right, "the right to keep and bear arms shall not be infringed," was the means to preserve and fulfill the need for a strong Militia. However, the reverse was never true, that the right was "granted" to fulfill the need for the Militia.

Grammar of the Second Amendment

The grammatical structure of the Second Amendment is sometimes presented as being mysterious. This contention is often intended to instill doubt in its straightforward meaning to substantiate a political position against the Second Amendment rather than a desire to determine the actual intent and context.

As the preamble to the Bill of Rights suggests, the amendments comprise declaratory ("declarative" in today's usage) and restrictive clauses. A declarative clause states a fact or argument. A restrictive clause is an essential modifier to a subject which cannot be eliminated without changing the meaning of the subject. In the Second Amendment, the first clause is declarative, and the second clause is restrictive.

1. A well-regulated militia is necessary to the security of a free state

2. The right of the people to keep and bear Arms shall not be infringed

These statements stand alone with very little confusion. Even taking them as stand-alone does not change the practical meaning of the Second Amendment. However, taken as declarative and restrictive clauses, the strength of the Second Amendment becomes clearer: to maintain a strong militia, that armed nation of free people, the palladium of security, it is essential that the right of the people to keep and bear arms not be infringed. Put another way, the right to keep and bear arms exists in any case, and the existence of the right is an imperative to the security of a free state.

The "confusing" statement about the Militia is not a limitation on Second Amendment rights; instead it is an expression of the extreme importance of Second Amendment rights for the protection of the States. Even without an understanding of the militia, this should be clear from the preamble of the Bill of Rights which states its goal to be one of limiting government, not peoples' rights.

In short, the right of the people to keep and bear arms is not to be infringed and the implicit personal right to arms for self-protection and self-provision is strengthened and reinforced by the need for a well-regulated militia to ensure the security of the state from threats within and without.

The implicit reasons for the right to keep and bear arms are not spelled out in the Second Amendment because in colonial America many people carried firearms in everyday life for hunting and protection from animals and hostile people, alike. An armed individual in society was not only accepted, but more likely expected. But it may be noted that Robert Whitehill, from Pennsylvania, who was against acceptance of the original Constitution because it did not contain a Bill of Rights, proposed the following amendment which explicitly addresses self-protection and self-provision that was so often unspoken:

> That the people have a right to bear arms for the defence of themselves and their own State, or the United States, or for the purpose of killing game; and no law shall be passed for disarming the people or any of them, unless for crimes committed, or real danger of public injury from individuals; (McMaster, 422)

Finally, another key to the grammatical structure of the Second Amendment is demonstrated in the state constitutions of Pennsylvania and Virginia. Written prior to the federal Constitution, the state bills of rights provide the basis for the language used in the federal Bill of Rights. The Second Amendment of the federal Constitution is a strong blend of the right to bear arms and militia philosophies from these two states:

The 1776 Pennsylvania Constitution, Chapter I, right XIII, states:

> That the people have a right to bear arms for the defence of themselves and the state; (Pennsylvania, *1776 Constitution*, 210)

and the Virginia Constitution of 1776, Section 13, states:

> That a well-regulated militia, composed of the body of the people, trained to arms, is the proper, natural, and safe defence of a free State; (General Assembly, 32)

The Second Amendment demonstrates an amalgam expressing that the values of both state constitutions should be protected; that the militia is necessary and is supported by free people able to keep and bear arms. This "cross-constitutional" influence is further evidenced by a change in the 1790 Pennsylvania Constitution, Article IX, Section XXI, created about the same time as the federal Bill of Rights, which uses the language "shall not be questioned" which is very similar to "shall not be infringed,"

That the right of the citizens to bear arms, in defence of themselves and the state, shall not be questioned. (Pennsylvania, *1790 Constitution*, 23)

Limitations to the Second Amendment

A well regulated Militia, being necessary to the security of a free State, the right of the people to keep and bear Arms, shall not be infringed.

Count the limitations written into the Second Amendment. Zero. Therefore, the duty aspect of the natural right to self-defense while bearing arms is the only potential bound to this right. As Sir William Blackstone was previously quoted,

For all of us have it in our choice to do every thing that a good man would desire to do; and are restrained from nothing, but what would be pernicious either to ourselves or our fellow citizens. (Blackstone, *Commentaries*, vol. 1, 140)

Just Bounds on the Right to Keep and Bear Arms

The only people who can justly be limited in their Second Amendment right are those who have broken their compact with society, and those incapable of maintaining a compact with society, and then only with the utmost care for the rights of the individual. Breaking the social compact is not simply an infraction of any law of society. Jaywalking does not break the social compact. It must be a significant and essentially irreconcilable breach of the Law of Nature and Nature's God which breaks the social compact, which John Locke has explained,

In transgressing the law of nature, the offender declares himself to live by another rule than that of reason and common equity, which is that measure God has set to the actions of men, for their mutual security, and so he becomes dangerous to mankind, the tye, which is to secure them from injury and violence, being slighted and broken by him, (Locke, 170)

Violent actors have, in general, broken the compact with society and conveyed that they would breach the duty aspect of their Second Amendment right. Being convicted of violent crimes of certain degree, society may reasonably abridge their right to keep and bear arms. It is fairly easy to say that murder, and most other violent felonies, would qualify one for this prohibition. Although there may be a sunset to the prohibition to allow for repentance and continued good behavior of the violator, just as there is in sentencing for crimes. Even some lesser forms of violence, not rising to the level of a felony, might be considered for prohibition in a just society. Yet there is a great tendency to let popular culture creep into the legal understanding of what constitutes violence breaching the social compact. Such culture creep lowers the bar for prohibition of Second Amendment rights so far as to subject individual rights to abridgement due to an isolated incidence of understandable violence, an unfounded allegation of violence, or even an allegation of the potential to commit violence at some future time – none of which breach the obligations of natural rights. By the standard of human nature suggested in the stories of Alfred Hitchcock – that anyone will become a murderer under certain circumstances – everyone would be stripped of Second Amendment rights simply for having the potential for murderous action.

The other category of individuals who might conceivably be limited in Second Amendment rights are those who do not have the mental ability to respect the duty aspect of the right. Small children are a prime example. While they have and can use the right of self-defense, until a certain level of maturity is reached, they may be deemed unfit to exercise the keeping and bearing of arms. Consider, however, that this level of maturity, often designated by age irrespective of maturity of ability, has varied throughout history, making it an artifact of popular culture. By the same token, the "mentally ill" may be determined, through thorough due process, to be unable to exercise the duty aspect of their Second Amendment right. But the standard for mental illness has likewise greatly varied across time and place, with each society being sure that they were doing the best for the individual and society, thereby making the definition of mental illness, and sometimes the science of it, deeply subject to popular culture. Definitions have also been altered and used politically to abridge Second Amendment rights from large groups of people without due process. In recent years, bureaucratic Federal rules have been leveraged to place those receiving Social Security benefits who are incapable of managing their own finances (Social Security Administration) on a list to deny them the right to purchase firearms, as if the inability to maintain complex finances constituted an adjudication of their mental capacity to manage a firearm for self-defense purposes. Similarly, veterans who have been appointed a fiduciary to handle Veteran's Administration payments and benefits, but not adjudicated as mentally unfit in any other capacity, have been globally denied their Second Amendment right to keep and bear arms (House of Representatives, 115th Congress).

The only other potentially valid restriction on the individual's right to keep and bear arms comes in terms of location. There are a few classes of public location, such as courtrooms, jails, legislative chambers, and secure government facilities, that may reasonably require temporary disarmament. For any such location there is a single absolute requirement and a secondary consideration for the temporary abridgement of the right to keep and bear arms. Any public offices or location restricting the individual right to keep and bear arms must assume responsibility for the individual's safety in a proactive and able capacity that is at least equal to the individual's capabilities. In such public locations there should also be secure facilities for individuals to safely store their firearms, otherwise the denial of rights at the location becomes a tacit denial of rights between the individual's abode or conveyance and the secure location prohibiting being armed.

Private Property and the Right to Bear Arms

One individual's right of private property used for private purposes competes with another individual's right to keep and bear arms such that private property ownership does not require protection for guests as is necessary for public property. Guests visit private property where firearms are forbidden at their own risk. That said, a rights-loving host should either provide for security or permit guests to provide their own.

Private property open to the public while prohibiting arms on premises should be responsible for patron safety, but because patrons visit by choice, the standard of protection need not be as high as for public facilities, or need not even exist. However, private business open to the public who deny patrons the right to be armed should be subject to civil suits and damages in court for negligence if a patron is exposed to danger and unable to mount their best self-defense, just as would be the case if the location had unsafe floors, electrical shock hazards, or ice on the sidewalk that led to injury.

Unjust Bounds – Popular Culture's Threat to the Second Amendment

The threat of popular culture to natural rights has some specific instances when it comes to the Second Amendment and carrying of arms: mode of carry, place of carry, type of arms, features of arms, limitations on group activities with firearms, and "maintaining public order." Popular culture continuously drives new, transient "norms" in each of these areas, leading to pressure on legislatures and courts to codify limitations on the Second Amendment. Time compounds the problem as popular culture changes, while the heaped, incoherent, limitations that have built-up remain and become the basis for expanded limitations until the right to keep and bear arms, is either gone or buried so deeply in caveats that it becomes impossible to practice.

The lack of consistency in time and place for these classes of restriction on the Second Amendment proves that they are based in popular culture and not timeless principle. At one time openly carrying a firearm was proper and carrying a concealed firearm was considered sinister, and at another time the opposite is true. Conversely, the culture of the Law of Nature and Nature's God is consistent in the rights of the individual and that individual's duty toward the rights of others. Society has the expectation of reasonable behavior within the bounds of natural rights. Society may hedge those bounds using social pressure, but society may not infringe the rights of an individual as a hedge of protection from a possible, but nonexistent, action.

Commentary and Legal Opinions on the Second Amendment

The text, history, and cultural context is all that is required to understand the Second Amendment. However, there exists a wealth of commentary and opinion from court cases which are worth mentioning as they provide a timeline of the generally ill effects of popular culture on the right to keep and bear arms. Judicial commentary and court opinions are just that, commentary and opinion. That commentaries and opinions regarding the Bill of Rights change over time is a clear identifier of the effect of popular culture, and its general proclivity to attempt to limit the foundational rights of Americans as established by the Declaration of Independence and codified in the Constitution.

The preeminent commentator on the Constitution of the early nineteenth century was Joseph Story, who has been cited liberally regarding the Constitution. His commentary on the Second Amendment from 1833 reads:[114]

> § 1889. The next amendment is: "A well regulated militia being necessary to the security of a free state, the right of the people to keep and bear arms shall not be infringed."

> § 1890. The importance of this article will scarcely be doubted by any persons, who have duly reflected upon the subject. The militia is the natural defence of a free country against sudden foreign invasions, domestic insurrections, and domestic usurpations of power by rulers. It is against sound policy for

---

[114] Section §1891 noting the history of the English Bill of Rights is not included here, having already been discussed under the history of the right to bear arms.

a free people to keep up large military establishments and standing armies in time of peace, both from the enormous expenses, with which they are attended, and the facile means, which they afford to ambitious and unprincipled rulers, to subvert the government, or trample upon the rights of the people. The right of the citizens to keep and bear arms has justly been considered, as the palladium of the liberties of a republic; since it offers a strong moral check against the usurpation and arbitrary power of rulers; and will generally, even if these are successful in the first instance, enable the people to resist and triumph over them. And yet, though this truth would seem so clear, and the importance of a well regulated militia would seem so undeniable, it cannot be disguised, that among the American people there is a growing indifference to any system of militia discipline, and a strong disposition, from a sense of its burthens, to be rid of all regulations. How it is practicable to keep the people duly armed without some organization, it is difficult to see. There is certainly no small danger, that indifference may lead to disgust, and disgust to contempt; and thus gradually undermine all the protection intended by this clause of our national bill of rights. (Story, *Commentaries*, vol. 3, 746-747)

Justice Story's commentary is brief and very straightforward, there is no hint that the subject is challenging to understand. There is no discussion about the "confusing" grammar and "hidden meaning" of phraseology. There is no discussion on limitations of arms. Furthermore, there is clear understanding that the Second Amendment is a right of the people and a palladium of liberty; that a key purpose in the right is to prevent the overreach of government, even more than the concern of foreign invasion. Story's greatest concern for the right is the waning public interest in the organization of the militia and the danger it might bring in keeping people properly armed. His foresight of the danger of indifference leading to disgust and then contempt for the right to keep and bear arms was prescient.

Thomas Cooley provides a commentary from 1880, post-Civil War and post-Emancipation.

> *The Constitution.* — By the second amendment to the Constitution it is declared that, " a well-regulated militia being necessary to the security of a free state, the right of the people to keep and bear arms shall not be infringed." The amendment, like most other provisions in the Constitution, has a history. It was adopted with some modification and enlargement from the English Bill of Rights of 1688, where it stood as a protest against arbitrary action of the overturned dynasty in disarming the people, and as a pledge of the new rulers that this tyrannical action should cease. The right declared was meant to be a strong moral check against the usurpation and arbitrary power of rulers, and as a necessary and efficient means of regaining rights when temporarily overturned by usurpation.
>
> *The Right is General.* — It might be supposed from the phraseology of this provision that the right to keep and bear arms was only guaranteed to the militia; but this would be an interpretation not warranted by the intent. The militia, as has been elsewhere explained, consists of those persons who, under the law, are liable to the performance of military duty, and are officered and enrolled for service when called upon. But the law may make provision for the enrolment of all who are fit to perform military duty, or of a small number only, or it may wholly omit to make airy provision at all; and if the right were limited to those enrolled, the purpose of this guaranty might be defeated altogether by the action or neglect to act of the government it was meant to hold in check. The meaning of the provision undoubtedly is, that the people, from whom the militia must be taken, shall have the right to keep and bear arms; and they need no permission or regulation of law for the purpose. But this enables the government to have a well-regulated militia; for to bear arms implies something more than the mere keeping; it implies the learning to handle and use them in a way that makes those who keep them ready

for their efficient use; in other words, it implies the right to meet for voluntary discipline in arms, observing in doing so the laws of public order.

Standing Army. — A further purpose of this amendment is, to preclude any necessity or reasonable excuse for keeping up a standing army. A standing army is condemned by the traditions and sentiments of the people, as being as dangerous to the liberties of the people as the general preparation of the people for the defence of their institutions with arms is preservative of them.

What Arms may be kept. — The arms intended by the Constitution are such as are suitable for the general defence of the community against invasion or oppression, and the secret carrying of those suited merely to deadly individual encounters may be prohibited. (Cooley, 271)

Just like Joseph Story's commentary, Cooley is reasonably brief and straightforward. The only discussion of grammar is to contradict the misconception that the Second Amendment is tied to militia participation, a belief that probably cropped up after the militia system was essentially gone by 1880[115] and misunderstood by the public, just as Joseph Story predicted 50 years earlier. Commensurate with that change, Cooley more explicitly than Joseph Story highlights that the right to keep and bear arms belongs to individuals and prescribes that public drilling with arms should be orderly.

New to the discussion with Cooley is a section on how arms may be carried under the Second Amendment, despite any mention of limitations within the amendment itself. Here Cooley adds a limitation on concealed arms to the United States Constitution based on a state court precedent from Tennessee in 1871 (Supreme Court of Tennessee, 165-201), which states that "the secret carrying of those suited merely to deadly individual

---

[115] As noted in the case that Cooley cited for limitation on what arms may be kept (Supreme Court of Tennessee, 184).

encounters may be prohibited" (Cooley, 271). Such would imply that open carrying of firearms suited merely for deadly individual encounters is constitutional, and perhaps even that secret carrying of arms suitable for military action is constitutional. Cooley does not suggest a limitation has been prescribed on the other end of the arms spectrum – large arms such as cannon, mortars and newer technologies, such as the Gatling gun, that were not available at the time of America's founding. By prescribing the one limitation and no others, Cooley essentially affirms that any arm suitable for defense against invasion or oppression is allowable, in any mode of carriage other than one narrow exception, as part of the individual right. As for Cooley's summary of a single state court case being extensible to the federal Second Amendment, his over-simplification is to his shame. Exercise of natural rights always has a line where it meets another's rights, but is never liable to the subjective whims of the majority or vociferous plurality spurred on by popular culture.

Moving to the present, the 2008 United States Supreme Court case, *District of Columbia v. Heller*, provides a rigorous review of the Second Amendment. The *Heller* Decision is noteworthy in its discussion tying historical references to modern recognition of the Second Amendment. Speaking for the majority, Justice Scalia made a thorough study of the history, context and grammar of the Second Amendment, keeping within the scope of the case before him. He did not, for instance, evaluate the history of the concealed carry of firearms or any requirement for licensure. To put the findings succinctly, the following passages from Scalia's opinion are presented to provide an overview. They amount to the common sense reading that an unbiased layperson would have for the Second Amendment.

> Constitutional rights are enshrined with the scope they were understood to have when the people adopted them, whether or not future legislatures or (yes) even future judges think that scope too broad. (*Heller*, 63)

In interpreting this text, we are guided by the principle that "[t]he Constitution was written to be understood by the voters; its words and phrases were used in their normal and ordinary as distinguished from technical meaning." (*Heller*, 3)

The Second Amendment is naturally divided into two parts: its prefatory clause and its operative clause. The former does not limit the latter grammatically, but rather announces a purpose. The Amendment could be rephrased, "Because a well regulated Militia is necessary to the security of a free State, the right of the people to keep and bear Arms shall not be infringed." See J. Tiffany, A Treatise on Government and Constitutional Law §585, p. 394 (1867); (*Heller*, 3)

Nowhere else in the Constitution does a "right" attributed to "the people" refer to anything other than an individual right. … What is more, in all six other provisions of the Constitution that mention "the people," the term unambiguously refers to all members of the political community, not an unspecified subset. (*Heller*, 6)

Putting all of these textual elements together, we find that they guarantee the individual right to possess and carry weapons in case of confrontation. This meaning is strongly confirmed by the historical background of the Second Amendment. We look to this because it has always been widely understood that the Second Amendment, like the First and Fourth Amendments, codified a pre-existing right. (*Heller*, 19)

We reach the question, then: Does the preface fit with an operative clause that creates an individual right to keep and bear arms? It fits perfectly, once one knows the history that the founding generation knew and that we have described above. That history showed that the way tyrants had eliminated a militia consisting of all the able-bodied men was not by banning the militia but simply by taking away the people's arms, enabling a select militia or standing army to suppress political opponents. This is what had occurred in

England that prompted codification of the right to have arms in the English Bill of Rights. (*Heller*, 25)

virtually all interpreters of the Second Amendment in the century after its enactment interpreted the amendment as we do. (*Heller*, 32)

Justice Scalia's majority opinion in *District of Columbia v. Heller* is very much in line with Joseph Story and the founding view of the Second Amendment. This is because, despite doing the work to review court precedent and refute the assertions of dissenting justices in the Supreme Court, Scalia looked to the law of the Constitution, as derived from the American Mind in the Law of Nature and Nature's God of the Declaration of Independence.

Chapter 9 –
The Fourth and Fifth Amendments

Amendment IV

> The right of the people to be secure in their persons, houses, papers, and effects, against unreasonable searches and seizures, shall not be violated, and no Warrants shall issue, but upon probable cause, supported by Oath or affirmation, and particularly describing the place to be searched, and the persons or things to be seized.

Amendment V

> No person shall be held to answer for a capital, or otherwise infamous crime, unless on a presentment or indictment of a Grand Jury, except in cases arising in the land or naval forces, or in the Militia, when in actual service in time of War or public danger; nor shall any person be subject for the same offence to be twice put in jeopardy of life or limb; nor shall be compelled in any criminal case to be a witness against himself, nor be deprived of life, liberty, or property, without due process of law; nor shall private property be taken for public use, without just compensation.

In short, the Fourth and Fifth Amendments say that no one can legally take someone's property without a just legal cause, due process, and in some cases, just compensation. There are only two[116] just legal causes for taking the property of another: payment of debts and reparation of wrongs. Payment of debts is a correction in property ownership, if handled in accordance with law or contract. Reparation is similar in that a debt created by unjust action is repaid through a transfer of property to the wronged individual.

John Locke summarized reparation in relation to crime as a right of an aggrieved party, along with the right of the society to punish a wrongdoer:

> two distinct rights, the one of punishing the crime for restraint, and preventing the like offence, which right of punishing is in every body; the other of taking reparation, which belongs only to the injured party ... (Locke, 172)

An injured party, and only the injured party, has a right to be compensated for losses at the hands of a wrongdoer.[117] Society has a right to exact punishment on a wrongdoer but does not have the right to a wrongdoer's property as part of that punishment. This fundamental founding philosophy of property has been forgotten from the American Mind.

Locke asserted even that a conquering power has no right to the property of a vanquished aggressor beyond reparation for losses, nor does the conqueror have any right to the property of the wife and children of the vanquished, they having not participated in the conflict.

> But because the miscarriages of the father are no faults of the children, and they may be rational and peaceable, notwithstanding the brutishness and injustice of the father; **the father, by his miscarriages and violence, can forfeit but his own life, but involves not his children in his guilt or destruction. His goods, which nature, that willeth the**

---

[116] Elimination of imminent external existential threat may be a rational cause for taking of property but is essentially is reversion to a state of nature and not a legal process.
[117] The Bible supports the position that only the injured party is to be compensated. See Exodus 22.

preservation of all mankind as much as is possible, hath made to belong to the children to keep them from perishing, do still continue to belong to his children: for supposing them not to have joined in the war, either through infancy, absence, or choice, they have done nothing to forfeit them: nor has the conqueror any right to take them away, by the bare title of having subdued him that by force attempted his destruction; … (Locke, 309, emphasis added)

So that he that by conquest has a right over a man's person to destroy him if he pleases, has not thereby a right over his estate to possess and enjoy it: for it is the brutal force the aggressor has used, that gives his adversary a right to take away his life, and destroy him if he pleases, as a noxious creature; but it is damage sustained that alone gives him title to another man's goods: for though I may kill a thief that sets on me in the highway, yet I may not (which seems less) take away his money, and let him go: this would be robbery on my side. His force, and the state of war he puts himself in, made him forfeit his life, but gave me no title to his goods. (Locke, 309-310)

Let the conqueror have as much justice on his side, as could be supposed, he has no right to seize more than the vanquished could forfeit: his life is at the victor's mercy; and his service and goods he may appropriate, to make himself reparation; but he cannot take the goods of his wife and children; they too had a title to the goods he enjoyed, and their shares in the estate he possessed: … (Locke, 310)

Civil Asset Forfeiture

Against this backdrop of the American Mind on property rights, the pernicious modern-day practice of "civil asset forfeiture" must be reviewed.

Civil asset forfeiture is a legal tool that allows law enforcement officials to seize property under the assertion that it was involved in criminal activity. The property owner need not have been involved in the criminal activity. No warrant need be issued, and civil asset forfeiture does not require conviction, charge, or even arrest, of the property owner. Simply, the property is blamed for involvement in a crime and thereby confiscated by law enforcement, to be used or sold to further their official activities. Property is also generally "equitably shared" among law enforcement, district attorney's offices and the court. Such conflict of interest has led many law enforcement agencies to regard civil asset forfeiture as an opportunity for revenue generation (Dewan). Return of property may be possible in courts, but the process is typically stacked against the property owner, requiring "proof of innocence" regarding alleged crimes, and legal costs, which add insult to injury and may be beyond the capability of many.

Civil asset forfeiture violates all the Constitutional and Lockean principles of property:

> Ignoring the right of people to be secure in their property against unreasonable searches and seizures.

> Seizing property without sworn statement of probable cause and not particularly describing the things to be seized.

> Depriving people of property without due process of law.

> Seizing private property for public use, without just compensation.

> Taking of "reparation" without being an injured party.

> Taking property as punishment, even punishment where no guilt has been found.

> Taking property in power as a conqueror from a vanquished foe.

> Taking property that belongs to the wife and children of an accused wrongdoer.

That civil asset forfeiture came to be a "lawful" practice in America boggles the mind. It has a very loose history in the seizure of ships used for smuggling under Admiralty law and a Prohibition Era analog for seizing vehicles from bootleggers, but it was the "war on drugs" instituted in the 1980s that brought the practice to modern use (Malcolm).

Egregious examples of civil asset forfeiture are not difficult to find. They range from a man having his life savings confiscated solely because he carried it in cash (Ingraham), to seizure of a disabled veteran's car because he lived with his son who had an arrest warrant, to seizure of a couple's home because their twenty-two-year-old son who lived with them was alleged to be selling drugs from the house, without their knowledge (Brown). Civil asset forfeiture has no standing in the philosophy of the American Mind and is so extremely counter to it that every American should firmly stand against it.

Eminent Domain

Apart from the war on drugs, civil asset forfeiture was probably just the next logical step from eminent domain, another "lawful" practice with a judicial history going back to 1879 (U. S. Department of Justice). Although eminent domain is "settled constitutional law" (*stare decisis*), it exhibits many of the noxious characteristics of civil asset forfeiture; the primary difference being that it has an established due process and provides just – at least in terms of fair market value – compensation for "condemned" property. Even so, it has been repeatedly abused, exemplified by the infamous 2005 "*Kelo* case" (U. S. Supreme Court, *Kelo*) in which a woman's home and property was condemned – a term of art, not a reflection of poor condition of the property – and taken for the "public good" to establish an office park for pharmaceutical giant, Pfizer, as part of a city revitalization effort under the auspices of the city of New London, Connecticut and a partnering nonprofit development corporation. In all, a total of fifteen properties were taken by eminent domain with the action upheld by the Connecticut Supreme Court in a 4-3 decision and by the United States Supreme Court in a 5-4 decision. To add further insult, the revitalization project fell through, leaving the condemned properties barren and undeveloped as recently as 2015 (Somin).

Popular culture has transformed American thought from seeking "public good" in the rights of the individual to seeking it in the collective, at the expense of individual rights; the wellspring of all public good. When a case for "public good" like the *Kelo* case arises, the legal system automatically looks within itself at the compounded legalese of multiple statutes and prior court precedents to build a legal argument to the exclusion of the source text, context, and rationale for the law. Cases then become not about what is righteous and true, but about winning the argument for "the public good," and the "rights of government."

Rather, such arguments should focus on the individual natural right to property and the context that the end of government as designed in the Declaration of Independence is to protect private property. John Locke laid out this premise as the American founders believed,

> The supreme power [government] cannot take from any man any part of his property without his own consent: for the preservation of property being the end of government, and that for which men enter into society, … nobody hath a right to take their substance or any part of it from them, without their own consent: without this they have no property at all; for I have truly no property in that, which another can by right take from me, when he pleases, against my consent. (Locke, 273)

Chapter 10 –
The Tenth
and Fourteenth Amendments

Clash of the Amendments

The Constitution is the basis of federal law and the Bill of Rights was added to constrain the Federal Government from interfering with the States and The People beyond its granted powers. The Tenth Amendment (Cobbett, vol. 26, 512, listed as Article 12) leaves all unenumerated powers with the states and the people, with the states having their own constitutions that often include bills of rights, for their citizens. This "compound republic" structure of the United States was intentional, as Hamilton outlined in *Federalist 51* (Hamilton, 282), protecting against concentration of power, and allowing the states to adapt to the needs and desires of their people, constrained only by the narrow federal authority of the Constitution. The United States Supreme Court validated this founding view of the first ten amendments to the federal Constitution in *Barron v. Baltimore* in 1833, upholding the view that the Bill of Rights applied only the Federal Government and not state governments (Peters, 243-251):

> Had the framers of these amendments intended them to be limitations on the powers of the state governments, they would have imitated the framers of the original constitution, and have expressed that intention. Had congress engaged in the extraordinary occupation of improving the constitutions of the several states by affording the people additional

protection from the exercise of power by their own governments in matters which concerned themselves alone, they would have declared this purpose in plain and intelligible language ... These amendments contain no expression indicating an intention to apply them to the state governments. (Peters, 250)

Furthermore, the Blaine Amendment, proposed as the sixteenth amendment to the Constitution in 1875, demonstrates the prevailing view of President Grant and the Congress that the Bill of Rights applied only to the Federal Government and not the States. The Blaine Amendment never made it out of the Senate and was therefore never presented to the States. It reads,

No State shall make any law respecting an establishment of religion, or prohibiting the free exercise thereof; and no money raised by taxation in any State for the support of public schools, or derived from any public fund therefor, or any public lands devoted thereto, shall ever be under the control of any religious sect; nor shall any money so raised or lands so devoted be divided between religious sects or denominations. (Congress, *Congressional Record*, 44th Congress, 5189)

The first clause of the Blaine Amendment is the same as the first clause of the First Amendment, except for the subject of restriction. In the First Amendment, Congress is restricted. In the Blaine Amendment, the States are restricted. Had the Bill of Rights been intended to apply to the States, the first clause of the Blaine Amendment would have been unnecessary.

However, a new era of constitutional tension regarding the compound republic began several years earlier with the Fourteenth Amendment (McDonald, 53-55), ratified in 1868. The Fourteenth Amendment was created in the wake of the Civil War, Emancipation, and the end of slavery, which was enshrined in the Thirteenth Amendment (McDonald, 53). Its intent was to stifle civil rights abuses that developed during Reconstruction following the Civil War.

The constitutional stressors within the Fourteenth Amendment, Sections 1 and 5, state:

> All persons born or naturalized in the United States, and subject to the jurisdiction thereof, are citizens of the United States and of the State wherein they reside. No State shall make or enforce any law which shall abridge the privileges or immunities of citizens of the United States; nor shall any State deprive any person of life, liberty, or property, without due process of law; nor deny to any person within its jurisdiction the equal protection of the laws.

> The Congress shall have the power to enforce, by appropriate legislation, the provisions of this article. (McDonald, 53-55)

Necessity of the Fourteenth Amendment

The citizenship clause of Section 1 of the Fourteenth Amendment was an absolute necessity for America to punctuate the end to slavery and ensure that the emancipated were accorded the legal rights of citizens and not left as "African immigrants" with no rights.[118] The remaining clauses were, perhaps, less necessary or equally in vain compared to the Declaration of Independence and Constitution which they amended. The final three clauses of Section 1 of the Fourteenth Amendment were, arguably, already covered in America's original founding documents:

> We hold these truths to be self-evident, that all men are created equal, that they are endowed by their Creator with certain unalienable Rights, that among these are Life, Liberty and the pursuit of Happiness.–That to secure these rights,

---

[118] Although there is considerable contention that "all persons born" in the United States unintentionally and fundamentally altered American citizenship beyond ensuring that former slaves were granted citizenship by granting citizenship to anyone born on American soil regardless of the parents' citizenship or loyalties. This question hinges on the phrase "subject to the jurisdiction thereof" which may be considered to exclude those born or naturalized who are under the jurisdiction of other powers.

Governments are instituted among Men, deriving their just powers from the consent of the governed, ...

Declaration of Independence

The Citizens of each State shall be entitled to all Privileges and Immunities of Citizens in the several States.

Constitution Article IV, Section 2

nor shall any person ... be deprived of life, liberty, or property, without due process of law;

Constitution, Fifth Amendment

Prior to the Fourteenth Amendment, the Constitution provided no direct statement of "equality," but "We the people" in the preamble and "any person," in the Fifth Amendment, implied all people – with the glaring exception of the great national sin of slavery[119] as upheld in the egregiously wrong *Dred Scott* case[120] (Howard, 393). But with slavery ended, and the citizenship clause of the Fourteenth Amendment, the Declaration and Constitution came into their God-ordained and intended fullness for the rights of mankind, prescribing justice for government apart from the remainder of the Fourteenth Amendment.

The Fourteenth Amendment's restatement of privileges and immunities, due process, and equality, when lined up with the Declaration and pre-existing Constitution, appears to be a direct indictment of the States' unwillingness, or incapability, to provide just due process for their citizens, thus requiring paternal intervention from the Federal Government. Such may have been true and necessary in the vanquished South, but it might have also been that application of the existing Constitution (including Thirteenth Amendment, ratified in 1865) with a simplified Fourteenth Amendment without punitive undertones would

---

[119] And it may be said, the lack of womens' suffrage.
[120] In *Dred Scott*, "a negro of the African race" was deemed to be excluded from "We the people" of the Declaration of Independence (Howard, 410).

have better restored the South to the Union and brought justice to emancipated slaves.

In addition to the potentially missed opportunity to better bring the South back into the fold of the Union, the long-lasting implication of (near) duplication of text in multiple places in the Constitution is that it leads to contention of different, or special, meaning based on the context in which it was implemented. Doing so is not dissimilar to citing legal precedent from court cases rather than the Constitution itself. It trends toward the abandonment of the foundational Constitution.

Restatement of rights of equality in the Fourteenth Amendment instead of "rehabilitation" of the original intent of the Constitution and Declaration also missed the opportunity to directly contradict and correct the erroneous conclusions of *Dred Scott* by an act of Congress. It is best to go to the original context, which in this case would be to look at the American Mind and see that "We hold these truths to be self-evident, that all men are created equal, that they are endowed by their Creator with certain unalienable Rights, that among these are Life, Liberty and the pursuit of Happiness," and to clarify the Constitution's assertion that "The Citizens of each State shall be entitled to all Privileges and Immunities of Citizens in the several States" and "nor shall any person ... be deprived of life, liberty, or property, without due process of law."

There is no way of knowing what would have been, of course. This is perhaps even too fine a point to put on such a great and multifaceted topic, but an undiluted Article IV, Section 2 and Fifth Amendment for all people seems stronger than divided amendments, one for "free America" and another for "emancipated America." Yet it is also clear in hindsight that neither the Fourteenth Amendment nor subsequent civil rights laws were satisfactory impetus to change hearts, minds and popular culture in the South and elsewhere.

Fallout of the Fourteenth Amendment

The Fourteenth Amendment was not significantly tested in court until the Supreme Court *Slaughterhouse* cases in 1873 (United States Supreme Court, *Slaughter-House Cases*, 36). The *Slaughterhouse* cases had nothing to do with the intent of the Fourteenth Amendment to protect emancipated slaves from State abuses. Instead, they focused on the application of Section 1 of the Fourteenth Amendment to protect the private New Orleans slaughterhouse industry from a City takeover under a newly enacted state law. The Supreme Court held that the Fourteenth Amendment Privileges or Immunities Clause affected only United States citizenship, not state citizenship and the "simple declaration that no State should make or enforce any law which shall abridge the privileges and immunities of citizens of the United States" (77) did not "transfer the security and protection of all the civil rights which we have mentioned, from the States to the Federal government," (77) stating further that to do otherwise would "fetter and degrade the State governments by subjecting them to the control of Congress in the exercise of powers heretofore universally conceded to them of the most ordinary and fundamental character" (78) and closing with, "We are convinced that no such results were intended by the Congress which proposed these amendments, nor by the legislatures of the States which ratified them" (78).

While it seems almost blasphemous today, this simple argument implying that the Fourteenth Amendment was intended to rectify wrongs done by States to emancipated slaves and others persecuted for their race or color, and was not intended to grow the scope of federal government in the face of the Tenth Amendment, seems very plain and straightforward in reasoning.

Perspective on the Clash of the Tenth and Fourteenth Amendments

Despite the narrow reading of the Fourteenth Amendment in the *Slaughterhouse* cases, there remained various interpretations of what was the Federal Government's power; to legislate and enforce equal protection under law with respect to race, color or previous condition of servitude, or a broader view that the Federal Congress gained the power to preemptively legislate conditions of equal protection.

The Civil Rights Act of 1875

In 1875, a bill was debated in the House of Representatives that brought the clash of the Tenth and Fourteenth Amendments, as well as issues of slavery, equality, individual rights and state sovereignty, to the forefront. This debate captured many of the issues surrounding the application of the Tenth and Fourteenth Amendments today. The debate covered the issue from all angles: federal law, state law, calls for equality and doing the "right thing," and sometimes citing law as a rationale to skirt doing the right thing, while at other times calling for the law to be ignored just to do the "right thing" by making another law. Yes, it is confusing, and it is in the midst of such confusing cross purposes that popular culture often overrides the culture of the American Mind.

The bill was known as the Civil Rights Act of 1875 (18 Stat. 335–337), entitled, *An Act to Protect all Citizens in their Civil and Legal Rights* (Congress, *Statutes 1873-1875*, 335). The act declared all persons within the jurisdiction of the United States to be entitled to the full and equal enjoyment of inns, public conveyances, and places of public amusement, and provided for punishment for the denial of such based on race, color or previous condition of servitude. Additionally, the act gave federal courts and the Supreme Court jurisdiction over all cases.

There were a number of points on which both major sides of the debate agreed. The chief being that only explicit grants of power by the Constitution are valid for the Federal Government[121] (*Appleton's Annual*, 158, 160) and that the Fourteenth Amendment did not apply beyond the narrow interpretation of protection of "privileges and immunities" relating

---

[121] Recall James Madison's criteria for constitutional law in the Alien and Sedition Acts discussion in Chapter 4 – *The Bill of Rights Clarifies the American Mind*.

to race or color by use of the *Slaughterhouse* opinion (*Appleton's Annual*, 158, 162). Both sides of the debate cited many of the same passages from the *Slaughterhouse* opinion in defense of their arguments. The debate, instead, focused on the extent to which Congress could go to protect "privileges and immunities" relating to race or color.

The crux of the argument was those in favor of *An Act to Protect all Citizens in their Civil and Legal Rights* claiming that the Federal Government, by the Fourteenth Amendment, had the power to legislate and enforce equal protection under the law if it was not instituted by a State, versus those against the act claiming that the Fourteenth Amendment, in giving power to Congress to legislate enforcement of the amendment, did not grant Congress the blanket power to preemptively or proactively legislate equal protection in the States. In short, the question on the Fourteenth Amendment was a question on the validity of the Tenth Amendment's reservation of powers for the States.

The Civil Rights Act of 1875 was passed by Congress and signed by President Grant but it was never well enforced and was ruled unconstitutional in the Supreme Court *Civil Rights Cases* in 1883, holding that Congress lacked authority under the Thirteenth and Fourteenth Amendments to regulate private business, only having authority to correct state law. These cases did not address the general constitutionality of rights to the use of inns, transportation, etc. (United States Supreme Court, *Civil Rights Cases*, 3-4). Effectively, the emotional arguments about equality and justice that should be in the hearts of men that were codified in the Civil Rights Act of 1875 were corrected to be what is right in a law, leaving the defects of men's behavior to the culture of the American Mind for correction, considering once more John Adams' quotation that "our Constitution was made only for a moral and religious people."

Incorporation Doctrine

The dispute over interpreting the Constitution to "do what is right" versus following the letter of the law to preserve the integrity of the Constitution is a far cry from what later happened with the development of the constitutional interpretation known as Incorporation Doctrine.

Ultimately, because of the Fourteenth Amendment, most of the federal rights contained in the Bill of Rights came to be applied to the States under the Incorporation Doctrine. This change of perspective in the Constitution has generally been viewed as being positive; targeting "State aggression" (United States Supreme Court, *Civil Rights Cases*, 17) upon emancipated slaves by some states, recognizing rights consistently across all of the states, and ensuring equal application of rights within states. Insofar as the Bill of Rights protects natural rights, the Incorporation Doctrine appears to make sense because natural rights should be protected within state governments in addition to the Federal Government, although it was intended at the founding for state constitutions to be the purview for protecting the majority of those rights.

Constitutional Repercussions of the Incorporation Doctrine

This extension of the Bill of Rights via a doctrine built on court precedent rather than considered debate by the people and their representatives in federal and state legislatures, has created some presumably unintended consequences. The Fourteenth Amendment as currently interpreted has effectively decimated the rights of States under the Tenth Amendment and concentrated power with unelected federal judges.

The beginnings of the Incorporation Doctrine can be traced to the 1897 *Chicago, Burlington and Quincy Railroad v. Chicago* (United States Supreme Court, *Chicago, Burlington and Quincy v. Chicago*, 226) and 1925 *Gitlow v. New York* (United States Supreme Court, *Gitlow*, 652) Supreme Court cases. More important than the details of these cases is the cultural thinking of that time, the Progressive Era[122] in America, that espoused not constitutional Federalism, but statism under control of the Federal Government, bringing about a fundamental change in the

---

[122] Refer to Glossary and Appendix: *Left, Center, Right – Framing Political Philosophies*.

application of justice from the *negative rights* of the Declaration of Independence and Constitution to *positive rights*. The natural rights of mankind as infinitely extended via the Tenth Amendment are negative rights, deemed negative because they exist without being created by man. Positive rights are those granted to society by government, only existing if explicitly listed in laws – like the grants of federal powers in the Constitution. Positive rights are subject to change by the government for "the good of society," "the common good," "to save just one life," or any other reason, amassing central power with the Federal State. All these arguments for incorporation seem to be some version of "doing the right thing," which is a nice, or perhaps, naïve, way of saying that "the ends justify the means." And it is always such an argument, even in a righteous argument for justice in an individual case, that erodes the larger volume of rights and justice for all.

The decimation of the Tenth Amendment happens largely via the judicial branch of the Federal Government with complicity, or ignorance, of the legislative branch. The scenario goes like this: A state makes a law regarding a right of the people of that state not related to federal law. That law is challenged in the state court system by people, eventually making its way to the state supreme court. The state supreme court makes a ruling and the law either stands or is overturned, leaving other states unaffected. This is where the case would have ended prior to the Fourteenth Amendment. With the Progressive Era Incorporation Doctrine, however, the same case became subject to appeal in the federal court system, all the way up to the United States Supreme Court, with the resulting court opinion becoming de facto law for all states.

In this judicial arrangement, the state court system is relegated to being a lower court system, and the state constitutional basis by which the state courts ruled became a mere background consideration to the federal Constitution and federal court precedent. As a result, the founders' fear of concentration of power in the Federal Government became realized, and rights were eroded as the Bill of Rights became viewed as a list of granted positive rights rather than natural negative rights.

Some may say this Federal control is necessary to ensure that states do not abridge people's rights.[123] That presumption implies there is some incapability of state legislatures, courts, and citizens of the states to effect justice that requires external intervention. The same presumption can also be true for the federal court system, which, in practice, answers to no particular body of citizens. It can also be said that the federal court system has to answer to the entire body of all citizens, often leading to pandering to popular culture and the mob-rule majority, rather than adherence to the Constitution and the culture defined by the Declaration of Independence.

Such "legislating" via court opinion is completely contrary to the intended and designed structure of American government. It is the people of each State who are responsible to right wrongs within their State, to elect new legislatures and seat courts that abide in the American Mind and Constitution. Then, only in the most egregious cases against the Law of Nature and Nature's God by a State is the intervention of the Federal Government warranted. As the maxim goes, "Don't make a Federal case out of it."

States as "Laboratories of Democracy"

Another saying relating to the Tenth Amendment is that States are the "laboratories of democracy." This idiom is often used as a pro-Tenth Amendment statement, implying that the States should be left alone to enact the laws wanted by their people. Unfortunately, that was neither the intent of the original use of the phrase, nor is it the practice of what happens today in America's current federally-driven court system.

States as the "laboratories of democracy" was coined as a Progressive dissention to the majority opinion in the 1932 *New State Ice Co. v. Liebmann* (United States Supreme Court, *New State Ice*, 262) by Justice Louis Brandeis. The majority opinion held that the New State Ice Company could not be prohibited from engaging in manufacturing and

---

[123] The same contention made in the overturned *Civil Rights Act of 1875*.

selling ice under a State licensing regime which intended to reduce "excess" ice in the market. Brandeis dissented, saying, in part:

> There must be power in the States and the Nation to remould, through experimentation, our economic practices and institutions to meet changing social and economic needs. I cannot believe that the framers of the Fourteenth Amendment, or the States which ratified it, intended to deprive us of the power to correct the evils of technological unemployment and excess productive capacity which have attended progress in the useful arts.
>
> To stay experimentation in things social and economic is a grave responsibility. Denial of the right to experiment may be fraught with serious consequences to the Nation. **It is one of the happy incidents of the federal system that a single courageous State may, if its citizens choose, serve as a laboratory; and try novel social and economic experiments without risk to the rest of the country.** This Court has the power to prevent an experiment. We may strike down the statute which embodies it on the ground that, in our opinion, the measure is arbitrary, capricious or unreasonable. We have power to do this, because the due process clause has been held by the Court applicable to matters of substantive law as well as to matters of procedure. But in the exercise of this high power, we must be ever on our guard, lest we erect our prejudices into legal principles. If we would guide by the light of reason, we must let our minds be bold. (311, emphasis added)

It should be plain enough, but Justice Brandeis was suggesting that States should be laboratories for social experiments so any experiments that go awry will not adversely affect other States, and, by implication, those deemed successful could then "scientifically" be promulgated to the remaining States. And in all of this, the Court, not the People, should be the arbiter of what is good and what is successful. The presumption of "laboratories of democracy" is not that States can do what they want per the Tenth Amendment, but rather that they are either guinea pigs to be used for testing by internal factions or outside organizations, or they are trying to establish "scientific law" from social or economic theory which then, because it is a "proven fact," must be federally applied to all states.

The majority opinion of *New State Ice Co. v. Liebmann* countered this progressive position in just a single sentence:

> A state law infringing the liberty guaranteed to individuals by the Constitution can not be upheld upon the ground that the State is conducting a legislative experiment. (262)

The Importance of Recognizing Tenth and Fourteenth Amendment Conflict

A lot of unraveling of history and court precedents must be done to get to the core issues when discussing the status of the Tenth Amendment. But the point is that, as cut and dry as the Incorporation Doctrine seems to be today, and as normal as Federal Government control of the civil rights agenda seems to be today, the arguments for Federal Government control are not so cut and dry when reviewing the meaning and context of the Tenth and Fourteenth Amendments.

Legal issues should always be approached from a constitutional perspective with the intent of the American Mind,[124] particularly under the present popular culture supporting judicial fiat as the means of establishing "law" and the automatic generalization of a single court opinion to have immediate and untested precedent over all laws in other States. Such practices were in no way intended by the founders, and the effect is especially egregious on liberty in today's 24-hour, instantaneous, distance-free society in which the impact of national "interest groups" (factions) quickly generate challenges at the federal level – either in the courts or Congress, often bypassing the will of the people of a State – to every state law, or even seeking to establish new law based on the outside court

---

[124] Refer back to Chapter 2 – *The Declaration of Independence is the American Mind* sections, Laws of Nature and Laws of Nature's God.

opinion. This process even surpasses the Progressive desire for "laboratories of democracy" by eliminating all elements of scientific method in favor of raw factional zeal.

No substantive call is being made for a change in the Fourteenth Amendment in America, and it will take a serious legal crisis or change in popular culture for reexamination of the Incorporation Doctrine. However, the Tenth Amendment still stands, and a balance of power needs to be reestablished between the States and Federal Government, and the People, as a check on statism. The Federal Government will not easily give up power, and State governments will also covet whatever power they can reclaim, so it is incumbent upon The People to maintain the American Mind to ensure the future of liberty.

APPENDIX

APPENDIX

The Fullness of Time – The Advent of Jesus Christ

Chapter 1 discussed the fullness of time for America, starting with the invention of the printing press. But the concept of "fullness of time" predates that by some 1,450 years with the coming of Jesus Christ.

Many Christians have placed their faith in Jesus Christ as their savior without an historical understanding of God's plan to bring Jesus into the world at a specific time and place where he could have the most effective earthly ministry. History lessons are not a requirement for salvation, but they can be instructive for both Christians and non-Christians to demonstrate the fulfillment of God's plan in history.

The conquest of Alexander the Great is a good place to pick up the story of the fullness of time for Christ. Alexander the Great was born in Greece and rose to power in 336 BC as the King of Macedonia. Within six years, Alexander had destroyed the Persian Empire which included ancient Israel and Babylon, where many Jews had been exiled 300 years earlier. By the time of his death in 323 BC, Alexander had conquered the known world and spread and enabled the free-thinking, reason-loving Greek Hellenistic culture throughout his empire.

In 63 BC the Romans conquered the despots ruling the remnants of Alexander's empire. At this time, the Roman Empire had no strong culture of its own, leaving Greek culture widespread in Roman vassal states. There were also too many Roman gods to force the empire into a singular form of worship, so people were free to practice any religion as long as they remained subservient to Caesar. The result was that Greek culture, one of freedom of thought and philosophical inquiry, and common usage of the highly descriptive Greek language, survived under Roman rule. At the time of Jesus' life,[125] these vestiges of Alexander's Greek empire remained pervasive from Spain to Palestine as part of the Roman empire. The Romans also established the Pax Romana, or Roman Peace, across the empire; and the system of roads used by Roman armies to maintain that peace were available for the free travel of subjects and citizens throughout the empire.

At the time of Christ, the vast majority of Jews remained spread throughout the Roman world from their days of exile under the Assyrians (722 BC) and Babylonians (586 BC). Some of the people from these Jewish diasporas retained Jewish Law and history. These Jews were awaiting the Messiah, the Christ, who would come and be the savior of the Jewish people.

And so it was the fullness of time as the Apostle Paul expressed in the Bible,

> But when the fullness of time had come, God sent forth his Son, born of woman, born under the law, to redeem those who were under the law, so that we might receive adoption as sons. (Galatians 4:4-5 ESV)

God appointed this time in history by spreading Jews across the known world, ready to receive the Messiah. He established a common language in Greek and a culture accepting of the study of new philosophies. God created peace through the Romans and enabled travel throughout the empire on Roman roads. He established an atmosphere in which freedom of religion existed, and, under the licentiousness of the Romans, created a climate in which many people sought universal truth. By the time of Jesus' ministry and the acts of the Apostles after Jesus' death and resurrection,

---

[125] Approximately 0 AD to 33 AD.

the known world was prepared to receive the good news of salvation through Jesus Christ.

The Christian's Relationship to Government

The big picture of a Christian's relationship to government is that there exists an incredible parallel between the truth of the gospel, in opposition to man-made religion, and liberty in the Law of Nature and Nature's God in opposition to popular culture-established and government-managed boundaries on licentiousness. These parallels might be easier to envision in diagram form:

Christianity		**Government/ Popular Culture**
Religion	⟷	Legalism
Freedom in Christ	⟷	Liberty
Salvation to Everlasting Life	⟷	Unalienable Rights

All people possess unalienable rights which can be left unexercised, but never taken away. All people have been offered salvation and everlasting life through the grace of Jesus Christ which may be rejected, but which cannot be taken away once accepted (John 10:9-10, 14, 27-28). When one accepts Jesus as Savior and becomes a Christian, they become free of the Law of the Old Testament (Galatians 4:4-7, 5:1) and from the certainty of death (2 Timothy 1:10; 1 Corinthians 15:20-22). As one accepts the liberty of the Law of Nature and Nature's God, one becomes free from the need for hedges on licentiousness required in popular culture, and the demand for government to police and enforce behavior that is not licentious.

Christians may choose to sin, just as one in liberty may choose licentiousness. But the ones truly believing, in either case, will not behave wrongly, and will turn from the practice when they realize an error. In the opposite sense, there will always be some who do not reach this understanding of liberty and grace. In Christianity, these are the people who value religion for the sake of religiosity; in society, these are the legalists. In both cases, these are people living in ignorance, falling short of their potential, or ones who seek power and control over others.

Christians are called to overcome the lovers of ignorance, religion, and power by growing in understanding and not being "carried about by every wind of doctrine, by the trickery of men, by craftiness in deceitful scheming" (Ephesians 4:13). This should likewise be true for all people regarding popular culture and government.

Obedience to Authority

Christians have, at times, been tested on the righteousness of the American Declaration of Independence and Revolution, or any action that challenges government. This is because the Bible, specifically the New Testament in which Christians believe, encourages obedience to governing authorities. The book of Romans declares that,

> Every person is to be in subjection to the governing authorities. For there is no authority except from God, and those which exist are established by God. Therefore whoever resists authority has opposed the ordinance of God; and they who have opposed will receive condemnation upon themselves. For rulers are not a cause of fear for good behavior, but for evil. Do you want to have no fear of authority? Do what is good and you will have praise from the same; for it is a minister of God to you for good. But if you do what is evil, be afraid; for it does not bear the sword for nothing; for it is a minister of God, an avenger who brings wrath on the one who practices evil. (Romans 13:1-4)

As with all Scripture and language, context is key to understanding the meaning of these four verses. The text in Romans 13 expresses the concept of obedience to governing authorities based on the truth that Christians are so free in Christ that the author of Romans felt the need to remind them to not take that freedom to an ungodly extreme. Romans 10:4 says, "For Christ is the end of the law for righteousness to everyone who believes." The pairing of Romans 10:4 and Romans 13:1-4 corresponds directly with Paul's explanation of how Christians should live with respect to their bodies, saying, "All things are lawful for me, but not all things are profitable. All things are lawful for me, but I will not be mastered by anything" (1 Corinthians 6:12); and in not causing others to stumble in their weakness of conscience, "All things are lawful, but not all things are profitable. All things are lawful, but not all things edify" (1 Corinthians 10:23). In short, because of their redemption through Jesus Christ, all things are lawful for a Christian, yet many things should not be done in respect for the will of God and desire to please Him, and in consideration of others. Christians are not to be anarchists or licentious. Christians should be civil.

This "recipe" should look familiar from the discussion of the Law of Nature and Nature's God. In the state of nature, people have complete liberty, but for one's own good, society maintains a common morality – which in Western Civilization has been the scriptural will of God – and people's unlimited unalienable rights meet with restriction only when they adversely impact the unlimited unalienable rights of another person. The "recipe" should also look very much like the "Great Commandment" of the Bible to love God and to love one's neighbor as one's self (Matthew 22:37-39). The Bible further concurs with this concept in James 1:25, "But one who looks intently at the perfect law, the law of liberty, and abides by it, not having become a forgetful hearer but an effectual doer, this man will be blessed in what he does." In essence, James is expressing the liberty-duty pairing of natural rights and revealed law.

Returning to the book of Romans, chapter 12, the author is speaking about how a Christian is to live. "Bless those who persecute you." "Do not be haughty in mind." "Be at peace with all men." These are all admonitions on how one should behave. Similarly, in Romans 13:1-4, the scripture tells Christians how both they and the governing authorities should behave. Because "all things are lawful," a Christian is able to disobey the call to bless those who persecute them, even if that is what they should do. Likewise, a governing authority, established by God, can disobey its righteous call from God. Romans 13 says, "For rulers are not a cause of fear for good behavior ..." What of a government that willingly and knowingly instills fear in the governed who are behaving well? The Pharaohs of Egypt went from appointing the Hebrew, Joseph, to be second in command in Egypt to enslaving all of Israel for 430 years. God raised up the Prophet Moses to bring freedom to Israel, and the heart of Pharaoh only grew harder against them, oppressing them more (Exodus). Were it true that followers of God must accept the authority of any government, Moses would have been wrong to oppose Pharaoh.

Furthermore, Romans 13 says the governing authority is "a minister of God, an avenger who brings wrath on the one who practices evil." If a governing authority that is called to stop evil, instead does or condones evil, it cannot be acting as a minister of God. In Luke 4:6, Satan cites his "domain" in the earth using the Greek word, *exousian*, a form of the same word, *exousiais* used for "authority" in Romans 13:1.[126] The difference between the passages is that Romans 13 adds a modifier, *huperechó*,[127] to that authority. That word, "governing" in the NASB translation, means surpassing or superior. Satan claimed the domain of the earth had been handed over to him[128] and he could give it away if he chose to, but he did not claim a surpassing, superior authority; he did not claim to have that authority in the will of God, to be "a minister of God." Therefore, it may be surmised that the author of Romans specifically meant that Christians should obey *huperechó* authorities, those acting within God's will and law.

---

[126] Strong's Greek 1849.
[127] Strong's Greek 5242.
[128] Strong's Greek 3680. Meaning it had been abandoned to Satan, or received through betrayal.

Proverbs 16:12 backs this up when it says, "It is an abomination for kings to commit wicked acts, for a throne is established on righteousness," and the story of King Ahab, Queen Jezebel, and the Prophet Elijah, provides an example of this in 1 Kings 21.

Christians are not to support or even ignore evil (Ephesians 6:10-17). Christians are called to obey just authorities, but an unjust authority which fails to work within its godly establishment may be righteously opposed.

Finally, this simple set of verses in Romans expresses the proper scope of civil government. "For rulers are not a cause of fear for good behavior, but for evil. … it is a minister of God, an avenger who brings wrath on the one who practices evil." God's purpose for government is to provide security for the people, avenging the good by bringing wrath to those who do evil.

Consider the analogy of military discipline. Soldiers are required to obey orders from superiors. A good solder executes orders expertly and without question. Yet soldiers must not, in fact may not, legally, obey illegal orders. Although there is a military hierarchy and the military seeks officers of character and discipline, it is possible for an officer to issue an unlawful command to a subordinate. For example, an order to mistreat prisoners, as defined under the Uniform Code of Military Justice, would be an illegal order. In this instance, were the subordinate to obey the illegal order, the subordinate would be violating the Uniform Code of Military Justice, and possibly also disobeying other lawful orders and their military oath. In the same way, a Christian is called to obey governing authorities when they are acting rightly, but a Christian may disobey governing authorities when those authorities call for unjust activity, assuming responsibility for their decision; and a Christian must disobey when a governing authority commands them to act contrary to the law of God. From this last principle comes the great maxim, "Rebellion to tyrants is obedience to God," which was proposed by Benjamin Franklin to be part of the Great Seal of the United States, and when rejected, it was espoused by Thomas Jefferson for his personal seal (Randolph, Title Page).

Biblical Consistency of the Declaration of Independence

Knowing then, how a Christian should respond to the governing authorities, is the Declaration of Independence consistent with the biblical counsel given to the Romans? John Quincy Adams answered that question:

> Thus their first movement [in the Declaration of Independence] is to recognise and appeal to the laws of nature and to nature's God, for their right to assume the attributes of sovereign power as an independent nation. (Adams, J. Q., 13)

In truth, the Declaration of Independence goes beyond a simple "I hope we are doing your will, God" appeal, fully explaining why the governance of King George III and the English Parliament were outside of their godly boundaries and why the local governance of the colonies, and the Continental Congress, representing the people of the colonies, were acting within godly authority in calling for independence. In effect, the Declaration of Independence is not an act of disobedience to the governing authority, it is a statement declaring in whom the proper governing authority actually resides, and why. The Declaration of Independence meets the exhortations of Romans 13 from the perspectives of both the governed and the government.

The governed people of the Colonies expressed why they believed they were righteous in their move to independence from the British governing authority, because the Declaration,

> Never advocates violence, only peaceful change to support God-given rights.

> Expresses that changing government should not be done lightly, but only with longsuffering.

> Lists 28 instances of ungodly governance, abuses, and oppressions by the King and Parliament as governing authorities that have created long suffering in the Colonies.

Explains that petitions to their British brethren for help in appealing to the King went unheard.

Expresses prayer for right standing before God in the decision for independence, "appealing to the Supreme Judge of the world for the rectitude of our intentions."

For the new government, the Declaration,

Defines what proper government is under the authority of God.

Outlines a change of government to a form supporting godly governance, not abandonment of civil government.

Puts the new independent United States of America into the hands of God to continue in His authority.

With the Declaration of Independence, America is set up to free man from the "divine right of kings" and other totalitarian regimes so man can be free to worship God and live in relationship to God. This is the freedom of Adam and Eve, or as close as one can get in broad society after the fall of Adam (Genesis 3).

Slaves, Obey Your Masters

Specific scriptures have long been misused to hold Christians in captivity and justify slavery by Christians. 1 Peter 2:13-20 states,

> Submit yourselves for the Lord's sake to every human institution, whether to a king as the one in authority, or to governors as sent by him for the punishment of evildoers and the praise of those who do right. For such is the will of God that by doing right you may silence the ignorance of foolish men. Act as free men, and do not use your freedom as a covering for evil, but use it as bondslaves of God. Honor all people, love the brotherhood, fear God, honor the king.

Servants,[129] be submissive to your masters with all respect, not only to those who are good and gentle, but also to those who are unreasonable. For this finds favor, if for the sake of conscience toward God a person bears up under sorrows when suffering unjustly. For what credit is there if, when you sin and are harshly treated, you endure it with patience? But if when you do what is right and suffer for it you patiently endure it, this finds favor with God.

The first paragraph (verses 13-17), reflects the same sentiments as Romans 13:1-4. The second paragraph goes further in the call for submission to authority, even so far as to tell slaves to obey their masters and for all to willingly submit to physical abuse for the glory of God. This is correct thinking on the individual level, which it addresses in context. Christians are to think of others as better than themselves (Philippians 2:3-4), to turn the other cheek to offense (Matthew 5:39), and to not cause unbelievers to stumble in conscience or have a reason to call Christians hypocritical (Romans 14:13, James 1:22, 1 Peter 2:12).

However, Christians are not called to simply be the helpless doormats of tyrannical rulers.[130] These words of Peter were never intended to be used for anything but an appeal to personal conscience when one is in difficult circumstances. Verse 18, however, was long used to claim that slavery was acceptable to God and to require slaves to obey their masters in fear, lest they fall under condemnation by God. This is incorrect and an evil use of this passage. A slave, who has no choice in the matter of his existence under a cruel master, may be forced to serve in a particular way, or he can choose to serve that master well, to the glory of God, and perhaps to the softening, even salvation, of the cruel master.[131] But neither choosing to serve well, nor the biblical call to do so, makes the circumstance of slavery right or good. In short, what exists is within the allowance of God's

---

[129] "Slaves" in some Bible versions, although "household servant" is most appropriate according to Strong's Greek 3610.
[130] Galatians 4:6-7, Galatians 5:1, Matthew 5:16, 1 Peter 2:9, 1 Peter 5:8-9
[131] See also Ephesians 6:5-9.

providence in a fallen world, but what exists is not necessarily what ought to be according to the will of God. This is also exemplified in 2 Peter 3:9,

> The Lord is not slow about His promise, as some count slowness, but is patient toward you, not wishing for any to perish but for all to come to repentance.

God wants no one to perish, but it is biblically clear that those who do not receive Jesus as Lord and savior will end up perishing (2 Peter 2:4-10).

With regard to the Declaration of Independence, the second part of verse 20 in 1 Peter 2, "But if when you do what is right and suffer for it you patiently endure it, this finds favor with God" is what the Colonies did, and Jefferson recorded, as, "all experience hath shewn, that mankind are more disposed to suffer, while evils are sufferable, than to right themselves..."

Finally, to maintain the context of the Apostle Peter's direction on obedience, he makes his own summary of its intent in 1 Peter 3:8-9, 16-17:

> To sum up, all of you be harmonious, sympathetic, brotherly, kindhearted, and humble in spirit; not returning evil for evil or insult for insult, but giving a blessing instead; for you were called for the very purpose that you might inherit a blessing.
>
> and keep a good conscience so that in the thing in which you are slandered, those who revile your good behavior in Christ will be put to shame. For it is better, if God should will it so, that you suffer for doing what is right rather than for doing what is wrong.

Despite being a call for individual behavior, this is what the Colonies did in their relationship to Britain. Imperfectly, perhaps, considering the Stamp Act riots, Boston Tea Party, and a few other instances, but greatly within the spirit of Peter's call for godly conduct.

My Kingdom is not of this World

> Jesus answered, "My kingdom is not of this world. If My kingdom were of this world, then My servants would be fighting so that I would not be handed over to the Jews; but as it is, My kingdom is not of this realm." (John 18:38)

It would be easy for Christians to ignore government and society by focusing on these words of Jesus, and some have. But Jesus is replying to Pontius Pilate's query about Jesus being a king. Jesus explains that his kingdom is, at that time, not in the world. Jesus never proclaimed earthly kingship and, in fact, told the crowds at Capernaum, "I must preach the kingdom of God to the other cities also, for I was sent for this purpose" (Luke 4:43).

Nor is the Kingdom of God a physical earthly kingdom.

> Now having been questioned by the Pharisees as to when the kingdom of God was coming, He answered them and said, "The kingdom of God is not coming with signs to be observed; nor will they say, 'Look, here it is!' or, 'There it is!' For behold, the kingdom of God is in your midst." (Luke 17:20-21)

Rather the Kingdom of God is within the gospel of Jesus Christ, which must be delivered by Christians who live in the world.

> This gospel of the kingdom shall be preached in the whole world as a testimony to all the nations, and then the end will come. (Matthew 24:14)

> Go therefore and make disciples of all the nations, baptizing them in the name of the Father and the Son and the Holy Spirit, teaching them to observe all that I [Jesus] commanded you; and lo, I am with you always, even to the end of the age. (Matthew 28:19-20)

Furthermore, Jesus recognized earthly government, telling his disciples to "render to Caesar the things that are Caesar's; and to God the things that are God's" (Matthew 24:21). If Christians were to live in a separate kingdom from earthly government, Jesus would neither have told his disciples to respect Caesar's tax nor go throughout the world to make disciples of all nations. Rather, Jesus quite literally says that Christians are to live with earthly government while seeking the things of God.

Jesus' Final Words on Government

Jesus indeed recognized earthly government, and he knew well the end of earthly government as he described in Mark 10:42:

> Calling them to Himself, Jesus said to them, "You know that those who are recognized as rulers of the Gentiles lord it over them; and their great men exercise authority over them."[132]

Yet, Jesus' thought as expressed in Mark 10:42 is incomplete. For in the that same thought, Jesus pronounced the truth of the American Mind and the culture that it created (Mark 10:43):

> But it is not this way among you, but whoever wishes to become great among you shall be your servant;

"But it is not this way among you..." This is what the American founders captured in the Declaration of Independence, Bill of Rights and Constitution. The American Mind is different. American government is different. It is not intended to "lord it over" people, it is meant to serve and protect the people at the individual level, and the American people are called to serve their neighbors, wherein the most basic service one can do is to respect the liberty of another.

---

[132] This statement echoes the sentiment of God, knowing what a government based on secular morality would bring to Israel as He spoke through the Hebrew Prophet, Samuel, when the people of Israel cried out for a king so they could be like the other nations (1 Samuel 8:10-13). Such was also evident in the religious government of the Jewish Sanhedrin that felt it expedient that one man – Jesus – should die for the good of a nation (John 11:50), which, while prophetic, was truly meant just for the good of the Sanhedrin's power over the nation.

Summary

Christians should not be trapped into being slaves of ungodly government because of misconstrued scripture and the false shame of religious hecklers. Nor should Christians depart from being salt and light in the world (Matthew 5:13-16), and spreaders of the gospel. And Christians must not be supporters of evil, be it due to selfish ambition, party spirit or lack of faith in God's plans. Christians should pray for God's kingdom to come (Matthew 6:10), and, as shown in Romans and Philippians, participate with justice and mercy in the world and its government to further God's kingdom and to bring others to faith by example. Finally, Christians are called to pray for all leaders, good and bad, as Paul wrote to Timothy,

> First of all, then, I urge that entreaties and prayers, petitions and thanksgivings, be made on behalf of all men, for kings and all who are in authority, so that we may lead a tranquil and quiet life in all godliness and dignity. This is good and acceptable in the sight of God our Savior, who desires all men to be saved and to come to the knowledge of the truth. (1 Timothy 2:1-4)

Left, Center, Right – Framing Political Philosophies

Declaration of the American Mind is about a timeless plan for individual liberty and duty to fellow man, it is not about political systems or politics. Unfortunately, the maintenance of liberty must, on the large scale, come through government by the people which, in the fallen state of Man, yields to politics and party spirit. To be able to mark a place from which to view the political wrangling of the world which largely seeks to destroy liberty, the topic of politics and political systems must be examined.

Left and Right

Unsurprisingly, the terms Left and Right as applied to political positioning arose out of the failed French Revolution and party spirit. One faction sat to the right of the king, the other to the left. There is no inherent value in which is left or right, nor is there great value in retracing politics of the Left and Right from the French Revolution because the effects are apparent in more recent history. The European Left and Right is easily identified from the era leading up to World War II.

European Left and Right

The European Left is the Communism of Lenin and Stalin,[133] while the European Right is the Fascism of Mussolini and Hitler.[134] Both the Left and Right in Europe are totalitarian socialist systems. These political systems exist along an axis of statism. Statism is the political form of collectivism, in which the state controls the Collective, that is, the body of the people. In communism, statism is under the guise of beneficence to the people as an equal whole. In fascism, statism is for the glory of the state, which claims a benevolent paternalism for the people. In between the two exist a variety of socialist forms, including "democratic socialism," but all forms are collectivist and statist despite use of any "democratic" appellation.

Under any form of collectivism, and therefore statism, the many (the Collective) will always sacrifice the individual on the altar of the good of the many. In practice, those in power will always sacrifice those not in power for the good of those in power, claiming it is for the good of all. A pure democracy is a form of collectivism because the rule of law changes with the whims of the majority ("the mob") and the majority always holds power. As the saying goes, democracy is two wolves and a sheep voting on what to have for dinner.

The statist, collectivist extremes of European Left and Right that existed prior to World War II remain the same today with the European Left currently largely in control and popular favor in Europe. Despite any modern favor, collectivism in all forms is anathema to the American Mind of the Declaration of Independence.

---

[133] Vladimir Lenin led the Bolshevik Revolution in 1917 that created the communist Soviet Union and Josef Stalin took power over the Soviet Union in 1924 after Lenin's death until his own death in 1953.

[134] Benito Mussolini was the dictator (technically Prime Minister) of fascist Italy from 1922 until his execution in 1945, and Adolf Hitler was the dictator (technically Chancellor then Führer) of fascist Germany from 1933 to 1945 when he committed suicide as Soviet forces approached his bunker in Berlin at the end of World War II.

American Left and Right

America has never had a European-style political Left or Right. The American Left and Right exist on a completely different axis, that of constitutionalism, perpendicular to totalitarian socialist European Left and Right. American Left and Right as we know it today did not really exist until the Twentieth Century. There had been generally opposing political forces during all periods of American History, but nothing so extreme as to attain the status of polar opposites. Instead it was factions supporting republicanism and democratic positioning – borne out of the conflict of slavery – that established the dubious distinctions of Left and Right in American politics. Still, American Left and Right reside on an axis of constitutionalism, ultimately rooted in the American Mind, rather than in European statism. Constitutionalism, as discussed throughout this book, is based in the rule of law of the Constitution, which itself derives from the American Mind of the Law of Nature and Nature's God of the Declaration of Independence.

Today, the American Left and Right struggle to continue in constitutionalism. Factions on the Left are seeking something resembling a pure democracy,[135] of late with a significant call for outright socialism, and in opposition the faction on the Right is seeking a republican government of representation and protection from the whims of mob-rule democracy and the totalitarianism of socialism. In the extremes, these positions are exemplified by "democratic socialism" and Progressivism on the Left – the steady progressive move from constitutional principles to European socialist statism, and libertarianism on the Right – seeking liberty to the extreme of ignoring the duty aspect of natural rights, ultimately ending in anarchy. In very recent times, the Right has also shown a willingness to forego constitutionalism in favor of European-style statism for short-term political gain.

---

[135] Refer to Republican Form of Government in Chapter 3 – *The Constitution Frames the Vision of the American Mind.*

Political Positioning

There are so many characteristics of political systems and so many different conceptions about what they mean that any discussion on the topic often devolves into a battle of equally ill-defined labels. The graphic of Figure 1 attempts to capture the key relationships and differences of major political systems without attempting to define every characteristic. The key takeaways here are:

1. The American system of constitutionalism operates on a perpendicular axis to European statism.

2. All forms of socialism are statist and lead to totalitarianism.

3. Throughout most, if not all of history, the only escape from totalitarianism has been violent revolution which has led to new forms of government that lead either to Anarchy or back to totalitarianism.

4. The American Revolution is unique in that the government was formed apart from violence, with thorough, peaceful, debate by democratically elected representatives, and power held by the people rather than autocratic leaders.

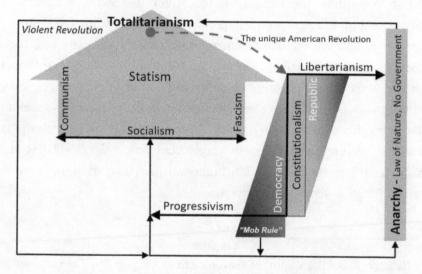

Figure 1. Summary of Major Political Systems

Forms of Totalitarianism

Totalitarianism is expressed here as if it were a curse, and it is. America fought for independence from a totalitarian government, the Monarchy of King George III. At other times and places totalitarianism has been called autocracy, dictatorship, military junta, empire, warlord rule, and even The People's Party. In all cases, totalitarianism is the end in which people have no rights other than those rights granted by the government – positive rights – which may be capriciously removed from either the individual or the collective. Totalitarian regimes may have a constitution, even a bill of rights, but neither protects the people and the people have no just political means to change their form of government.

The Character of the Constitution

The diagram in Figure 1 brings to light a number of characteristics of a constitutional government in comparison to the political structures adjacent to it: Libertarianism and Progressivism. America's Constitution is based in law and morality. In fact, the rule of law follows morality, because without morality, there can be no consistency in law or no valid reason for it to be followed. The value of morality also degrades as Libertarianism and Progressivism depart from America's Constitution. With Libertarianism, the duty aspect of rights erodes until man returns to a state of nature in anarchy. With Progressivism, morality dies under the philosophy of "the end justify the means" to institute policies of "social justice" and other trojan horse policies for the abrogation of individual rights and redistribution of property. The economics of capitalism are also reflected in Libertarianism and Progressivism. Capitalism is the economics of individual liberty, so the less capitalistic a society is, the less individual liberty will be available to the people. Libertarianism protects capitalism until reaching the extreme when capitalism cannot exist under growing cartels, cronyism and monopolies working against free markets. On the Progressive end, capitalism becomes similarly subsumed by state or state-sponsored cronyism.

Progressivism or Libertarianism as the End of Constitutionalism

If Libertarianism goes too far, it is more likely than Progressivism to self-correct as people recognize the need for some government, and, having no competing form, return to the Constitution. However, if morality based in Nature's God is completely abandoned, Libertarianism is just as likely as Progressivism to end in totalitarianism under emergent warlords or a foreign power after a quick trip through anarchy.

Progressivism and outright Socialism are far greater threats to the American Constitution than the anarchistic extreme of Libertarianism. Progressivism, after all, is the intentional slow, steady, movement from the Constitution to Socialism. Progressivism dismisses the Declaration of Independence as a "once and done" document that gave America independence, but which holds no relevance for today. Progressivism trades "Life, Liberty & Pursuit of Happiness" for "opportunity and fairness," where the outcome of opportunity is predetermined – the end justifies the means – and fairness is prescribed by the whims of the majority, not by morality or the justice of Nature's God. Progressivism views the Constitution as a "living document," whose meaning changes based on present conditions, popular culture, and "scientific" understanding, all as viewed by the majority. "Democracy" is the watchword of Progressivism and Socialism as means to keep one foot on the Constitution for conversation's sake while striving for majority rule. Progressivism seeks collectivism over individual liberty and is therefore anathema to the American Mind of the Declaration of Independence.

Center on the American Mind

The proper political Center between the Left and Right of American politics is constitutionalism based in the Declaration of Independence. Simply, the Center for America is its true culture, a culture that yet remains but is heavily burdened by popular culture, propaganda and opinion from a largely statist world. If all American's were Centrists of the American Mind, Americans would be living the proverbial American Dream in liberty and equality with their neighbors. At this time in America there is no strong Center, and this is the reason so many feel the country is adrift – because, to the visible horizon of mankind, America is adrift. To those with hope in Divine Providence, the apparent decline of America need not be viewed as a permanent decline. Better still, the way for every individual to respond to present circumstances in America is to respond as we have always been called to respond – living in the American Mind of the Declaration of Independence with *Nature's God, Man's Creator, Supreme Judge of the World,* and *Divine Providence.*

The Cause of Revolution

On July 3, 1776, a day after the Continental Congress passed the Resolution on Independence and the day before it passed the Declaration of Independence, John Adams wrote home to his wife, Abigail. His tone one of both relief that the people had come to proclaim independence, and resolve that it must now be won in conflict.

> When I look back to the year 1761, and recollect the argument concerning writs of assistance in the superior court, which I have hitherto considered as the commencement of this controversy between Great Britain and America, and run through the whole period from that time to this, and recollect the series of political events, the chain of causes and effects, I am surprised at the suddenness as well as greatness of this revolution. (Adams, C. F., *Letters*, 191)

King George III came to power on October 25, 1760. The French and Indian War ended in 1763, after which King George III and the British Parliament laid their focus on recouping war losses by way of the colonies (Scott, 48-49), and restraining the growing colonial mind for self-governance. Therefore, Adams lays the blame for American revolution directly upon the actions and policies of King George III and his Parliament despite acts of oppression by his grandfather, King George II (Jefferson, Summary, 15-16).

The writs of assistance of which Adams wrote were general search warrants issued by the British and used capriciously to search for crimes, especially concerning smuggling in navigation and trade. In 1761, James

Otis, a Boston lawyer, challenged the legality of writs of assistance (Tudor, 63). Britain rejected his challenge and upheld the writs. It was, from Adams' perspective, the oppressive act which set the tone for American independence.

Thomas Jefferson, in his pamphlet, *Summary of Rights in British America*, agreed much with Adams, quickly highlighting the oppressions prior to King George III and then prefacing that present monarch's tyranny by stating,

> That thus have we hastened through the reigns which preceded his majesty's, during which the violations of our right were less alarming, because repeated at more distant intervals than that rapid and bold succession of injuries which is likely to distinguish the present from all other periods of American story. Scarcely have our minds been able to emerge from the astonishment into which one stroke of parliamentary thunder has involved us, before another more heavy, and more alarming, is fallen on us. Single acts of tyranny may be ascribed to the accidental opinion of a day; but a series of oppressions, begun at a distinguished period, and pursued unalterably through every change of ministers, too plainly prove a deliberate and systematical plan of reducing us to slavery. (Jefferson, *Summary*, 17-18)

In *Summary of Rights in British America*, Jefferson cited the specific laws associated with his list of grievances. In the Declaration of Independence, the grievances were made general, being known by the people at the time, and being understandable in America as tyranny in the general sense, without citation.

The acts of tyranny by the British King and Parliament, even when punitive, may have seemed right to the King and Parliament as they sought to maintain their power.[136] But it was exactly that desire to retain power,

---

[136] The source for many of the subsequent comments on the grievances of the Declaration expresses this perception even to the point of apology.

against the Laws of Nature and Nature's God – the law which disproves the divine right of kings – and against the right of the people to govern themselves, which made the acts tyrannical. Even without a detailed explanation, the cause of revolution was just that which was declared in the Declaration of Independence: the equality of man and the truth of the Law of Nature and Nature's God. This highlights the rationale for the grievances of the Declaration of Independence – to state the truth of the matter, not just one side of an argument – to make a case by reason. When reason is unrequited, argument takes on the character of "my truth" versus "your truth," and proper reason, as part of the Law of Nature, gives way to the state of war. Such was the impasse between Britain and America.

The 28 Grievances of the Declaration of Independence

There are twenty-eight grievances, or charges, listed in the Declaration of Independence. They are all targeted at King George III, as the authority in charge, but many reference actions that were initiated by Parliament. The first twelve are principally grievances about laws made locally by American legislatures and assemblies that the King vetoed (Fisher, 262) for exhibiting too much independence in the colonies and a lack of respect for the authority of Parliament.

The thirteenth grievance provides an umbrella for nine subsequent grievances highlighting acts of Parliament, saying that the King "combined [with Parliament] to subject" the colonial Americans "to jurisdiction foreign to our own constitution."

The twenty-third through twenty-seventh grievances are based on the King's actions in declaring war on America, sending troops and ships to halt rebellion, and engaging in military actions including battles at Lexington and Concord, Bunker Hill, the occupation of Boston, and the burning of fleets in Portland, Maine and Norfolk, Virginia. By these actions the King had abdicated his authority for governing the colonies (Fisher 261).

The final grievance closes these prior charges by stating that the American people had petitioned the King to rectify the conditions of the grievances and that he was a tyrant, unfit for authority, having not worked for peaceful resolution (Fisher, 262).[137]

Detail and Comments on the 28 Grievances

1. He has refused his Assent to Laws, the most wholesome and necessary for the public good.

British colonial governors were the primary executive for laws created in the colonies. However, the King had authority to veto any law, even months or years after a law was in place, sometimes without reason (Fisher, 264).

2. He has forbidden his Governors to pass Laws of immediate and pressing importance, unless suspended in their operation till his Assent should be obtained; and when so suspended, he has utterly neglected to attend to them.

In some cases, the King "preemptively vetoed" laws, disallowing governors to approve laws on certain topics, requiring months or years for royal assent or veto, both of which were sometimes ignored, leaving the desired colonial law unapproved and unactionable. One such example was a 1769 law disallowing New York to create lotteries, often used to raise money for public purposes, without direct royal assent (Fisher, 270-271).

3. He has refused to pass other Laws for the accommodation of large districts of people, unless those people would relinquish the right of Representation in the Legislature, a right inestimable to them and formidable to tyrants only.

As the populations of colonies expanded into previously uninhabited areas, the natural process was to bring representation to those people in the

---

[137] A number of the acts of Parliament were overturned, but always due to consideration for what was best for Britain rather than in consideration of protest and petitions.

assemblies. Britain refused many such expansions, notably in Virginia, Massachusetts, New Hampshire, New York and New Jersey (Fisher, 273), leaving those people unrepresented as the natural right of man in society prescribes (Locke, 289-290).

4. He has called together legislative bodies at places unusual, uncomfortable, and distant from the depository of their public Records, for the sole purpose of fatiguing them into compliance with his measures.

The Boston legislature had been removed by the Governor to Cambridge as an act of spite for the colonists wanting the King's troops removed from Boston during elections (Wells, 256), and at another time to Housatonic, quite a distance from Boston (Wells, 395). Similarly, the South Carolina legislature had been moved to Beaufort from Charleston to quell disturbances after repeal of the Stamp Act (Fisher, 274).

5. He has dissolved Representative Houses repeatedly, for opposing with manly firmness his invasions on the rights of the people.

The King notably dissolved the Virginia legislature in 1765 in response to Patrick Henry's resolutions against the Stamp Act and his speech saying, "Caesar had his Brutus, Charles I. his Cromwell, and George III. may profit by their example." In 1768, the legislatures of Massachusetts, South Carolina and Virginia were dissolved for circulating a Massachusetts letter urging patriots in all colonies to unite against the British Government (Fisher, 274).

6. He has refused for a long time, after such dissolutions, to cause others to be elected; whereby the Legislative powers, incapable of Annihilation, have returned to the People at large for their exercise; the State remaining in the mean time exposed to all the dangers of invasion from without, and convulsions within.

The refusal to reinstate legislatures was a natural consequence of their dissolution, with the British rationale being to keep the colonies in check of rebellion. However, the natural effect was to make them more rebellious because they were less able to protect themselves.

7. He has endeavoured to prevent the population of these States; for that purpose obstructing the Laws for Naturalization of Foreigners; refusing to pass others to encourage their migrations hither, and raising the conditions of new Appropriations of Lands.

Without naturalization, which took seven years and was only naturalization to a single colony, a person could not own or trade in commerce associated with ships, could not obtain title to land, and could not pass on property to children via inheritance (Fisher, 276-277). The southern colonies, especially, being large and less populated, wanted to offer naturalization to immigrants (Fisher, 279).

8. He has obstructed the Administration of Justice, by refusing his Assent to Laws for establishing Judiciary powers.

Long before the Constitution, the colonies understood the need for the three branches of government, including a judiciary. That the King refused the establishment of local judiciaries and did not provide fit justice through his own government, left the colonists stranded in legal proceedings. For example, a 1768 North Carolina law established superior courts, provisions of which the King would not enact. The King's governor established courts on his own authority, but the colonial assembly refused to vote salaries for the unwanted judges, resulting in no courts operating in North Carolina from 1773 until 1776 (Fisher 279-280).

9. He has made Judges dependent on his Will alone, for the tenure of their offices, and the amount and payment of their salaries.

Until 1773, the King and the colonies were at loggerheads over the appointment and compensation of judges. The King held the power to appoint judges, and so the colonial assemblies held firm in controlling compensation as a means to "impeach" judges who did not serve justice. In 1773, the King, via the Massachusetts governor, took over the compensation of the judges of that colony, resulting in the grievance (Fisher, 280-281).

> 10. He has erected a multitude of New Offices, and sent hither swarms of Officers to harrass our people, and eat out their substance.

This charge refers principally to four new admiralty courts established at Boston, complete with commissioners of customs to enforce the King's trade laws and reduce smuggling brought about by them. The harassment of the colonists by these courts and commissioners was exacerbated by conflict of interest stemming from their salaries being paid through the duties and forfeitures that they imposed (Fisher, 281-282).

> 11. He has kept among us, in times of peace, Standing Armies without the Consent of our legislatures.

The practice of Britain, and the practice in the American colonies was not to retain standing armies in times of peace. Once the French and Indian War had ended in 1763, there was no longer a need for standing armies. Some British troops and the colonial militias could protect the colonies and the British Navy was always protecting commerce on the seas. Therefore, for the King to retain standing armies was a sign of power and control of the colonies rather than protection of them.

> 12. He has affected to render the Military independent of and superior to the Civil power.

This charge is presumed to refer to the appointment of General Gage as Governor and commander-in-chief of Massachusetts in 1774 (Fisher, 284). Gage was appointed to implement the Intolerable Acts[138] as

---

[138] In response to the Boston Tea Party, the British Parliament and King instituted a series of acts to purposely oppress the American colonies, particularly Massachusetts and the city of Boston. The British called these five acts the Coercive Acts because they were intended to be punitive. In America they were collectively known as the Intolerable Acts, and they were the final causes leading to bloodshed. The five Intolerable Acts were, the Boston Port Act, the Administration of Justice Act, the Massachusetts Government Act, the Quartering Act, and the Quebec Act.

punishment for the Boston Tea Party, and in making the appointment, King George essentially showed the colonists that he considered them property and not fellow countrymen with the British.

13. He has combined with others to subject us to a jurisdiction foreign to our constitution, and unacknowledged by our laws; giving his Assent to their Acts of pretended Legislation:

The Acts of Parliament, with approval by the King, were some of the most reproachful grievances in the Declaration of Independence. That combination of powers, impressing their will on the colonial Americans three thousand miles away, was an intolerable breach of liberty and justice to Americans.

14. For Quartering large bodies of armed troops among us:

The quartering of troops in the homes, businesses and properties of the colonists was an affront to the strongly held value of personal property and privacy. King George implemented and intensified the quartering act which brought about this complaint.

The Quartering Act (14 G3 c54)[139] had long been part of British law in America. By the 1765 Act, the colonies were required to provide barracks and some support for British soldiers.[140] In 1766 the Quartering Act was expanded to include the use of hotels and empty buildings. Then, on June 2, 1774, the Quartering Act was expanded as the final act of the Intolerable Acts, requiring the boarding of soldiers in private homes with the occupants. So egregious was this final Act that the third amendment to the American Constitution was passed to ensure it could never happen again (England and Great Britain, vol. 13, 695).

---

[139] The laws under the monarchs of England were denoted by the year of reign, abbreviation for the reigning monarch, and chapter number of the act created.
[140] The New York Suspending Act.

15. For protecting them, by a mock Trial, from punishment for any Murders which they should commit on the Inhabitants of these States:

This charge stems from the Administration of Justice Act.

The Administration of Justice Act (14 G3 c39) of May 20, 1774 was passed with the rationale of supporting British administration of justice in Massachusetts after the Boston Tea Party. One of the Intolerable Acts, it provided that magistrates or any British subject supporting, or accused of, crimes during the administration of justice in Massachusetts, could be tried in England rather than face unfavorable juries in the colony. However, because this was a punitive measure in response to the Boston Tea Party, made explicitly to encourage British suppression of riots and rebellion, it was viewed in America as the "Murder Act," enabling those accused of murders in quashing rebellion to escape to England where they would be unlikely to face punishment (England and Great Britain, vol. 13, 673).

16. For cutting off our Trade with all parts of the world:

The Boston Port Act and Prohibitory Act were the sources of this charge.

The Boston Port Act closed the port of Boston and demanded that the city's residents pay for the tea dumped into Boston Harbor during the Boston Tea Party on December 16, 1773. While the Boston Tea Party was a rebellious and costly act, it was perpetrated by a small group of people without foreknowledge of the general population. For the King to close an entire port using military might and essentially hold innocent city residents hostage until a third-party, the East India Company, was repaid, was a coercive, tyrannical act and was the first of what were to be called the Intolerable Acts. The Boston Port Act (14 G3 c19) became law on March 31, 1774 (England and Great Britain, vol. 13, 655).

The Prohibitory Act halted all trade in American ports, whether by American ship or foreign traders. The Prohibitory Act was passed by Parliament on December 21, 1775 and appears at 16 G3 c5 in the British Statues at Large (England and Great Britain, vol. 14, 86-87).

17. For imposing Taxes on us without our Consent:

Because King George set out to recoup losses from the French and Indian War on the backs of the American colonists, taxation was a regular and contentious grievance between the King and colonists.

The Sugar Act (4 G3 c15), also known as the American Revenue Act, was passed on April 5, 1764. The British had just completed the French and Indian war in 1763, spending much on their colonial interests, and saw the expiration of the 1733 Molasses tax in 1763 as an opportunity for revenue from broader taxation and stricter enforcement. Parliament claimed it to be for raising revenue for the protection and security of the colonies, taxing molasses imports, a number of other goods, and also some exports. Many Americans saw the tax as a culprit in causing an economic downturn after the war and also as a case of taxation without representation which would lead to more taxes (England and Great Britain, vol. 12, 235).

The Stamp Act (5 G3 c12) of March 22, 1765 resulted in America's first specific grievance of taxation without representation. It required a tax on every piece of paper used in the colonies to pay for British defense of the frontier. Unlike prior taxes Britain had levied as duties for the regulation of commerce, the Stamp Act created direct taxes for raising of revenue. The precedent set by such taxation caused an uproar in the American colonies, ultimately leading to its repeal in 1766 (Great Britain, 179).

The Townshend Acts (7 G3 c46, c47) were passed on November 20, 1767 and effected a vast number of indirect taxes on goods imported into the American colonies including glass, lead, paints, paper and tea. The indirect taxes, as import duties, were a replacement tactic after the failure of the Stamp Act. Due to the uproar from the American people, most duties were later rescinded, only tea was retained as a way for Britain to exert their right to tax commerce into America (England and Great Britain, vol. 12, 672-683).

The Tea Act was an act of cronyism by the British in support of the nearly bankrupt East India Company. It became law on May 10, 1773 and the British legal citation was 13 G3 c44 (England and Great Britain, vol. 13,

432-435). The Tea Act gave the East India Company the exclusive right to sell tea directly in the American colonies and restored a lapsed refund of duties, making tea from the company far less expensive than any other in the colonies. The King and Parliament did not expect any problems from America as it actually made tea prices lower in the colonies. However, the people of Massachusetts, already being disgusted with capricious taxation by the crown, saw the inequitable taxation and favoritism of the Tea Act as another affront. Perhaps also, there were by this time colonists who were looking for an opportunity to challenge the British. In that climate, the Sons of Liberty, a secret American patriot group, staged the Boston Tea Party by dressing as Mohawk Indians, boarding three East India Company vessels, and dumping all of the tea cargo into Boston Harbor on December 16, 1773.

18. For depriving us in many cases, of the benefits of Trial by Jury:

Breach of due process was incorporated as punishment into several of the tax acts and in punitive acts stemming from rebellion. Such breaches of English law in the colonies further convinced Americans that their brotherly ties were being severed with the British.

The Stamp Act not only prescribed a direct tax on paper goods from ship's logs to playing cards, it also required that those accused of violating it be tried in Admiralty Courts which exercised jurisdiction over maritime offenses and were conducted without a jury (Great Britain, 203). Similarly, the Prohibitory Act called for evaluation of the status of seized vessels, cargo and crew to be carried out in British Admiralty Courts without jury.

19. For transporting us beyond Seas to be tried for pretended offences

The Arson in Royal Dockyards Act (12 G3 c24) of 1772 prescribed a sentence of death for those convicted of arson or other crimes in dockyards and harbors throughout the British kingdom. The Act was targeted at colonial mischief and held a clause allowing for any trial connected with the Act to be held in England. Not only would a Colonial accused of a crime be unable to bear the cost of taking legal counsel to England, they would be removed from the opportunity to be judged by a jury of their peers in America. (England and Great Britain, vol. 13, 302).

20. For abolishing the free System of English Laws in a neighbouring Province, establishing therein an Arbitrary government, and enlarging its Boundaries so as to render it at once an example and fit instrument for introducing the same absolute rule into these Colonies:

The Quebec Act (14 G3 c83) was the last of the Intolerable Acts, and it was squarely aimed at angering Massachusetts and the northern colonies by currying favor with the French in Quebec as a prelude to war. Instituted on October 7, 1775, the Quebec Act enlarged Canada into what is now Ohio, Indiana, Illinois, Michigan, Wisconsin and Minnesota. It also established Roman Catholicism, which was anathema to the Church of England, as lawful in that territory. In addition to the effective closure of vast swaths of territory to American expansion, the capricious and pernicious nature of the Act inflamed American sentiments. (England and Great Britain, vol. 13, 789-794)

21. For taking away our Charters, abolishing our most valuable Laws, and altering fundamentally the Forms of our Governments:

The Massachusetts Government Act (14 G3 c45) was enacted along with the Administration of Justice Act on May 20, 1774. This Intolerable Act truly was intolerable to the inhabitants of Massachusetts. It revoked the colony's 1691 charter, deeming it flawed and incompatible with the laws of Britain. The Act eliminated the annual election of a panel that sat in an advisory capacity to the Governor of the colony, replacing them with members appointed by the King. It gave greater power to the British governor and effectively eliminated the town meetings which had always been the lifeblood of community and government in Massachusetts (England and Great Britain, vol. 13, 682).

22. For suspending our own Legislatures, and declaring themselves invested with power to legislate for us in all cases whatsoever.

The removal of legislatures to inconvenient locations was a grievance against the King, and the King went further at times, completely disbanding colonial legislatures, notably with the Declaratory, New York Suspending, and Prohibitory Acts.

The Declaratory Act (6 G3 c12) was passed in response to American reaction to the Stamp Act, on the very day the Stamp Act was repealed, March 18, 1766. The Declaratory Act declared the power of Parliament and the King over the colonies, saying, Parliament had "full power and authority to make laws and statutes of sufficient force and validity to bind the colonies and people of America, subjects of the crown of Great Britain, in all cases whatsoever," and "That all resolutions, votes, orders, and proceedings, in any of the said colonies or plantations, ... to make laws and statutes as aforesaid ... are hereby declared to be, utterly null and void to all in purposes whatsoever" (England and Great Britain, vol. 12, 480).

The New York Suspending Act (7 G3 c59) became law on July 2, 1767 in response to New York's unwillingness to quarter British soldiers per the existing Quartering Act. The Act suspended the legislature of New York until such time as it complied with the required quartering (England and Great Britain, vol. 12, 701).

> 23. He has abdicated Government here, by declaring us out of his Protection and waging War against us.

The Prohibitory Act was, to the British, a severe punishment to the rebellious colonies, putting the two on a war footing as enemies (Force, *American Archives*, ser. 4, vol. 4, 378). To America, that war footing was a breach of the protection that a government must provide to its people. It was the King abdicating his authority over America and placing the colonies in the position of a being separate nation to be conquered. It was, to America, and even some in Parliament (Gordon, 236), a statement that America was independent of Britain.

> 24. He has plundered our seas, ravaged our Coasts, burnt our towns, and destroyed the lives of our people.

As the American Revolution slowly unfolded, the abandonment of America as a charge of King George became complete. In that transition, the King treated American people, towns, and business as enemies to be vanquished (Fisher, 296).

25. He is at this time transporting large Armies of foreign Mercenaries to compleat the works of death, desolation and tyranny, already begun with circumstances of Cruelty & perfidy scarcely paralleled in the most barbarous ages, and totally unworthy the Head of a civilized nation.

As the King ravaged the coastline, he also transported some 12,000 Hessian mercenaries to fight the American colonists (Greene, 139-140).

26. He has constrained our fellow Citizens taken Captive on the high Seas to bear Arms against their Country, to become the executioners of their friends and Brethren, or to fall themselves by their Hands.

In addition to treating all American ships as enemy vessels, the Prohibitory Act allowed the American crews aboard such ships to be impressed into service for the British, resulting in them being forced to fight against their American brethren. A number of ministers in Parliament were against such a provision, protesting it with language similar to that which Jefferson adopted in the Declaration: "Because we reject with indignation that clause of this bill, which by a refinement in tyranny, and in a sentence worse than death, obliges the unhappy men, who shall be made captives in this predatory war, to bear arms against their families, kindred friends and country; and, after being plundered themselves, to become accomplices in plundering their brethren" (Gordon, 237).

27. He has excited domestic insurrections amongst us, and has endeavoured to bring on the inhabitants of our frontiers, the merciless Indian Savages, whose known rule of warfare, is an undistinguished destruction of all ages, sexes and conditions.

While British law maintained slavery in the colonies, British Lord Dunmore, the royal governor of Virginia, offered freedom and weapons to all slaves who joined the British side and then mocked the equality of the Declaration of Independence by extoling his gesture of emancipation. Additionally, the British encouraged Indian groups to fight the colonists. (Fisher, 297-298).

28. In every stage of these Oppressions We have Petitioned for Redress in the most humble terms: Our repeated Petitions have been answered only by repeated injury. A Prince whose character is thus marked by every act which may define a Tyrant, is unfit to be the ruler of a free people.

The final grievance is also the summary. Americans had petitioned many times throughout the reign of King George III for redress of perceived wrongs. Most petitions went unheard. Those that appear on the surface to have been addressed, such as repeal of the Stamp Act, were re-exerted in other acts like the Townshend Acts, always to the benefit of British concerns. The King had abandoned his charge; America was independent based on his actions as much as in the words of the Declaration of Independence.

Who Christians Are in Christ

Note to Non-Christians

To the non-Christian reading this, please consider the joy that the Christian believer has in understanding their place with God,

> For God so loved the world, that He gave His only begotten Son, that whoever believes in Him shall not perish, but have eternal life. For God did not send the Son into the world to judge the world, but that the world might be saved through Him. (John 3:16-17)

Consider also that the same gift is freely offered to you,

> if you confess with your mouth Jesus as Lord, and believe in your heart that God raised Him from the dead, you will be saved; for with the heart a person believes, resulting in righteousness, and with the mouth he confesses, resulting in salvation. (Romans 10:9-10)

Scriptures Expressing Who Christians are in Christ

For Christians to be culture-bearers for the American Mind, it is important that they understand their own identity "in Christ" as a person saved by grace.

> For our citizenship is in heaven, from which also we eagerly wait for a Savior, the Lord Jesus Christ. (Philippians 3:20)

Christian faith says that when one accepts Jesus as Lord and Savior they are reborn, becoming a new creation, and are indwelled by the Holy Spirit of God, having new life, becoming children of God, and will be raised to eternal life with God.

> Jesus answered, "Truly, truly, I say to you, unless one is born of water and the Spirit he cannot enter into the kingdom of God. That which is born of the flesh is flesh, and that which is born of the Spirit is spirit. (John 3:5-6)

> Therefore if anyone is in Christ, he is a new creature; the old things passed away; behold, new things have come. (2 Corinthians 5:17)

> Do you not know that you are a temple of God and that the Spirit of God dwells in you? (1 Corinthians 3:16)

> But God, being rich in mercy, because of His great love with which He loved us, even when we were dead in our transgressions, made us alive together with Christ (by grace you have been saved). (Ephesians 2:4-5)

> But as many as received Him, to them He gave the right to become children of God, even to those who believe in His name. (John 1:12)

> But if the Spirit of Him who raised Jesus from the dead dwells in you, He who raised Christ Jesus from the dead will also give life to your mortal bodies through His Spirit who dwells in you. (Romans 8:11)

Christianity is not about "getting things," it is about being in a personal relationship with God, the Creator of Heaven and Earth (Genesis 1:1), the same "Nature's God" referred to in the Declaration of Independence. The good news, the Gospel of Jesus Christ, is that in establishing a relationship with God by accepting Jesus as Lord and Savior, the Christian gains the eternal and temporal "benefits package." The following Bible verses are just a sampling of who Christians are as a new creation in Christ.

See how great a love the Father has bestowed on us, that we would be called children of God; and such we are. ... Beloved, now we are children of God, and it has not appeared as yet what we will be. We know that when He appears, we will be like Him, because we will see Him just as He is. (1 John 3:1, 2)

These things I have written to you who believe in the name of the Son of God, so that you may know that you have eternal life. (1 John 5:13)

For we are His workmanship, created in Christ Jesus for good works, which God prepared beforehand so that we would walk in them. (Ephesians 2:10)

He made Him who knew no sin to be sin on our behalf, so that we might become the righteousness of God in Him. (2 Corinthians 5:21)

Be anxious for nothing, but in everything by prayer and supplication with thanksgiving let your requests be made known to God. And the peace of God, which surpasses all comprehension, will guard your hearts and your minds in Christ Jesus. (Philippians 4:6-7)

For you have not received a spirit of slavery leading to fear again, but you have received a spirit of adoption as sons by which we cry out, "Abba! Father!" The Spirit Himself testifies with our spirit that we are children of God, and if children, heirs also, heirs of God and fellow heirs with Christ. (Romans 8:15-17)

for God gave us a spirit not of fear but of power and love and self-control. (2 Timothy 1:7 ESV)

Therefore there is now no condemnation for those who are in Christ Jesus. For the law of the Spirit of life in Christ Jesus has set you free from the law of sin and of death. (Romans 8:1-2)

For He rescued us from the domain of darkness, and transferred us to the kingdom of His beloved Son, in whom we have redemption, the forgiveness of sins. (Colossians 1:13-14)

He himself bore our sins in his body on the tree, that we might die to sin and live to righteousness. By his wounds you have been healed. (1 Peter 2:24)

For if by the transgression of the one, death reigned through the one, much more those who receive the abundance of grace and of the gift of righteousness will reign in life through the One, Jesus Christ. So then as through one transgression there resulted condemnation to all men, even so through one act of righteousness there resulted justification of life to all men. For as through the one man's disobedience the many were made sinners, even so through the obedience of the One the many will be made righteous. (Romans 5:17-19)

Resist the devil and he will flee from you. (James 4:7)

But in all these things we overwhelmingly conquer through Him who loved us. (Romans 8:37)

I can do all things through Him who strengthens me. ... And my God will supply all your needs according to His riches in glory in Christ Jesus. (Philippians 4:13, 19)

and He who searches the hearts knows what the mind of the Spirit is, because He intercedes for the saints according to the will of God. And we know that God causes all things to work together for good to those who love God, to those who are called according to His purpose. (Romans 8:27-28)

For this is the love of God, that we keep His commandments; and His commandments are not burdensome. For whatever is born of God overcomes the world; and this is the victory that has overcome the world – our faith. (1 John 5:3-4)

Glossary

The glossary provides meaning in context for select terms in the book. The definitions, where possible, are taken from Webster's *An American Dictionary of the English Language* from 1857 or *Webster's New International Dictionary of the English Language* from 1911. The simple understanding that many terms, such as *socialism* and *black market* did not exist in the context of today's meanings, or even exist at all in these sources, should not be overlooked by the reader. Nor should the reader overlook explicit use of religious reference in definitions such as "coming of our Savior" in the definition of *advent*.

aboriginal – An original inhabitant. The first settlers in a country are called aboriginals. (Webster, *American Dictionary*)

abortion – 1. Act of giving premature birth; specif., the expulsion of the human fetus prematurely, particularly at any time before it is viable, or capable of sustaining life; miscarriage. In medicine *abortion* is by some used of the expulsion of the fetus during the first three months of pregnancy, later expulsion occurring before the time of viability being then called a *miscarriage*. An expulsion occurring after the fetus is viable, but before the normal time, is generally termed *premature delivery* or labor. In law, the term abortion usually implies criminality in producing *miscarriage*; the latter term denoting any premature birth irrespective of its cause. (Webster, *International Dictionary*)

advent – A coming; appropriately, the coming of our Savior. (Webster, *American Dictionary*)

Age of Discovery – The period roughly from the beginning of the 15th century to the middle of the 17th century, characterized by extensive seafaring exploration by Europeans.

anarchy – Want of government; a state of society when there is no law or supreme power, or when the laws are not efficient; political confusion. (Webster, *American Dictionary*)

antifederalist – One who, at the formation of the constitution of the United States, opposed its adoption and ratification. (Webster, *American Dictionary*)

autocracy – 1. Independent power; supreme, uncontrolled authority. 2. Sole right of self-government in a state. (Webster, *American Dictionary*)

black market – Illegal trade in controlled or scarce commodities or goods. A black market may be immoral, such as in the trade of child pornography, or it may be moral, such as in the trade of food under an oppressive government.

blessing – 1. Benediction; a wish of happiness pronounced; a prayer imploring happiness upon another. 2. A solemn prophetic benediction. 3. Any means of happiness; a gift benefit, or advantage. 4. Among the Jews, a present; a gift. (Webster, *American Dictionary*)

Christ – The Anointed; an appellation given to the Savior of the world, and synonymous with the Hebrew Messiah. (Webster, *American Dictionary*)

collectivism – The theory of the collectivists. It is practically equivalent to socialism. (Webster, *International Dictionary*)

Committee of Correspondence – committees in the American colonies appointed to correspond and cooperate on approaches to self-governance in the face of British tyranny, ultimately leading to selection of the Continental Congress by colonial governments.

committee of the whole – A meeting of a complete assembled body using modified rules based on committee rules.

communism – 1. A system of social organization in which goods are held in common; – the opposite of the system of private property. 2. A system of social organization where large powers are given to small political units, or communes; communalism. 3. Any theory or system of social organization involving common ownership of the agents of production, and some approach to equality in the distribution of the products of industry; unformulated socialism. (Webster, *International Dictionary*)

Confucianism – The principles of morality taught by Confucius and his disciples, forming the basis of the Chinese jurisprudence and education. It is based upon ancestor worship, teaching that the source of all true devotion and morality is filial piety, which enjoins veneration of the authors of one's family as the genii of its perpetuity and welfare. (Webster, *International Dictionary*)

Continental Congress – The formal gathering of representatives of the American colonies to address British tyranny and define a structure for self-governance of the united states of America. There were eleven sessions of the Continental Congress between September 5, 1774 and January 11, 1785. (Lanman, *Dictionary*, 533)

culture – A particular state or stage of advancement in civilization; the characteristic attainments of a people or social order. (Webster, *International Dictionary*)

defamation – The uttering of slanderous words with a view to injure another's reputation; the malicious uttering of falsehood respecting another which tends to destroy or impair his good name, character, or occupation. (*Webster, American Dictionary*)

deism – The doctrine or creed of a deist; the belief or system of religious opinions of those who acknowledge the existence of one God, but deny revelation. (Webster, *American Dictionary*)

democracy – Government by the people; a form of government in which the supreme power is lodged in the hands of the people collectively, or in which the people exercise the powers of legislation. (Webster, *American Dictionary*)

democratic socialism – Socialism under the guise of being a democratically managed government, but necessarily run by "managers," with control beyond that addressable by the body of the people.

diaspora – Lit., "Dispersion," – applied collectively: **a** To those Jews who, after the Exile, were scattered through the Old World, and afterwards to Jewish Christians living among heathen. (Webster, *International Dictionary*)

dictum – An authoritative saying or assertion. (Webster, *American Dictionary*)

1. An authoritative statement; dogmatic saying; apothegm. 2. *Law.* A judicial opinion expressed by judges on points that do not necessarily arise in the case, and are not involved in it, or one in which the judicial mind is not directed to the precise question necessary to be determined to fix the rights of the parties. A dictum does not have the binding force upon subsequent or inferior courts that is accorded to an adjudication. (Webster, *International Dictionary*)

ethics – 1. The doctrines of morality; the science of moral duty. 2. A system of moral principles; a system of rules for regulating the actions of men. (Webster, *American Dictionary*)

federal – 1. Pertaining to a league or contract; derived from an agreement or covenant. 2. Consisting in a compact between parties, chiefly between states or nations; founded on alliance by contract or mutual agreement. (Webster, *American Dictionary*)

federalist – An appellation, in America, given to the friends of the Constitution of the United States, at its formation and adoption, and to the political party which favored the administration of President Washington. (Webster, *American Dictionary*)

gentile – 1. Pertaining to pagans or heathens. (Webster, *American Dictionary*)

gospel – A revelation of the grace of God to fallen man through a Mediator. (Webster, *American Dictionary*)

habeas corpus – A writ for delivering a person from false imprisonment or for removing a person from one court to another, &c. (Webster, *American Dictionary*)

Hellenism – Greek character, spirit, or civilization; esp., the type of culture represented by the ideals of the classical Greeks, as in their regard for athletic vigor and grace, their cultivation of the arts and sciences, their devotion to civic social organization, and their social and ethical attitude exemplified in the caution, "Nothing too much," or "Temperance in all things." (Webster, *International Dictionary*)

honor – 1. The esteem due or paid to worth; high estimation or praise. 2. A testimony of esteem; any expression of respect or of high estimation by words or actions. 3. Dignity; exalted rank or place; distinction; fame. 4. Reverence; veneration. 5. Reputation; good name. 6. True nobleness of mind; magnanimity. 7. An assumed appearance of nobleness; scorn of meanness, springing from the fear of reproach, without regard to principle, 8. Any particular virtue much valued; as bravery in men, and chastity in females. (Webster, *American Dictionary*)

idiom – 1. A mode of expression peculiar to a language; peculiarity of expression or phraseology. 2. The genius or peculiar cast of a language. (Webster, *American Dictionary*)

integrity – 1. Wholeness; entireness; unbroken state. 2. The entire, unimpaired state of any thing, particularly of the mind; moral soundness or purity; incorruptness; uprightness; honesty; probity. 3. Purity; genuine, unadulterated, unimpaired state. (Webster, *American Dictionary*)

jubilee – 1. Among the Jews, every fiftieth year, being the year following the revolution of seven weeks of years, at which time all the slaves were liberated, and all lands which had been alienated during the whole period reverted to their former owners. This was a time of great rejoicing. 2. A season of great public joy and festivity. (Webster, *American Dictionary*)

Judeo-Christian – relating to the tenets of Jewish and Christian teachings and philosophy as defined by the Bible.

judicial fiat – A capricious and often arbitrary decree promulgated by a judge, notably in a scenario in which the judge lacks legal or constitutional authority. See also *dictum*.

justice – 1. The virtue which consists in giving to every one what is his due; practical conformity to the laws and to principles of rectitude in the dealings of men with each other; honesty; integrity in commerce or mutual intercourse. 2. Impartiality; equal distribution of right in expressing opinions; fair representation of facts respecting merit or demerit 3. Equity; agreeableness to right 4. Vindictive retribution; merited punishment 5. Right; application of equity. (Webster, *American Dictionary*)

For justice, defined by the Institutes of Justinian, as the constant and perpetual will of securing to every one his right, includes the whole duty of man in the social institutions of society, toward his neighbor. (Adams, 70)

Ku Klux Klan – A secret political organization in the Southern States, active for several years after the close of the Civil War, and having for its chief aim the repression of the political power of the freedmen; – called also Ku-Klux Klan. After this organization had come to be chiefly made up of the more restless and lawless elements and had committed numerous outrages, the government, in 1871, by the passage of the Enforcement Act (popularly known as the Ku-Klux Act or Force Bill) took steps to suppress it, and thereafter its activity gradually ceased. (Webster, *American Dictionary*)

The Ku Klux Klan found resurgence as a white protestant supremacist organization in 1915 with the movie, *The Birth of a Nation*, which was screened in President Woodrow Wilson's Whitehouse, and became a significant force in racism against blacks and bigotry against Catholics and other minority groups.

libel – 1. A defamatory writing, L. *libellus famosus*. Any book, pamphlet writing, or picture containing representations, maliciously made or published, tending to bring a person into contempt or expose him to public hatred and derision. (Webster, *American Dictionary*)

licentious – 1. Using license; indulging freedom to excess; not restrained by law or morality; [applied to persons.] 2. Exceeding the limits of law or propriety, as acts. SYN. Unrestrained; uncurbed; uncontrolled; unruly; riotous: ungovernable; wanton; profligate; dissolute; lax; loose; sensual; impure; unchaste; lascivious; immoral. (Webster, *American Dictionary*)

liturgy – In a general sense, the established formulas for public worship, or the entire ritual for public worship in those churches which use written forms. (Webster, *American Dictionary*)

magistrate – A public civil officer, invested with the executive or judicial authority, or some branch of it. (Webster, *American Dictionary*)

memorial – 1. That which preserves the memory of something; any thing that serves to keep in memory. 2. Any note or hint to assist the memory. 3. A written representation of facts, made to a legislative or other body as the ground of a petition, or a representation of facts accompanied with a petition. (Webster, *American Dictionary*)

Messiah – Christ, the Anointed; the Savior of the world. (Webster, *American Dictionary*)

morality – 1. The doctrine or system of moral duties, or the duties of men in their social character; ethics. 2, The practice of the moral duties; virtue. 3. The quality of an action which renders it good. (Webster, *American Dictionary*)

nationalism – The state of being national; nationality. (Webster, *American Dictionary*)

In the modern sense, nationalism is often characterized by undiscriminating devotion to one's country to the exclusion of principles and morals.

negative rights – Liberties. Rights not created by man. The type of right existing without requirement for positive acknowledgement by an authority.

oath – A solemn affirmation or declaration, made with an appeal to God for the truth of what is affirmed. (Webster, *American Dictionary*)

patriot – A person who loves his country, and zealously supports and defends it and its interests. (Webster, *American Dictionary*)

patriotism – Love of one's country; the passion which aims to serve one's country. (Webster, *American Dictionary*)

populism – A political principle or movement emphasizing a focus on the will and role of "the people," tending to pander to individual complaints and greed to draw allegiance, often at the expense of sound principles.

positive rights – Entitlements. Those rights which are prescribed by an authority and obligating others to act respecting the one asserting the right.

posterity – 1. Descendants; children, children's children, &c, indefinitely; the race that proceeds from a progenitor. 2. In a general sense, succeeding generations. (Webster, *American Dictionary*)

privateer – A ship or vessel of war owned and equipped by a private man or by individuals, at their own expense, and having a commission from government to seize or plunder the ships of an enemy in war. (Webster, *American Dictionary*)

progressive – One seeking a steady political and governmental transition from constitutionalism to socialism.

Progressive Era – the period from roughly 1890 to 1920 characterized by social activism based in identities rather than principles and seeking steady constitutional reforms toward socialism.

[divine] providence – In theology, the care and superintendence which God exercises over his creatures; hence, also, God viewed in this relation. (Webster, *American Dictionary*)

religion – 1. Religion, in a comprehensive sense, includes a belief in the being and perfections of God, in the revelation of his will to man, in man's obligation to obey his commands, in a state of reward and punishment and in man's accountableness to God; and also, true godliness or piety of life, with the practice of all moral duties. 2. Religion, as distinct from theology, is godliness or real piety in practice. 3. Religion, as distinct from virtue or morality, consists in the performance of the duties we owe directly to God, from a principle of obedience to his will. 4. Any system of faith and worship. (Webster, *American Dictionary*)

remonstrance – 1. Show; discovery; [obs.] 2. Expostulation; strong representation of reasons against a measure. 3. Pressing suggestions in opposition to a measure or act. 4. Expostulatory counsel or advice; reproof. (Webster, *American Dictionary*)

Renaissance – the period in European history covering the 14th to 17th centuries transitioning from the Middle Ages to the Enlightenment, characterized by a resurgence of literature, music, art and philosophy.

right – 5. Just claim; legal title; ownership; the legal power of exclusive possession and enjoyment, 6. Just claim by courtesy, customs, or the principles of civility and decorum. 7. Just claim by sovereignty; prerogative. 8. That which justly belongs to one. ... 10. Just claim; immunity; privilege; as, the *rights of citizens*, 11. Authority; legal power. (Webster, *American Dictionary*)

secularism – Secular humanism. A political or religious philosophy favoring complete separation of theistic religion from public and governmental affairs, often characterized by a devotion to science and unprovable scientific theory.

slander – 1. A false tale or report maliciously uttered, and tending to injure the reputation of another; defamation. (Webster, *American Dictionary*)

social justice – A philosophy of justice in which justice, or fairness, is weighted by real, perceived or asserted wrongs felt by one party or class against real, perceived or imagined privileges of another party or class, administered directly by society or demanded of the judicial system apart from established law or principle.

Social Security – the "social safety net" program of the United States Federal Government paid for by a tax on earned income and providing regular payments starting at retirement age as set by the government.

socialism – A political theory or philosophy of social and governmental organization in which the means of production and distribution of goods and services is owned collectively by the people and held in trust by the government which plans and controls the economy and which, historically, has always devolved into statism and totalitarianism.

statism – A form of collectivism in which individuals are forced to be subservient to government and where all claims of purpose are made in the name of the state to the detriment of individual rights. Statism is the typical end of both fascism and socialism at the onset of complete totalitarianism.

strawman argument – A form of argument that portends to represent a common sense point but which is really a false, fallacious, or incomplete argument against the point in question.

theocracy – A form of government which is run, or controlled, by unelected religious leaders exerting economic, political and social control based on religious dictates.

Tory – The name given to an adherent to the ancient constitution of England and to the ecclesiastical hierarchy. In *America*, during the Revolution, those who opposed the war, and favored the claims of Great Britain, were called tories. (Webster, *American Dictionary*)

totalitarianism – A political end under which the state has no limit of authority, and controls, or seeks to control, all aspects of public and private life.

tyranny – 1. Arbitrary or despotic exercise of power; the exercise of power over subjects and others with a rigor not authorized by law or justice, or not requisite for the purposes of government. Hence, tyranny is often synonymous with cruelty and oppression. 2. Cruel government or discipline. 3. Unresisted and cruel power. 4. Absolute monarchy cruelly administered. (Webster, *American Dictionary*)

usurp – To seize and hold in possession by force or without right. (Webster, *American Dictionary*)

virtue – 3. Moral goodness; the practice of moral duties and the abstaining from vice, or a conformity of life and conversation to the moral law. 4. A particular moral excellence. (Webster, *American Dictionary*)

viz. – A contraction of *videlicet*; to wit, that is, namely. (Webster, *American Dictionary*)

Western Civilization – the civilization of the western hemisphere, characterized by European Christendom and deriving from Greek and Roman culture.

Whig – One of a political party which had its origin in England in the seventeenth century, in the reign of Charles I. or II. Those who supported the king in his high claims were called tories, and the advocates of popular rights were called whigs. During the revolution in the *United States*, the friends and supporters of the war and the principles of the revolution were called whigs, and those who opposed them were called tories and royalists. (Webster, *American Dictionary*)

Sources

Adams, Charles Francis. *Familiar Letters of John Adams and His Wife Abigail Adams During the Revolution*. Hurd and Houghton, New York, 1875, https://books.google.com/books?id=fYEEAAAAYAAJ.

Adams, Charles Francis. *The Works of John Adams, Second President of the United States*. vol. 3, Little, Brown and Company, Boston, 1865, https://books.google.com/books?id=2ps8AAAAIAAJ.

Adams, Charles Francis. *The Works of John Adams, Second President of the United States*. vol. 9, Little, Brown and Company, Boston, 1854, https://books.google.com/books?id=-Wh3AAAAMAAJ.

Adams, Charles Francis. *The Works of John Adams, Second President of the United States*. vol. 10, Little, Brown and Company, Boston, 1856, https://books.google.com/books?id=fWt3AAAAMAAJ.

Adams, John. *A Defence of the Constitutions of Government of the United States of America*. Edmund Freeman, Boston, 1788, https://books.google.com/books?id=ialXAAAAcAAJ.

Adams, John Quincy. *The Jubilee of the Constitution*. Samuel Colman, New York, 1839, https://books.google.com/books?id=w325tHxgmJkC.

Appleton's Annual Cyclopaedia and Register of Important Events of the Year 1875. vol. 15, D. Appleton and Company, New York, 1876, https://books.google.com/books?id=U3bXAAAAMAAJ.

Appleton's Cyclopaedia of American Biography. vol. 1, James Grant Wilson and John Fiske, editors, D. Appleton and Company, New York, 1888, https://books.google.com/books?id=AbALAAAAIAAJ.

Appleton's Cyclopaedia of American Biography. vol. 2, James Grant Wilson and John Fiske, editors, D. Appleton and Company, New York, 1887, https://books.google.com/books?id=WH4lAQAAMAAJ.

Appleton's Cyclopaedia of American Biography. vol. 4, James Grant Wilson and John Fiske, editors, D. Appleton and Company, New York, 1888, https://books.google.com/books?id=400WAAAAYAAJ.

Appleton's Cyclopaedia of American Biography. vol. 5, James Grant Wilson and John Fiske, editors, D. Appleton and Company, New York, 1888, https://books.google.com/books?id=YmrhAAAAMAAJ.

Appleton's Cyclopaedia of American Biography. vol. 6, James Grant Wilson and John Fiske, editors, D. Appleton and Company, New York, 1889, https://books.google.com/books?id=MNEi1tF6VRIC.

Authority. *Laws of the Territory of the United States North-West of the Ohio*. W. Maxwell, Cincinnati, 1796, https://books.google.com/books?id=83JPAQAAIAAJ.

Baldwin, Simeon E. *The Constitution of the United States, with References to Judicial Decisions, &c., prepared for the Use of the Yale Law School*. Hoggson & Robinson, New Haven, 1875, https://books.google.com/books?id=nbdBAAAAYAAJ.

Bancroft, George. *History of the United States of America from the Discovery of the Continent*. Author's last revision, vol. 4, D. Appleton & Company, New York, 1885, https://books.google.com/books?id=UT9FAQAAMAAJ.

Bancroft, George. *History of the United States of America from the Discovery of the Continent*. Author's last revision, vol. 6, D. Appleton & Company, New York, 1888, https://books.google.com/books?id=b7oTAAAAYAAJ.

Bellamy, D., Marchant, J., Gordon. *A New Complete English Dictionary*. 2nd Ed., J. Fuller, London, 1760, https://books.google.com/books?id=zRxWAAAAYAAJ.

Blackstone, Sir William. *An Analysis of the Laws of England*. 6th ed., Clarendon Press, Oxford, 1771, https://books.google.com/books?id=Q8sDAAAAQAAJ.

Blackstone, Sir William. *Commentaries on the Laws of England*. Book the First. Clarendon Press, Oxford, 1765, https://books.google.com/books?id=faZFAAAAcAAJ.

Blackstone, Sir William. *Commentaries on the Laws of England*. Book the Fourth. 5th ed. John Exshaw, Henry Saunders, et. al., Dubline, 1773, https://books.google.com/books?id=jQU0AQAAMAAJ.

British National Archives, "Britain and the Slave Trade," http://www.nationalarchives.gov.uk/slavery/pdf/britain-and-the-trade.pdf, accessed 12 Aug 2019.

Brown, Pamela. "Parents' house seized after son's drug bust." CNN, 8 Sep 2014, https://www.cnn.com/2014/09/03/us/philadelphia-drug-bust-house-seizure/, accessed 23 Jun 2018.

Cates, William L. R. *A Dictionary of General Biography*. 2nd ed., Longmans, Green and Co., London, 1875, https://books.google.com/books?id=h5dQAAAAYAAJ.

Charles II. *The Famous Old Charter of Rhode-Island*. I. H. Cady, Providence, 1842, https://books.google.com/books?id=ZjQBAAAAYAAJ.

Chitty, J. *A Treatise on the Game Laws and on Fisheries*. vol. 1, W. Clarke and Sons, London, 1812, https://books.google.com/books?id=CZA9AAAAYAAJ.

Cicero, M. T. *M. T. Cicero His Offices, Or His Treatise Concerning the Moral Duties of Mankind*. Translated by William Guthrie, T. Waller, London, 1755, https://books.google.com/books?id=F2VjAAAAcAAJ.

Cobbett, William. *Cobbett's Political Register*. vol. 11, from January to June, 1807, Richard Ragshaw, London, 1807, https://books.google.com/books?id=gCM8AAAAIAAJ.

Cobbett, William. *Cobbett's Political Register*. vol. 26, from July to December, 1814, G. Houston, London, 1814, https://books.google.com/books?id=G8s7AQAAMAAJ.

Columbus, Christopher. "The Will of Christopher Columbus." *The Authentic Letters of Christopher Columbus*, compiled by William Eleroy Curtis, vol. 1, no. 2, Field Columbian Museum, Chicago, 1895, https://books.google.com/books?id=Mvt1AAAAMAAJ.

Columbus, Christopher. *The Journal of Christopher Columbus (During His First Voyage, 1492-93)*. Translation and introduction by Clements R. Markham, Chas. J. Clark, London, 1893, https://books.google.com/books?id=2mvK60VAdCcC.

Congress. *Congressional Record: Containing the Proceedings and Debates of the Forty-fourth Congress, First Session; also Special Session of the Senate*. vol. 4, Government Printing Office, Washington, 1876, https://books.google.com/books?id=SZZZpRn0iiwC.

Congress. *Executive Documents Printed by Order of the House of Representatives during the Second Session of the Forty-first Congress, 1869-'70*. Government Printing Office, Washington, 1870, https://books.google.com/books?id=T1hHAQAAIAAJ.

Congress. *Journal of the House of Representatives of the United States at the Second Session of the Tenth Congress in the Thirty Third Year of the Independence of the United States*. The Congressional Journals of the United States Part 1 of the National State Papers of the United States Series, 1789-1817, The Journal of the House of Representatives, Thomas Jefferson Administration 1801-1809, vol. 8, Tenth Congress, Second Session, November, 1808 - March, 1809, Reprint by Michael Glazier, Inc., Wilmington, Delaware, Original Printing by A. & G. Way,

Washington City, 1808,
https://books.google.com/books?id=H2YuAAAAIAAJ.

Congress. *Laws of the United States of America from the 4th of March, 1789, to the 4th of March 1815.* vol. 2, John Bioren and W. John Duane, Philadelphia, and R. C. Weightman, Washington City, 1815, https://books.google.com/books?id=I1krAQAAMAAJ.

Congress. *Laws of the United States of America from the 4th of March, 1789, to the 4th of March 1815.* vol. 4, John Bioren and W. John Duane, Philadelphia, and R. C. Weightman, Washington City, 1816, https://books.google.com/books?id=o8NgAAAAcAAJ.

Congress. *Register of Debates in Congress: Comprising the Leading Debates and Incidents of the Second Session of the Eighteenth Congress.* vol. 10, part 2, Gales & Seaton, 1834, https://books.google.com/books?id=bWC_RP90sSUC.

Congress. *The Statues at Large of the United States from December, 1873, to March, 1875 and Recent Treaties, Postal Conventions, and Executive Proclamations.* vol. 18, part 3, Government Printing Office, Washington, 1875, https://books.google.com/books?id=mmA2AQAAMAAJ.

Cooke, George Willis. *Ralph Waldo Emerson: His Life, Writings, and Philosophy.* 2nd ed. James R. Osgood and Company, Boston, 1882, https://books.google.com/books?id=ky1IAAAAIAAJ.

Cooley, Thomas McIntyre. *The General Principles of Constitutional Law in the United States of America.* Little, Brown, and Company, Boston, 1880, https://books.google.com/books?id=VbpVAAAAYAAJ.

Continental Congress. *The Declaration by the Representatives of the United Colonies of North America, now met in Congress at Philadelphia; setting forth the causes and necessity of their taking up arms.* Declaration principally authored by Thomas Jefferson, The London Association, London, 1774, https://books.google.com/books?id=TqRhAAAAcAAJ.

Continental Congress. *Journal of the Proceedings of Congress, Held at Philadelphia, from September 5, 1775, to April 30, 1776.* Philadelphia, 1778, https://books.google.com/books?id=bY9KAAAAMAAJ.

Cutler, William Parker and Cutler, Julia Perkins. *Life Journals and Correspondence of Rev. Manasseh Cutler, LLD.* vol. 1, Robert Clarke & Co., Cincinnati, 1888, https://books.google.com/books?id=HRAXAAAAYAAJ.

Davies, Charles Stewart. "Address Delivered at Portland on the Decease of John Adams and Thomas Jefferson, August 9, 1826." *Memorial Addresses on Adams and Jefferson, from the Aldine Collection*, 1826, https://books.google.com/books/?id=hR9EAQAAMAAJ.

Davis, Henry. *The Works of Plato.* vol. 2, Henry G. Bohn, London, 1849, https://books.google.com/books?id=WlVRAAAAYAAJ.

Department of State. *Catalogue of the Papers of the Continental Congress. Bulletin of the Bureau of Rolls and Library of the Department of State.* no. 1, September, 1893, Department of State, Washington, 1893, https://books.google.com/books?id=nA84AQAAMAAJ.

Deshler, Charles D. "How the Declaration was Received in the Old Thirteen." *Harper's New Monthly Magazine*, vol. 85, no. 506, July, 1892, pp. 165-187, https://books.google.com/books?id=VEtOAQAAMAAJ.

Dewan, Shaila. "Police Use Department Wish List When Deciding Which Assets to Seize." *The New York Times*, 9 Nov 2014, https://www.nytimes.com/2014/11/10/us/police-use-department-wish-list-when-deciding-which-assets-to-seize.html, accessed 28 Jul 2018.

Editor. "National Standards and Emblems." *Harper's New Monthly Magazine*, vol. 47, no. 278, July, 1873, pp. 171-181, https://books.google.com/books?id=NUtOAQAAMAAJ.

Edwards, Jonathon. "Sinners in the Hands of an Angry God. A Sermon." July 8, 1741, Lumisden and Robertson, Edinburgh, 1745, https://books.google.com/books?id=aBxdAAAAcAAJ.

Elliot, Jonathan. *The Debates in the Several State Conventions on the Adoption of the Federal Constitution*. 2nd ed., vol. 2, Jonathan Elliot, Washington, 1836, https://books.google.com/books?id=SLoxAQAAMAAJ.

Elliot, Jonathan. *The Debates in the Several State Conventions on the Adoption of the Federal Constitution*. 2nd ed., vol. 3, Jonathan Elliot, Washington, 1836, https://books.google.com/books?id=ijEMAQAAMAAJ.

Elliot, Jonathan. *The Debates in the Several State Conventions on the Adoption of the Federal Constitution*. 2nd ed., vol. 4, Jonathan Elliot, Washington, 1836, https://books.google.com/books?id=KVgSAAAAYAAJ.

Elliot, Jonathan. *Journal and Debates of the Federal Convention*. vol. 4, Jonathan Elliot, Washington, 1830, https://books.google.com/books?id=-gtAAAAAYAAJ.

England and Great Britain. *The Statutes at Large of England and of Great Britain: from Magna Carta to the Union of the Kingdoms of Great Britain and Ireland*. In Twenty Volumes, vol. 12, From 1 George III, A.D. 1760 – To 7 George III, A.D. 1767, Edited by John Raithby, George Eyre and Andrew Strahan, London, 1811, https://books.google.com/books?id=-opKAAAAYAAJ.

England and Great Britain. *The Statutes at Large of England and of Great Britain: from Magna Carta to the Union of the Kingdoms of Great Britain and Ireland*. In Twenty Volumes, vol. 13, From 8 George III, A.D. 1768 – To 14 George III, A.D. 1774, Edited by John Raithby, George Eyre and Andrew Strahan, London, 1811, https://books.google.com/books?id=cotKAAAAYAAJ.

England and Great Britain. *The Statutes at Large of England and of Great Britain: from Magna Carta to the Union of the Kingdoms of Great Britain and Ireland*. In Twenty Volumes, vol. 14, From 15 George III, A.D. 1775 – To 19 George III, A.D. 1779, Edited by John Raithby,

George Eyre and Andrew Strahan, London, 1811, https://books.google.com/books?id=9I9KAAAAYAAJ.

Finch, John Bird. *The People Versus the Liquor Traffic.* edited by Samuel D. Hastings, Frank J. Sibley, Publishing Agent, Literature Com. R. W. G. Lodge, I. O. of G. T., Chicago, 1883, https://books.google.com/books?id=rIDaAAAAMAAJ.

Fisher, Sydney George. "The Twenty-Eight Charges against the king in the Declaration of Independence." *The Pennsylvania Magazine of History and Biography*, vol. 31, no. 3, 1907, pp. 257-303, https://www.jstor.org/stable/20085387.

Foote, William Henry. *Sketches of Virginia, Historical and Biographical.* William S. Martien, Philadelphia, 1850, https://books.google.com/books?id=bm4U1ZRZKDQC.

Force, Peter. *American Archives: Fourth Series, Containing A Documentary History of the United States of America.* vol. 1, M. St. Clair Clark and Peter Force, Washington, December, 1837, https://books.google.com/books?id=ZU0MAQAAMAAJ.

Force, Peter. *American Archives: Fourth Series, Containing A Documentary History of the United States of America.* vol. 4, M. St. Clair Clark and Peter Force, Washington, April, 1843, https://books.google.com/books?id=lEwMAQAAMAAJ.

Force, Peter. *American Archives: Fifth Series, Containing A Documentary History of the United States of America.* vol. 1, M. St. Clair Clark and Peter Force, Washington, April 1848, https://books.google.com/books?id=VWxAAAAAcAAJ.

Force, Peter. *The Declaration of Independence, or Notes on Lord Mahon's History of the American Declaration of Independence.* G. Willis, London, 1855, https://books.google.com/books?id=y252AAAAMAAJ.

Franklin, Benjamin. *Memoirs of the Life and Writings of Benjamin Franklin, LL.D.* vol. 1, Henry Colburn, London, 1818, https://books.google.com/books?id=RpoEAAAAYAAJ.

Franklin, Benjamin. *Memoirs of the Life and Writings of Benjamin Franklin, LL.D.* vol. 2, compiled by William Temple Franklin, printed for Henry Colburn, London, 1818, https://books.google.com/books?id=YmMFAAAAQAAJ.

Gales, Joseph. *Annals of Congress. The Debates and Proceedings in the Congress of the United States.* vol.1, Gales and Seaton, Washington, 1834, https://books.google.com/books?id=Gq8XAQAAMAAJ.

General Assembly of Virginia. *The Revised code of the Laws of Virginia.* vol. 1, Thomas Ritchie, Richmond, 1819, https://books.google.com/books?id=VVhRAAAAYAAJ.

Gillies, John. *Aristotle's Ethics and Politics.* vol. 2, 3rd edition, T. Cadell and W. Davies, London, 1813, https://books.google.com/books?id=yGsMAAAAYAAJ.

Gordon, William. *The History of the Rise, Progress, and Establishment of the Independence of the United States of America.* vol. 2, William Gordon, London, 1788, https://books.google.com/books?id=3quxGuqXjOAC.

Great Britain. *The Statutes at Large: From the Magna Charta, to the End of the Eleventh Parliament of Great Britain, Anno 1761 [Continued].* vol. 26, edited by Danby Pickering, Joseph Bentham, Cambridge, 1764, https://books.google.com/books?id=0L4uAAAAIAAJ.

Greene, George Washington. "The Hessian Mercenaries of our Revolution." *The Atlantic Monthly,* vol. 35, No. 207, H. O. Houghton and Company, Boston, January, 1875, https://books.google.com/books?id=ralOAQAAMAAJ.

Hamilton, A., Jay, J., Madison, J. *The Federalist, on the New Constitution; Written in 1788.* A New Edition, Benjamin Warner,

Philadelphia, 1818,
https://books.google.com/books?id=ujhWAAAAYAAJ.

Hamilton, Alexander. *The Official and Other Papers of the Late Major-General Alexander Hamilton.* vol. 1, New York and London, Wiley & Putnam, 1842, https://books.google.com/books?id=8aCn-BLIYf8C.

Hay, George, as Hortensius. *An Essay on the Liberty of the Press.* Reprinted by Samuel Pleasants, Junior, Richmond, 1803, https://books.google.com/books?id=92kFAAAAQAAJ.

Holland, Josiah G. *History of Western Massachusetts. The Counties of Hampden, Hampshire, Franklin, and Berkshire.* vol. 1, Parts 1 and 2, Samuel Bowles and Company, Springfield, 1855, https://books.google.com/books?id=aiBMAAAAYAAJ.

Holland, Josiah G. *The Life of Abraham Lincoln.* Gurdon Bill, Springfield, 1866, https://books.google.com/books?id=rk_fL3GTeycC.

House of Representatives. "Veterans 2nd Amendment Protection Act." 115th Congress, 1st Session, Report 115-33, March 10, 2017, https://www.congress.gov/115/crpt/hrpt33/CRPT-115hrpt33.pdf.

Howard, Benjamin C. *Reports of Cases Argued and Adjudged in the Supreme Court of the United States, December Term, 1856.* vol. 19, William M. Morrison and Company, Washington, D. C., 1857, https://books.google.com/books?id=6yKHlu6xFu4C.

Ingraham, Christopher. "A 64-year-old put his life savings in his carry-on. U.S. Customs took it without charging him with a crime." *The Washington Post*, May 31, 2018, https://www.washingtonpost.com/news/wonk/wp/2018/05/31/a-64-year-old-put-his-life-savings-in-his-carry-on-u-s-customs-took-it-without-charging-him-with-a-crime/, accessed 23 Jun 2018.

Irving, Washington. *The Life and Voyages of Christopher Columbus.* Abridged and arranged by the author, N. and J. White, New York, 1834, https://books.google.com/books?id=EaE-AAAAYAAJ.

Janney, Samuel M. *The life of William Penn: with selections from his correspondence and autobiography.* Lippincott, Grambo & Co., Philadelphia, 1852, https://books.google.com/books?id=fwxvAAAAMAAJ.

Jefferson, Thomas. "A Summary View of the Rights of British America: Set Forth in Some Resolutions Intended for the Inspection of the Present Delegates of the People of Virginia, Now in Convention. By a Native, and Member of the House of Burgesses." 2nd ed. Clementina Rind, Williamsburg, re-printed for G. Kearsly, London, 1774, https://books.google.com/books?id=oaVbAAAAQAAJ.

Jefferson, Thomas. "Letter to John Adams, April 4, 1819." *The Historical Magazine, and Notes and Queries Concerning the Antiquities, History and Biography of America.* Second Series, vol. 1, Henry B. Dawson, Morrisania, N.Y., 1867, https://books.google.com/books?id=A3wFAAAAQAAJ.

Jefferson, Thomas. *Memoirs, Correspondence, and Private Papers of Thomas Jefferson, Late President of the United States, Now First Published from the Original Manuscripts.* Thomas Jefferson Randolph, editor, vol. 1, Henry Colburn and Richard Bentley, London, 1829, https://books.google.com/books?id=_g5AAAAcAAJ.

Jefferson, Thomas. *The Writings of Thomas Jefferson.* Edited by H. A. Washington, vol. 1, Taylor & Maury, Thorne & Co., New York, 1853, https://books.google.com/books?id=Q2ISAAAAYAAJ.

Jefferson, Thomas. *The Writings of Thomas Jefferson.* Edited by H. A. Washington, vol. 3, Taylor & Maury, Thorne & Co., New York, 1853, https://books.google.com/books?id=3WQSAAAAYAAJ.

Jefferson, Thomas. *The Writings of Thomas Jefferson.* Edited by H. A. Washington, vol. 4, Taylor & Maury, Washington D.C., 1854, https://books.google.com/books?id=sCUWAAAAYAAJ.

Jefferson, Thomas. *The Writings of Thomas Jefferson.* Edited by H. A. Washington, vol. 7, Taylor & Maury, Washington D.C., 1854, https://books.google.com/books?id=zjtEAQAAMAAJ.

Jefferson, Thomas. *The Writings of Thomas Jefferson.* Edited by H. A. Washington, vol. 8, Taylor & Maury, Washington D.C., 1854, https://books.google.com/books?id=QzRLAAAAYAAJ.

Jefferson, Thomas. *The Writings of Thomas Jefferson.* Edited by H. A. Washington, vol. 9, Riker, Thorne & Co., New York, 1854, https://books.google.com/books?id=szNEAQAAMAAJ.

KGW Staff, "Food Cart Closing Due to Threats from Occupy ICE PDX Protesters, Owners Say." July 25, 2018, KGW8, https://www.kgw.com/article/news/local/food-cart-closing-due-to-threats-from-occupy-ice-pdx-protesters-owners-say/283-576480995, accessed 25 July, 2018.

Lancaster, Edward M. *A Manual of English History: For the Use of Schools.* American Book Company, Printed by H. S. Barnes & Company, New York, 1877, https://books.google.com/books?id=lVUXAAAAYAAJ.

Lanman, Charles. *Dictionary of the United States Congress and the General Government.* 5th ed., T. Belknap and H. E. Goodwin, Hartford, 1868, https://books.google.com/books?id=zcUTAAAAYAAJ.

Lee, John Adams. *The Shot Heard Round the World, from Lexington to Yorktown.* The John Adams Lee Publishing Company, Boston, 1892, https://books.google.com/books?id=awVQAAAAYAAJ.

Lee, Richard Henry. *Letters from The Federal Farmer to The Republican.* Letter XVIII, Lee Family Digital Archive, housed at Stratford Hall, https://leefamilyarchive.org/papers/essays/fedfarmer/18.html, accessed 15 May 2018.

Lempriere, John. *Biblioteca Classica: Or, A Classical Dictionary.* vol. 1, third New York edition, enlarged by Charles Anthon, G. And C. and H.

Carvill, New York, 1831,
https://books.google.com/books?id=xeE_AAAAYAAJ.

Lewis, John. *A Complete History of the Several Translations of the Holy Bible and New Testament, into English, both in MS. and in Print*. 2nd edition, H. Woodfall, London, 1739,
https://books.google.com/books?id=YbVVAAAAYAAJ.

Lincoln, Abraham. "Presidential Address to the New Jersey Legislature." *The History, Civil, Political & Military of the Southern Rebellion*, written by Orville J. Victor, vol. 1, James D. Torrey, New York, 1861,
https://books.google.com/books?id=XrFYAAAAMAAJ.

Linn, William. *The Life of Thomas Jefferson, Author of the Declaration of Independence, and Third President of the United States*. 3rd ed., Andrus, Woodruff, & Gauntlett, Ithaca, 1843,
https://books.google.com/books?id=4noEAAAAYAAJ.

Lloyd, Thomas. *The Congressional Register; or History of the Proceedings and Debates of the House of Representatives of the United States of America*. vol. 1, Harrisson and Purdy, New York, 1789,
https://books.google.com/books?id=Ea9bAAAAQAAJ.

Locke, John. *Two Treatises of Government*. Awnsham and John Churchill, London, 1698,
https://books.google.com/books?id=7kwUAAAAQAAJ.

Luther, Martin. *First Principles of the Reformation, Or, The Ninety-five Theses and the Three Primary Works of Dr. Martin Luther*. Translation and commentary by Henry Wace and C. A. Buchheim, John Murray, London, 1883, https://books.google.com/books?id=OFFHAQAAMAAJ.

McDonald, W. J. *Constitution of the United States of America with the Amendments Thereto*. Government Printing Office, Washington, 1873,
https://books.google.com/books?id=VrgtAAAAYAAJ.

Madison, James. "Day of Thanksgiving." *Niles' Weekly Register*, vol. 8, March to September 1815, Il. Niles, Baltimore, 1815, https://books.google.com/books?id=gJE-AAAAYAAJ.

Madison, James. *Debates on the Adoption of the Federal Constitution in the Convention Held at Philadelphia in 1787*. Revised and Newly Arranged by Jonathan Elliot, Complete in One Volume, vol. 5, Supplementary to Elliot's Debates, J. B. Lippincott Company, Philadelphia, 1891, https://books.google.com/books?id=oU1GAQAAMAAJ.

Madison, James. *Letter of Marque carried by Captain Millin of the American privateer Prince of Neufchatel*. Constitution Society Popular Pages, permanent record cited as Public Record Office in Richmond, Surrey, UK; High Court of Admiralty HCA32/1342, https://www.constitution.org/mil/lmr/1812amer1.htm, accessed 10 May 2018.

Madison, James. *The Papers of James Madison, Purchased by Order of Congress*. Superintended by Henry D. Gilpin, vol. 2, J. & H. G. Langley, New York, 1841, https://books.google.com/books?id=VGASAAAAYAAJ.

Madison, James. *Religious Freedom. A Memorial and Remonstrance*. Lincoln & Edmands, Boston, 1819, https://books.google.com/books?id=AlJgAAAAcAAJ.

Madison, James. *Selections from the Private Correspondence of James Madison, from 1813 to 1836*. J. C. McGuire, Washington, 1859, https://books.google.com/books?id=tZpPAQAAIAAJ.

Madison, James. *The Writings of James Madison*, vol. 3, G. P. Putnam's Sons, 1902, https://books.google.com/books?id=YWQSAAAAYAAJ.

Malcolm, John. "Civil Asset Forfeiture: Good Intentions Gone Awry and the Need for Reform." The Heritage Foundation, 20 Apr 2015, https://www.heritage.org/crime-and-justice/report/civil-asset-forfeiture-good-intentions-gone-awry-and-the-need-reform, accessed 23 Jun 2018.

Maltby, Charles. *The Life and Public Services of Abraham Lincoln.* Daily Independent Steam Power Print, Stockton, California, 1884, https://books.google.com/books?id=ZDRCAAAAIAAJ.

McMaster, John Bach and Stone, Frederick Dawson, editors. *Pennsylvania and the Federal Constitution, 1787-1788.* Historical Society of Pennsylvania, Lancaster, 1888, https://books.google.com/books?id=7lgSAAAAYAAJ.

Members. *The Christian Observer, Conducted by Members of the Established Church.* For the Year 1817 being the Sixteenth Volume, Samuel Whiting, New York, 1818, https://books.google.com/books?id=k543AQAAMAAJ.

Mill, John Stuart. *On Liberty.* 2nd ed., John W. Parker and Son, London, 1859, https://books.google.com/books?id=AjpGAAAAcAAJ.

Moncure, Daniel Conway. *The Writings of Thomas Paine.* vol. 1, 1774-1779, G. P. Putnam's Sons, New York and London, 1894, https://books.google.com/books?id=zp4rAQAAMAAJ.

Montesquieu, Charles de Secondat, baron de. *The Spirit of Laws.* vol. 2, 6th ed., translated by Thomas Nugent, F. Wingrave, London, 1793, https://books.google.com/books?id=sU_KnWV4YaoC.

Morse, Jedidiah. *Annals of the American Revolution.* Oliver D. Cooke & Sons, Hartford, 1824, https://books.google.com/books?id=TbquJQo5Ic0C.

Morton, John S. *A History of the Origin of the Appellation Keystone State.* Claxton, Remsen & Haffelfinger, Philadelphia, 1874, https://books.google.com/books?id=A1Q_AQAAMAAJ.

Nicolay, John G. "Lincoln's Gettysburg Address." *The Century Magazine*, vol. 97, new series vol. 25, November 1893 to April 1894, p. 596-608, The Century Co., New York, 1894, https://books.google.com/books?id=t7xAAQAAMAAJ.

Noble, Rev. S. *The Divine Law of the Ten Commandments Explained.* Simpkins, Marshall, and Co., London, 1848, https://books.google.com/books?id=phxgAAAAcAAJ.

Paine, Thomas. *The American Crisis.* R. Carlile, London, 1819, https://books.google.com/books?id=jUVHAQAAMAAJ.

Paine, Thomas. *Common Sense.* W. and T. Bradford, Philadelphia, 1776, https://books.google.com/books?id=1YhbAAAAQAAJ.

Peabody, Selim Hobart, editor. *American Patriotism: Speeches, Letters, and Other Papers which Illustrate the Foundation, the Development, the Preservation of the United States of America.* American Book Exchange, New York, 1880, https://books.google.com/books?id=oaIChfaeg3kC.

Penn, William. *A Collection of the Works of William Penn,* vol. 1, Printed and sold by the assigns of J. Sowle, London, 1726, https://books.google.com/books?id=F-NBAQAAMAAJ.

Pennsylvania Constitutional Convention. *The Constitution of the Commonwealth of Pennsylvania.* Zachariah Poulson, Junior, Philadelphia, 1790, https://books.google.com/books?id=so81AQAAMAAJ.

Pennsylvania Constitutional Convention. "The Constitution of Pennsylvania, 1776." *The Register of Pennsylvania,* vol. 4, edited by Samuel Hazard, William F. Geddes, Philadelphia, 1829, https://books.google.com/books?id=Lg4QAQAAMAAJ.

Pennsylvania Legislature. *Laws of the Commonwealth of Pennsylvania: From the Fourteenth Day of October, One Thousand Seven Hundred.* vol. 5, John Bioren, Philadelphia, 1812, https://books.google.com/books?id=h6IzAQAAMAAJ.

Peters, Richard. *United States Reports: Cases Adjudged in the Supreme Court,* Baron v. the Mayor and City Council of Baltimore, vol. 32, Peters vol. 7, January Term 1833, Desilver, Jun. and Thomas, Philadelphia, 1833, https://books.google.com/books?id=a3k-AAAAYAAJ.

Phillips, Wendell. *The Constitution A Pro-Slavery Compact*, 3rd ed., American Anti-Slavery Society, New York, 1856, https://books.google.com/books?id=yhu09hOUdOYC.

Ralph, James (A Lover of Truth and Liberty). *The History of England, During the Reigns of K. William, Q. Anne and K. George I.: With an Introductory Review of the Reigns of the Royal Brothers, Charles and James.* vol. 2, Daniel Browne, London, 1746, https://books.google.com/books?id=IitDAAAAcAAJ.

Randolph, Sarah N. *The Domestic Life of Thomas Jefferson.* Harper & Brothers, New York, 1871, https://books.google.com/books?id=IP8TJneA4SwC.

Rippon, John. *The Baptist Annual Register for 1801 and 1802.* Button and Conder, London, 1802, https://babel.hathitrust.org/cgi/pt?id=nyp.33433069134116.

Roosevelt, Theodore. *The Naval War of 1812.* vol. 2, G. P. Putnam's Sons, New York and London, 1900, https://books.google.com/books?id=qkNJAAAAIAAJ.

Rush, Benjamin. "The Defects of the Confederation." *American Patriotism: Speeches, Letters and Other Papers which Illustrate the Foundation, the Development, The Preservation of the United States of America*, vol. 1, compiled by Selim H. Peabody, American Book Exchange, New York, 1880, https://books.google.com/books?id=qf4-AQAAMAAJ.

Rush, Benjamin. *Essays, Literary, Moral and Philosophical.* Thomas and William Bradford, Philadelphia, 1806, https://books.google.com/books?id=xtUKAAAAIAAJ.

Schaff, Philip. *Church and State in the United States; Or, The American Idea of Religious Liberty and Its Practical Effects.* Reprinted from the Papers of the American Historical Association, vol. 2, No. 4, Charles Scribner's Sons, New York, 1888, https://books.google.com/books?id=McQfAAAAMAAJ.

Scott, David B. *A Manual of History of the United States.* Collins & Brother, New York, 1860, https://books.google.com/books?id=C289AAAAYAAJ.

Sheridan, Thomas. *A Complete Dictionary of the English Language both with Regard to Sound and Learning to which is Prefixed a Prosodial Grammar.* 2nd ed., C. Dilby, London, 1789, https://books.google.com/books?id=VJ5XAAAAYAAJ.

Smith, Adam. *An Inquiry into the Nature and Causes of the Wealth of Nations.* vol. 1, W. Strahan and T. Cadell, London, 1776, https://books.google.com/books?id=td1SAAAAcAAJ.

Smith, Adam. *An Inquiry into the Nature and Causes of the Wealth of Nations.* vol. 2, W. Strahan and T. Cadell, London, 1776, https://books.google.com/books?id=mt1SAAAAcAAJ.

Smith, Adam. *The Theory of Moral Sentiments.* 2nd edition, A. Millar, London, 1761, https://books.google.com/books?id=xVkOAAAAQAAJ.

Social Security Administration. "20 CFR Part 421, [Docket No. SSA-2016-0011], RIN 0960-AH95, Implementation of the NICS Improvement Amendments Act of 2007." Federal Register, vol. 81, no. 243, Monday, December 19, 2016, https://www.gpo.gov/fdsys/pkg/FR-2016-12-19/pdf/2016-30407.pdf.

Somin, Ilya. "The story behind Kelo v. City of New London – how an obscure takings case got to the Supreme Court and shocked the nation." 29 May 2015, *The Washington Post*, https://www.washingtonpost.com/news/volokh-conspiracy/wp/2015/05/29/the-story-behind-the-kelo-case-how-an-obscure-takings-case-came-to-shock-the-conscience-of-the-nation/, accessed 23 Jun 2018.

Sparks, Jared. *The Writings of George Washington.* vol. 3, Harper and Brothers Publishers, New York, 1847, https://books.google.com/books?id=HL4OAAAAYAAJ.

Sparks, Jared. *The Writings of George Washington*. vol. 12, John B. Russell, Boston, 1837,
https://books.google.com/books?id=qy2nqT6FnLMC.

Sprigle, Ray. "Justice Black Revealed As Ku Klux Klansman." *Pittsburgh Post-Gazette*, September 13, 1937, pg. 1,
http://pgdigs.tumblr.com/image/30869087306, retrieved August 24, 2018.

Story, Joseph. *Commentaries on the Constitution of the United States*. vol. 3, Hilliard, Gray and Company, Boston, 1833,
https://books.google.com/books?id=1CATAAAAYAAJ.

Strong, James. *The Exhaustive Concordance of the Bible*. Hodder and Stoughton Limited, Madison, NJ, 1890,
https://books.google.com/books?id=Png7AQAAMAAJ.

Supreme Court of Tennessee. "The State v. Andrews." *Reports of Cases Argued and Determined in the Supreme Court of Tennessee, for the Years, 1871-2*, vol. 3, Joseph B. Heiskell, Reporter, Jones, Purvis & Co. Nashville, 1872, https://books.google.com/books?id=iuAzAQAAMAAJ.

Supreme Court of the United States. "Slaughter-House Cases." *Cases Argued and Adjudged in the Supreme Court of the United States, December Term, 1872*. vol. 16, reported by John William Wallace, W. H. & O. H. Morrison, Washington, D. C., 1873,
https://books.google.com/books?id=DkgFAAAAYAAJ.

Supreme Court of the United States. *District of Columbia v. Heller*. June 26, 2008, United States Supreme Court: Opinions,
https://www.supremecourt.gov/opinions/07pdf/07-290.pdf.

Supreme Court of The United States. *U.S. Reports: Schenck v. United States, 249 U.S. 47 (1919)*. Retrieved from the Library of Congress, https://cdn.loc.gov/service/ll/usrep/usrep249/usrep249047/usrep249047.pdf, accessed 27 Jul 2018.

Supreme Court of The United States. *U.S. Reports: Gitlow v. New York, 268 U.S. 652 (1924)*. Retrieved from the Library of Congress, https://cdn.loc.gov/service/ll/usrep/usrep268/usrep268652/usrep268652.pdf, accessed 27 Jul 2018.

Supreme Court of The United States. *U.S. Reports: New State Ice Co. v. Liebmann, 285 U.S. 262 (1931)*. Retrieved from the Library of Congress, https://cdn.loc.gov/service/ll/usrep/usrep285/usrep285262/usrep285262.pdf, accessed 27 Jul 2018.

Supreme Court of the United States. "Civil Rights Cases." *United States Reports Volume 109 - Cases Adjudged in the Supreme Court at October Term, 1883*. vol. 109, reported by J. C. Bancroft Davis, Banks & Brothers, New York and Albany, 1884, https://books.google.com/books?id=q-EGAAAAYAAJ.

Supreme Court of the United States. "Chicago, Burlington and Quincy v. Chicago." *United States Reports Volume 166 - Cases Adjudged in the Supreme Court at October Term, 1896*. vol. 166, reported by J. C. Bancroft Davis, Banks & Brothers, New York and Albany, 1897, https://books.google.com/books?id=K-w_AAAAYAAJ.

Supreme Court of the United States. *U. S. Reports: Everson v. Board of Education, 330 U. S. 1 (1947)*. Retrieved from the Library of Congress, https://cdn.loc.gov/service/ll/usrep/usrep330/usrep330001/usrep330001.pdf, accessed 27 Jul 2018.

Supreme Court of The United States. *U.S. Reports: Engel v. Vitale, 370 U.S. 421 (1962)*. Retrieved from the Library of Congress, https://cdn.loc.gov/service/ll/usrep/usrep370/usrep370421/usrep370421.pdf, accessed 27 Jul 2018.

Supreme Court of The United States. *U.S. Reports: Brandenburg v. Ohio, 395 U.S. 444 (1969)*. Retrieved from the Library of Congress, https://cdn.loc.gov/service/ll/usrep/usrep395/usrep395444/usrep395444.pdf, accessed 27 Jul 2018.

Supreme Court of the United States. *"Kelo et. al. v. City of New London et. al."* United States Reports 545, October term 2004, 469-523, https://www.supremecourt.gov/opinions/boundvolumes/545bv.pdf, accessed 23 Jun 2018.

Tamburin, Adam. "ACLU of Tennessee sues Mt. Juliet over police seizure of veteran's BMW." *Tennessean*, 5 Jun 2018, https://www.tennessean.com/story/news/2018/06/05/aclu-mt-juliet-police-civil-asset-forfeiture-unconstituational/675294002/, accessed 23 Jun 2018.

"Thanksgiving Day Proclamations 1789–Present." *What So Proudly We Hail*, https://www.whatsoproudlywehail.org/curriculum/the-american-calendar/thanksgiving-day-proclamations-1789-present, accessed 23 Jun 2018.

The Holy Bible. Authorized King James Version, Thomas Baskett, Printer to the King's most Excellent Majesty, London, 1759, https://books.google.com/books?id=3XlaAAAAYAAJ.

Tocqueville, Alexis de. *Democracy in America*. vol. 1, third American edition, edited by John Canfield Spencer, translated by Henry Reeve, George Adlard, New York, 1839, https://books.google.com/books?id=e8IOEkLM6KsC.

Tocqueville, Alexis de. *Democracy in America*. vol. 2, edited by Francis Bowen, translated by Henry Reeve, Sever and Francis, Cambridge, 1863, https://books.google.com/books?id=FMwrPn6t-VkC.

Trump, Donald J. "President Donald J. Trump Proclaims Thursday, November 23, 2017, as a National Day of Thanksgiving." https://www.whitehouse.gov/presidential-actions/president-donald-j-trump-proclaims-thursday-november-23-2017-national-day-thanksgiving/, accessed 23 Jun 2018.

Tudor, William. *The Life of James Otis, of Massachusetts*. Wells and Lilly, Boston, 1823, https://books.google.com/books?id=sb1BAQAAIAAJ.

United Press International. "Justice Black Dies at 85; Served on Court 34 Years." *New York Times* archive, On This Day September 25, 1971, https://archive.nytimes.com/www.nytimes.com/learning/general/onthisday/bday/0227.html, retrieved August 24, 2018.

United States. *The Laws of the United States of America.* vol. 1, Richard Folwell, Philadelphia, 1796, https://books.google.com/books?id=nWpZAAAAYAAJ.

United States Department of Justice. "History of the Federal Use of Eminent Domain." The United States Department of Justice, https://www.justice.gov/enrd/history-federal-use-eminent-domain, accessed 23 Jun 2018.

United States Department of Veteran's Affairs. "America's Wars." The United States Department of Veteran's Affairs, https://www.va.gov/opa/publications/factsheets/fs_americas_wars.pdf, accessed 18 Aug 2019.

Virginia, *Governor's Message and Annual Reports of the Public Officers of the State, of the Board of Directors, and of the Visitors, Superintendents, and Other Agents of Public Institutions or Interests of Virginia.* William F. Ritchie, Richmond, 1851, https://books.google.com/books?id=MvJFAQAAMAAJ.

Washington, George. "First Inaugural Address." *Journal of the First Session of the Senate of the United States of America*, printed by order of the Senate of the United States, Gales & Seaton, Washington, 1820, https://books.google.com/books?id=5t9DAQAAMAAJ.

Washington, George. *Washington's Farewell Address to the People of the United States.* Published for the Washington Benevolent Society of the County of Gloucester, Printed by George Sherman, Trenton, 1812, https://books.google.com/books?id=StXTAAAAMAAJ.

Washington, George. *The Writings of George Washington from the Original Manuscript Sources 1745-1799.* vol. 26, January 1, 1783 - June 10, 1783, John C. Fitzpatrick, Editor. Prepared under the direction of the

United States George Washington Bicentennial Commission and published by authority of Congress, United States Government Printing Office, Washington, 1938, https://books.google.com/books?id=i-o7AAAAIAAJ.

Webster, Daniel. "Eulogy on Adams and Jefferson." *American Patriotism: Speeches, Letters and Other Papers which Illustrate the Foundation, the Development, The Preservation of the United States of America*, vol. 1, compiled by Selim H. Peabody, American Book Exchange, New York, 1880, https://books.google.com/books?id=qf4-AQAAMAAJ.

Webster, Noah. *An American Dictionary of the English Language.* Abridged from the Quarto Edition of the Author, Revised and Enlarged by Chauncey A. Goodrich, J. B. Lippincott & Co., Philadelphia, 1857, https://books.google.com/books?id=V_8YAAAAYAAJ.

Webster, Noah. *The American Spelling Book.* 7th ed. Isaiah Thomas and Ebenezer T. Andrews, Boston, 1793, https://books.google.com/books?id=NTRcAAAAQAAJ.

Webster, Noah. *Webster's New International Dictionary of the English Language.* W. T. Harris, Editor in Chief, F. Sturges Allen, General Editor, G. Bell & Sons, London, 1911, https://books.google.com/books?id=1n3FLI97mDkC.

Weems, Mason L. *The Life of William Penn, the Settler of Pennsylvania.* Uriah Hunt, Philadelphia, 1829, https://books.google.com/books?id=_x06AAAAcAAJ.

Wells, William V. *The Life and Public Services of Samuel Adams.* vol. 1, Little, Brown and Company, Boston, 1866, https://books.google.com/books?id=TIoTAQAAMAAJ.

Williams, Charlotte. *Hugo Black – A Study in the Judicial Process.* Johns Hopkins Press, Baltimore, 1950, https://books.google.com/books?id=XGYaAAAAYAAJ.

Williams, Edwin. *The Addresses and Messages of the Presidents of the United States, Inaugural, Annual, and Special, from 1789 to 1846.* vol. 1, Edward Walker, New York, 1846, https://books.google.com/books?id=dm0FAAAAQAAJ.

Williams, Roger. *The Bloudy Tenent of Persecution for Cause of Conscience Discussed: and Mr. Cotton's Letter Examined and Answered.* Edited for The Hanserd Knolls Society by Edward Bean Underhill, J. Haddon, London, 1848, https://books.google.com/books?id=634rAAAAYAAJ.

Wilson, James. *The Works of the Honourable James Wilson, L.L.D.* Published under the Direction of Bird Wilson, vol. 1, Bronson and Chauncey, Philadelphia, 1804, https://books.google.com/books?id=UlxHAAAAYAAJ.

Wirt, William. *Sketches of the Life and Character of Patrick Henry.* Revised ed., Mack, Andrus & Co. Ithaca, N.Y., 1847, https://books.google.com/books?id=uF9gAAAAcAAJ.

Witherspoon, John. *The Works of the Rev. John Witherspoon.* vol. 3, 2nd edition, William W. Woodward, Philadelphia, 1802, https://books.google.com/books?id=moQrAAAAYAAJ.

Index